The English Farm

The English
Farm

Ralph Whitlock

J. M. Dent & Sons Ltd
London & Melbourne

First published 1983
Text © Ralph Whitlock 1983

Planned and edited by Tigerlily Ltd., 34 Marshall Street, London W1

This book is set in 11/13 Linotron Sabon
Printed and made in Great Britain by
The Pitman Press Ltd., Bath, for
J. M. Dent & Sons Ltd.,
Aldine House, 33 Welbeck Street, London W1M 8LX

British Library Cataloguing in Publication Data

Whitlock, Ralph
  The English farm.
  1. Farms—England—History
  I. Title
  338.1'0942   S455

  ISBN 0–460–04584–9

Contents

Acknowledgments

The author and publishers would like to thank the following museums, institutions, agencies and photographers for permission to reproduce illustrations and for supplying photographs:

Institute of Agricultural History and Museum of English Rural Life, University of Reading: title and contents pages; pages 13 (bottom), 25, 28, 33, 38, 50, 60, 70, 75, 79, 83, 103, 104, 105, 106 (right), 113, 119, 123, 128, 135, 142, 148, 153, 159, 163, 164, 182, 184, 186, 187, 190, 191, 195, 200, 201, 202, 204, 205 (top), 210.

Rothampsted Agricultural Station: pages 62, 154, 165, 170, 172; colour plates 2–4, 7.

University of Cambridge, Committee for Aerial Photography: pages 23, 35, 40, 41, 48, 69, 90, 94, 133.

The British Library: pages 64, 80, 84; colour plate 1.

BBC: pages 47, 67.

Farmers Weekly: pages 225, 230; colour plates 11–15, 17, 18.

The Tate Gallery: colour plates 5, 6.

John Tarlton and *The Field:* half title and contents pages; also pages 12, 14, 16, 17, 97, 207, 235, 236, 237, 242.

John Topham and *The Field*: pages 14 (bottom), 15, 224, 238 (bottom).

Fox Photos and *The Field*: pages 8 (left), 205 (bottom), 238 (top), 244.

The Field: pages 8 (right), 9 (top & bottom), 10, 11, 13, 18, 19, 20, 63, 86, 99, 106 (left), 122, 141, 173, 176, 196, 197, 209, 215, 216, 219, 234.

National Museum of Wales: pages 56–57.

S & O Mathews: colour plate 8.

Fotobank/England Scene: colour plates 9, 10, 16.

Country People

Country Sights

Country Landscapes

1. Neolithic Farmers

Archaeologists are generally agreed that agriculture was introduced to Britain by early Neolithic invaders who arrived about BC 3500 equipped with well-established farming techniques and a useful range of cultivated crops and domestic livestock. Much research has been devoted to the logistics of such a formidable enterprise. Cattle, sheep, pigs and dogs would not only have had to be safely transported but assured of a food supply when they arrived. Seed corn would have needed protection against damage by sea water during the voyage.

Early examples of both boats made of skins on wooden frames, similar to curraghs or coracles, and of dug-out craft have been discovered, studied and found adequate for transporting the entire stock-in-trade of a Neolithic farmer across stretches of sea. Indeed, evidence accumulates that at least some of these Neolithic men were intrepid seafarers. In the colonization of Britain, for instance, they did not necessarily take the shortest sea route by the Straits of Dover. Some landed on the Dorset coast and farther west, and it has been suggested that some may have come direct from Iberia.

It may reasonably be supposed that the clans which set out, with all their possessions, from harbours on the Continent, were not venturing entirely into the unknown. Unencumbered menfolk had doubtless made exploratory voyages before and were aware of what awaited them on the other side. Probably they knew that the land was sparsely populated with semi-nomadic hunters and food gatherers, and it is possible that advance parties had gone ahead to make preparations—including perhaps the accumulation of stocks of food against the coming winter—for the selected season would no doubt have been late summer, after the harvest had been gathered but before autumn gales increased the hazards of the journey. Nor, of course, are we dealing with one expedition. It is reasonable to assume that a number of colonizing enterprises, perhaps quite independent of one another, occurred over a lengthy period. There was plenty of room. Britain was relatively empty—emptier than it would ever be again.

Shropshire coracle of skins on wooden frame. Neolithic immigrants probably came to Britain about BC 3500 in similar but larger craft.

It would be satisfying now to turn to a settlement established by these early farming and seafaring ancestors and to study their way of life and how they settled down in their new environment. Unfortunately we cannot. The best examples of Neolithic settlements belong to the late Neolithic period, separated from the arrival of our pioneers by perhaps 1,500 or 2,000 years—a period as long as the Christian era. A lot can happen in such a vast panorama of centuries.

Skara Brae, in the Orkneys, is one of the best-preserved Neolithic settlements in Britain, for the reason that it was for centuries buried by drifting sand. Also, in the absence of timber on that windswept shore, it was constructed of stone slabs. Not only are the walls of the houses (in places five to eight feet thick) made of stone but so is the internal furnishing. There are stone-built bed platforms, stone store-cupboards, stone hearths, stone-paved alleyways connecting the houses, and even stone-built privies, a domestic feature rare in England until 3–400 years ago. These remarkable edifices, dating from comparatively late in the Neolithic period, cannot be taken as typical of domestic architecture in earlier centuries. It seems likely, anyhow, that along the south coast of England, the sites which marked the natural landfalls of the immigrants have all since been claimed by the encroaching sea.

Britain was originally a forest country. The statement that in early times a squirrel could travel via tree-tops from the Severn Estuary to the Wash without ever descending to the ground has often been repeated, but it nevertheless graphically illustrates the ecology of the land. It was long assumed that the chalk downlands were an exception and that, free from trees, they formed natural highways into the heart of the country. The immigrants, it was thought, drove their flocks and herds along the South Downs or North Downs, or followed the chalk uplands of Dorset to Salisbury Plain, and thence, by the ancient track which we know as the Icknield Way, moved diagonally across England to Norfolk and Lincolnshire. But palaeobotanical investigations of pollen and of prehistoric snail shells has revealed a much more complex pattern—one which indicates that settlement of these areas was more difficult. It shows for instance that the environs of Avebury, in the heart of the chalk country, was well-developed woodland in the centuries preceding the arrival of the Neolithic farmers. So, questionable as 'natural highways' may be, evidence suggests that from time to time Mesolithic hunters deliberately cleared areas of forest by fire in order to improve the grazing for deer, aurochs and other animals on which they largely depended for food, and this may have helped to clear a path for the new immigrants.

An intensively excavated site which has given its name to the culture of the early Neolithic settlers is Windmill Hill, about a mile north-west of Avebury, in north Wiltshire. The site is a low hill crowned by three concentric earthworks and a sprinkling of round barrows. The main period of occupation seems to have been around BC 2500, but there are traces of earlier settlement about BC 3000. Windmill Hill is one of the earliest farming centres known in England, but it immediately presents a conundrum. Here

Earthworks at Windmill Hill, one of Britain's earliest farm communities.

have been found traces of cultivated fields and evidence of a large population of farm animals, with their human attendants, but no signs of human dwellings. Where did the people live? Two alternatives suggest themselves. One is that the early Neolithic farmers were semi-nomadic, much as primitive agriculturists are in certain parts of the world today. In parts of Africa, for example, where a rotation or slash-and-burn system of agriculture is logical and reasonably effective, the tribe arrives in a particular locality and clears an area by cutting and burning the undergrowth and the smaller trees. Larger trees are often ring-barked, for felling later. When rain has washed the ashes into the soil, the seed of a food crop is planted by means of a dibbing-stick. Alternatively, the seed can be scattered broadcast. (Stubs and roots in the soil can be ignored, there being no mechanical devices for them to interfere with at either sowing or harvesting.) The yields from the first harvest after clearing are usually excellent. In the second year they diminish considerably, so the site is generally abandoned and the tribe moves on. Their migrations are, however, planned and regular, not haphazard. After a period of years established by tradition, generally in Africa from seven to ten but sometimes up to fifteen to eighteen, they return to the first site and repeat the process. What they have done is, in effect, to establish a fixed rotation of crops on the same principle as that employed by European farmers who intersperse periods of crop-bearing with occasional years of fallow.

Archaeological evidence for a slash-and-burn system, alternatively known by its German name of *Brandwirtschaft*, has been gathered from a number of prehistoric sites in northern Europe. It could well have been the system favoured at Windmill Hill. The periodic migrations of tribes employing it are approximately circular, with the result that the people are never very far from their tribal centre, though sometimes in one direction, sometimes in another. Windmill Hill can be visualized as such a centre, its inhabitants making do with the simplest and flimsiest huts, perhaps mere shelters of animal skins over a timber framework. (The climate of England is thought to have been somewhat warmer, though perhaps wetter, than at present.)

However, there is another possible solution to the problem. The potentialities of chalk cob, a traditional building material in chalk districts, have been largely ignored by archaeologists. The material seems to have been last used for house building shortly before or during World War One. Numerous cottages and farm buildings constructed of it still survive, as do elderly people who have seen it made or even helped in its preparation. The method, as they describe it, was to assemble heaps of rubbly chalk on a level site. As water was thrown over a heap, a group of men trod it methodically, working it into a kind of stiff paste. From time to time animal hair, chaff and chopped straw were tossed in to give the mixture consistency and adhesion. While this was going on the workers may have chanted a Mudwallers' Song such as a correspondent from Brittany stated he had heard there under similar circumstances. A wall was built up in layers some twelve to eighteen inches deep—that being the limit that could be reached before the semi-liquid material started to collapse under its own weight—and was allowed to set for two or three days before the next layer was added.

Much Neolithic housing would have been temporary skin-covered frames similar to these and suitable to semi-nomadic farmers.

Chalk cob is exceptionally durable. It defies fire, water and shock, but it does need to be capped with thatch. 'Keep its head dry and it will last for ever,' say the experts. Once the capping thatch is removed or allowed to deteriorate, rain soon penetrates and frosts cause rapid disintegration. The traditional treatment then is to cart away the chalk rubble to spread over cultivated fields, as a kind of marling. Even a substantial building can thus disappear within a few days. Unless it has been reinforced by upright timbers set in post-holes at the time of building (an unnecessary refinement) no one would know that it had ever existed. Nineteenth-century cottages and farm buildings usually had foundations of flints, though some were built without them. These flints, too, would be dispersed when the building was demolished, for use again elsewhere. Thus the technique of making and using chalk cob or clay cob is one which our Neolithic ancestors might well have possessed; and if so, they could have built for themselves quite substantial houses, and no archaeologist would be any the wiser.

Interior walls of surviving chalk cob cottages are often constructed of wattle and daub, the making of which is another technique probably understood in the Stone Age. They were certainly adept at wickerwork, which they used for lining storage pits and doubtless for fashioning traps and cages. Wicker eel stages surviving in parts of Ulster from about 6,000 years ago are very similar to those in use there today. Wands of willow and hazel, the two trees most frequently used in such work, could have been cut easily by the sharpened stone tools at the disposal of Neolithic men.

Earlier the custom was mentioned of ring-barking and burning large trees when land was cleared. Men of the tribe would return, perhaps several years later, when the tree was satisfactorily dead, and proceed to deal with it by means of flint axes and fire. An experiment by archaeologists in Denmark showed that three men attacking a tree one foot in diameter with flint axe-blades mounted on wooden hafts were able to fell it in half-an-hour. Further calculations showed that the clearing of a woodland acre occupied by trees of that size would take one man 96 hours. The timber retaining-wall of an early Neolithic long barrow (dated about BC 3240) at Fussells Lodge, near Salisbury, is built of whole or split tree-trunks between one and three feet in diameter. Such a barrow would have taken about 5,000 man-hours to construct.

Flint, chipped and fashioned to a variety of shapes, can be a very versatile substance. By Neolithic farmers and their wives it was used to make hoes, adzes, scrapers, boring tools, picks and even saws and sickles, as well as axes. Not far from Windmill Hill, at a site known as South Street, ploughmarks earlier than BC 2810 have been found under a long barrow. Presumably these were made by a wooden plough of a type known in Europe before that date, but examples of what appear to be stone plough-shares have occasionally been found. Some cultivation of the soil would doubtless have been by the digging-stick, on which an angled projection was sharpened and then hardened by fire. Antlers, which would be found quite commonly when the stags had shed them, were widely used as picks.

The grain crops grown on the small cleared plots were mainly emmer wheat and barley. An analysis of grain imprints found on pottery at Windmill Hill shows 91.6% of wheat and 8.4% of barley. Similar proportions have been found through archaeological work on other Neolithic sites. We do not know whether these cereals were grown as pure stands or as a mixed crop.

Detailed examination of the stomach contents of sacrificed corpses found in Danish bogs has revealed the presence of certain seeds which we regard as weeds, such as persicaria, corn spurrey and camelina (Gold of Pleasure), in quantities which suggest they may have been cultivated, though there is as yet no conclusive evidence. No doubt Neolithic households appreciated wild fruits, such as blackberries, raspberries, rose hips and wild cherries, and perhaps made use of a number of salad plants, including water-cress, goutweed, sorrel, young hawthorn leaves, wild garlic and the seeds of mallow. At Windmill Hill traces were also found of crab-apple pips, flax seeds (probably used for food) and hazel-nuts. Casualties from eating poisonous fungi mistaken for mushrooms were probably not unknown. Wild honey was no doubt valued exceedingly, but we do not know what proportion of that luxury, and of cultivated barley and other crops, was used for making fermented drink, though we may suspect that the ratio may have been quite high.

The British climate presents farmers with the perpetual problem of growing and storing enough food in five or six months to sustain themselves and their livestock for the next six or seven months. Two methods of storing were practised in prehistoric times. One was in granaries raised above ground level on staddle stones or similar devices, to protect the grain against vermin. The other was in pits, tightly sealed over to retain the carbon dioxide produced by the grain, thus preventing the action of destructive bacteria. The first is well suited to grain required for consumption at intervals during the winter; the second to the preservation of seed corn not wanted till the following spring. Both methods were employed at a later period, but we have little information about Neolithic practice. Nor do we know whether the grain was stored in ears or was first threshed. Some of it was parched, presumably in ovens, a process which helped to preserve grains intended for eating but rendered them useless as seed corn.

The earliest method of preparing grain for food was pounding it with a stone crusher on a flat rock. To the Neolithic people, however, belongs the invention of the saddle quern, a saddle-shaped rock and a stone roller, between which the grain was crushed. The flour produced could be used in a kind of porridge or as unleavened bread, probably baked on heated stones. But wheat and other cereals, grown in small fields hardly more than garden plots, were subsidiary sources of food. The Neolithic farmers of Windmill Hill and other early sites enjoyed a diet mainly of meat and milk. They relied heavily on their flocks and herds; at Windmill Hill only 3.9% of the food-bones examined were those of wild animals, mostly red deer.

Analysis of the animal bones at Windmill Hill before the enclosures were constructed shows 66% cattle, 16% pig, 11.7% sheep and goats and 2.2% dogs. In the primary levels of the enclosure ditches, representing a somewhat later period, the proportions of food-bones are 60% cattle, 24.8% sheep and goats, and 15.2% pigs. At a much later stage, on the margins of the Bronze Age, the ratios are 61.2% cattle, 14.3% sheep and goats, and 24.5% pigs. The picture is thus one of a remarkably stable economy over a very long

period. Cattle were, however, not necessarily so preponderant in all Neolithic farming communities. At Durrington Walls, on Salisbury Plain, where an exhaustive study of the bones of food animals has been made, the proportions were 26% cattle, 2% sheep and 63% pigs. Durrington Walls appears to have been a community of pig-farmers, in contrast to the cattle ranchers of Windmill Hill. (The analysis is for the late Neolithic period and so should be compared with the third set of figures for Windmill Hill, quoted above.) The comparative paucity of sheep at both sites is interesting. Sheep require open pasture for grazing, whereas pigs in particular, but also cattle, thrive in well-wooded country.

The Neolithic settlers from continental Europe almost certainly brought with them their own cattle, which were a kind of Shorthorn, of the species *Bos longifrons*. Undoubtedly, though, they found the forests of Britain inhabited by the aurochs or urus (*Bos primigenius*), the great wild ox. (According to Julius Caesar, the bulls stood more than six feet high at the shoulders.) Some authorities think that *Bos longifrons* may also have lived wild in British woodlands. Whatever their origins, there must have been much interbreeding between the two species as it would have been

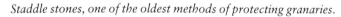

Staddle stones, one of the oldest methods of protecting granaries.

29

impossible for Neolithic herdsmen to keep their cows away from the great forest bulls, even if they had wanted to.

A similar difficulty exists in differentiating between domestic and wild pigs. There was, in fact, probably no difference. Semi-wild pigs rooted and grubbed for their living in the woods, as they did on the rubbish-heaps of London in Tudor times. They were lean, long-snouted, bristle-backed scavengers, very different from our modern baconers.

Sheep, which were certainly brought over by the settlers—as no wild sheep survived in Britain to Neolithic times—were small, agile creatures, probably something like the semi-wild Soay. As already noted, they were few in number and would have been kept for meat or milk, for weaving had not yet been invented. Archaeologists find it almost impossible to distinguish between many of the bones of sheep and goats.

Dog bones investigated at Windmill Hill are of a rather small animal, similar to a fox terrier. Such dogs could have been of little use for herding, they may have been kept as pets or for food.

Of wild animal bones found at Windmill Hill, red deer are the most numerous, and these were considerably larger than the modern red deer of Scotland. Roe deer, also larger than the modern type, were present too.

For a person conditioned to present-day living standards, life on a Neolithic farm would be rough but not unbearable. Food was reasonably plentiful at most seasons, though with a preponderance of meat and an extreme scarcity of sweet things. The chief deprivation would be clothes, for without weaving, these early farming people had to make do with skins, though, as we know, furs can be comfortable. In most respects each community would have been self-sufficient, and for much of the time people must have busied themselves supplying the necessities of life. Tools and implements had to be made and sharpened, pottery manufactured, hides scraped and cured, livestock slaughtered, jointed and cooked, crops sown and harvested, grain and perhaps other seeds processed, fires kept burning or rekindled, huts built. An exception to the general self-sufficiency would be the supply of best-quality flints, which are found only in certain districts. Quite early in the period flint-mines were developed, as at Findon (Sussex), Harrow (Middlesex), Easton Down (Wiltshire) and Grime's Graves (Norfolk), supplying flints to other parts of the country, presumably through the agency of itinerant traders.

A problem which exercises the minds of modern students probably more than it did Neolithic Britons is water supply, for the water table in much of Britain was considerably higher then than it is now. It has been estimated, for example, that on the chalk downland near Shaftesbury, Dorset, the water table has dropped by about 150 feet since Roman times. So streams which are now mere rivulets, especially in summer, would have been full at all seasons, and upland valleys which are now waterless probably had brooks. We can imagine stockmen from the hilltop enclosures taking their animals down to the valley mornings and evenings to drink.

In appearance these Neolithic people were small and dark, belonging to a long-headed race often referred to as Iberian. While we do not know what language they spoke it is thought to have belonged to the Hamitic family and was perhaps akin to Basque. Religion must have played an important part in their lives. It was the Neolithic tribes who began the monumental works of Avebury, Arbor Low, Callernish, Stonehenge and large numbers of impressive long barrows and megaliths; although the more grandiose stages were accomplished after the arrival of the first Bronze Age immigrants. It seems legitimate to surmise that their religion was closely connected with the new techniques on which Neolithic culture was based, the domestication of livestock and the cultivation of crops. Fertility, of flocks and herds and of the soil, was of supreme importance and the study of current rural customs, many of them of immense antiquity, supplies clues to what went on.

The revels of May Day (Beltane) have all the hallmarks of original fertility rituals. Imbolc, the February quarter-day, marked the beginning of the lambing season; Lammas, the threshold of harvest. Most of the primitive religions of Europe have a common element in the worship of the Earth Mother, who gave life to the seed committed to her. Memories of her are evoked by the images of corn dollies, or kern babies, subjects of a recently revived vogue. Traditionally, the corn dolly, representing the goddess of harvest, was fashioned of the last stalks of corn cut at harvest-time. After occupying the place of honour at the Harvest Home feast, the corn dolly was kept by the hearth until ploughing was resumed after the winter solstice. She was then taken to the fields and ceremoniously buried beneath the first furrow, in readiness for fulfilling her role in producing the harvest that was to come. As the archaeologist, Jacquetta Hawkes, observes, 'I do not think it is allowing the imagination too great liberty to say that the faith, for it is very truly a faith, which made the New Stone Age communities labour to drag, raise, pile thousands of tons of stone and earth, was in resurrection, the resurrection of their corn and beasts, of themselves. They laid their dead in the dark, earth-enclosed chamber with something of the same conviction with which they cast the seed corn into the soil.'

2. The Bronze Age

Although the Neolithic farmers were accustomed to visits by travelling traders who dealt in quality flints from well-established flint mines, at a date which used to be estimated at about BC 1800 but which has been forced steadily back by more recent archaeological evidence, these pedlars produced from their wicker baskets something new and exciting. Its impact on the wondering customers is not difficult to imagine.

Displaying glittering bronze daggers, brooches and tools, the trader would explain that here was a new kind of 'stone' which did not need sharpening by chipping when its edges grew blunt. One could just rub it against a rough stone until it was as good as new. Or, if it broke, the farmer could keep it till the pedlar next called, and he would then, by his secret arts, use it to fashion something new. A knife could be refashioned into an axe-head; hoops for a wooden bucket could be broken down to make rings and ornamental pins. Though the source of the new material and the method of its manufacture would have been for a long time beyond the understanding of the farmer and his family, they would in time come to appreciate that the bronze was obtained by melting certain rocks and mixing the molten stuff together. As far as the British Isles were concerned, the magic stones were to be found in Cornwall and southern Ireland. The miners and metal-workers of the new Age knew how to identify the ore-bearing rocks and how to extract the metals by subjecting them to great heat. They had worked out the ideal proportions of copper and tin (90% of copper and 10% tin) for making the best bronze, and they understood how to make the hardest type of bronze by using copper ore contaminated by arsenic. They also worked with gold.

The itinerant traders now became craftsmen as well. As they travelled from place to place they carried, probably in panniers on the backs of donkeys or ponies, the tools for metal-working and a small stock of bronze, some of it probably in the form of discarded tools for melting down. Arriving at a farm or village, they would set up camp, build a small furnace and produce whatever the farmers wanted and were willing to pay for. The tradition of the travelling Irish tinker may well have its roots in those far-off days.

At first the new inventions brought nothing but benefits to the farmers. Previously they had harvested their crops by plucking off the ears laboriously by hand or, at the best, by cutting the stems with heavy and apparently rare flint sickles. Now the bronze sickle enabled them to speed up harvesting operations and so defy the weather. Discovering that grass could also be cut by these curved, sharp-edged tools, they learned how to conserve it as hay,

Victorian farm worker using a sickle as did his Bronze Age ancestors.

thus vastly increasing their capacity for feeding livestock during winter. At the same time the improved harvesting methods encouraged them to grow their crops on larger acreages. The scene was set for a rapid expansion of agriculture, and of the agricultural population.

Unfortunately for the Stone Age inhabitants of Britain, similar developments had already occurred in continental Europe, and in the less hospitable lands of central Europe tribes armed with bronze were on the move, searching for new areas of settlement. By around BC 2000 some of them had reached the shores of the English Channel and the North Sea and, embarking on boats and rafts as the Neolithic peoples had done long before, had crossed to Britain. Among the earliest and most formidable Bronze Age immigrants to Britain were tribes of people whom archaeologists have labelled the Beaker Folk, after their characteristic pottery which featured red, flat-bottomed drinking vessels or beakers. They came from central Europe and were taller, fairer and more heavily built than the Neolithic farmers they found here. They came not all at once but in several waves, and not in particularly large numbers, though the evidence suggests that they took over as an alien aristocracy much as the Normans would do 2,000 years later.

When such an event occurs, everyone other than the conquerors takes a step down in the social scale. Some intermarriage takes place between the new rulers and the upper classes of the former régime, but more and more individuals are pressed down into the lower strata. And the lowest level of all, to judge from developments in innumerable other lands and eras, soon consists of slaves. The folklore of rural Britain, and especially of the Celtic west and north, abounds in references to dark, furtive little people who lived in remote caves, bogs and forests and who sometimes ventured timidly to the outskirts of farms and villages after dark. In these scared little folk we can perhaps detect the pitiful remnants of our Stone Age farmers.

To aggravate the situation, around BC 1000 the climate, which was warmer and drier than at present, began to deteriorate. While the increasing incidence of cool, damp summers, of hill mists and winter rains created problems for lowland farmers, it spelt ruin for those on the hills, as on Dartmoor, who were forced to abandon their little farms and seek refuge wherever they could. Their cereal crops would no longer ripen on the rain-sodden soils. This meant competing not only with the farmers already in possession but with new immigrants from the Continent. The last few centuries of the Bronze Age were therefore a period of turmoil and violence. The numerous hill-forts which had their origin in this period (though many of them were enlarged and refortified in later ages) testify to the dangers of the times.

Line of earthwork thought to be the boundary of a Bronze Age ranch, meandering across the landscape in Hampshire.

Against this increasingly turbulent background the cycle of the seasons unfolded its eternal drama, with men planning and working to win their harvests. As often happens, progress was most pronounced in time of war, men presumably being stimulated by the challenges and exigencies of events, and although the Bronze Age was ushered in by the discovery of metal-working, the changes it produced occurred mainly towards the end of the period; the early centuries were relatively tranquil.

At least some of the early Bronze Age immigrants seem to have been pastoral rather than agricultural. Steep-sided, narrow-bottomed ditches which lead apparently aimlessly across the downlands of Wiltshire and Hampshire and the wolds of East Yorkshire are interpreted by some authorities as the boundaries of ranches. In some instances they enclose hundreds of acres and represent the earliest territorial divisions of land, other than for arable purposes, known in Britain. Smaller enclosures, of less than an acre, which seem to be associated with them may be cattle corrals. An alternative suggestion is that the ditches were originally fenced lanes along which cattle could be driven without trespassing on the cultivated land on either side.

To whatever extent the so-called Celtic Shorthorn (*Bos longifrons*) contributed to the herds of Neolithic farmers—and some authorities think it was not a very large contribution—considerable numbers of them were introduced from the Continent during the Bronze Age. They were small cattle, about midway between the modern Kerry and Dexter, and resembling the Jersey in build. By the end of the Bronze Age this type of cattle was dominant and all-purpose, being used for milk, meat and draught. The meagre evidence of a few hairs attached to hides in bogs and burials suggest that they were reddish-brown in colour, though some may have been white or white-marked, as ancestors of the white cattle known to have existed in Celtic times.

Sheep seem to have been at least as numerous as cattle and to have been, on the whole, much the same as the Neolithic stock. At the Shetland site of Jarlshof, however, two types have been identified. One is the light, fragile, big-horned sheep of the Soay type; the other a larger, heavier animal. With the introduction of weaving, the number of sheep seems to have increased, as might be expected. The discovery of colanders at a few Bronze Age sites suggests that the ewes may have been milked and the milk made into cheese.

During the Bronze Age the pig declined in numbers and importance, probably because of the reclamation of forest land for cultivation. By the end of the period it was quite scarce, though the small, long-legged pig of central

Europe had been imported. In the *Mabinogion*, the fourteenth-century collection of ancient scraps of Welsh poetry, legends and other literature, there is a possible reference to one such importation. A character in one of the stories says, 'I have heard there have come to the south some beasts, such as were never known in this island before . . . They are small animals, and their flesh is better than the flesh of oxen . . . Swine they are now called . . . half-hog, half-pig.'

An important addition to the farm's livestock during the Bronze Age was the horse. Wild horses of pony type apparently lived in Britain in Neolithic times but were probably not domesticated. Horse bones found at a few New Stone Age sites, particularly in Wales, are considered evidence that the animals were hunted and eaten. Towards the end of the era horses were ridden and drew the chariots of the aristocracy, but it is unlikely that any of these valuable animals were used for farm work.

In addition to the bronze sickle, already mentioned, one of the most important of the new bronze tools was the celt or axe-head. The various stages of its development have been traced. First a primitive bronze axe-head was forced at right-angles through a wooden handle, exactly as stone axe-heads had been. Then one limb of a V-shaped rod was cleft, and the axe-head inserted and bound in, the longer limb of the rod serving as a handle. Then the metal itself was shaped to fit around a wooden handle and finally, the base of the axe was made hollow, to form a socket for fitting over a handle. The bronze sickle underwent a similar transition.

Simultaneously, new techniques were developed to improve the hardness and cutting power of bronze implements, which by the end of the period were very efficient indeed. Using celts, adzes, saws, boring tools and other accessories of the carpenter's trade, Bronze Age artisans became skilful in the use of wood, both for building and for making implements. One of their achievements was a light, wooden plough, capable of gouging a groove through loose, friable soil. The earliest draught animals were most probably women, but later oxen were the power units. Replicas of these ploughs, made by archaeologists and tested on similar soils, have shown them to be versatile and reasonably efficient tools, within their limitations. Experimenting with one of them, I found it possible to produce a kind of shallow furrow, though the implement was hardly designed with that in mind. About BC 750, however, one of the great steps forward in the history of British agriculture occurred when farmers from the Rhineland introduced a bronze ploughshare and revolutionized the techniques of land cultivation. An early example, found in East Yorkshire, is not unlike a modern

The breast plough was an early device for cultivating land.

ploughshare. Socketed, it fits over the end of a wooden plough-beam, to which it was fastened by bronze rivets. So much importance was attached to this invention by contemporary farmers that the name of a hero, Hu Gadarn, who is said to have been the first man to plough a furrow in British soil, is still preserved in ancient Welsh legends.

Of equal importance in the field of human progress, though of less significance agriculturally, was the introduction of the wheel. Wheeled carts and waggons are a convenience about the farm, but it is possible to manage without them. The farmers of Devonshire are said to have managed with only sledges and panniers until the middle of the eighteenth century, and the empire of the Incas is an example of a powerful civilization which made no use at all of the wheel. Wheeled vehicles require a firm, hard surface to function efficiently, and firm, hard surfaces were a scarce commodity in Devonshire in winter throughout most of history.

The first wheels were solid, made either of rings cut from tree-trunks or of several segments fastened together. Obviously they were very heavy and cumbersome, and the development of spoked wheels, made possible by metal tools, was an enormous improvement. The first spoke-wheeled vehicles were war chariots, which are known to have had a light timber-and-wicker superstructure. Farm carts and waggons came later, though they are thought to have been in use before the end of the Bronze Age. It is suggested that they may have had rawhide tyres, which would shrink and tighten as they dried, strengthening the wheels.

Until the introduction of the metal ploughshare and the turning of the first furrow, the most efficient way of cultivating a field was to run a wooden plough through it in one direction and then cut it across at right angles. This procedure gave an advantage to roughly rectangular or square fields. Bronze Age farmers also apparently liked their fields to be of a size which could be ploughed or harvested in a day, a preference which exists in the Scottish Highlands today. The fields, the outlines of which may still be detected on hill slopes in many parts of Britain, were often on terraces and were bounded by ditches and/or banks which were probably surmounted by live hedges. Whether the terraces, like later lynchets, were deliberately man-made or resulted naturally from ploughing methods is still a matter for controversy.

Most fields were situated within easy distance of farmsteads, and in at least one instance that pattern can be linked with a programme for manuring the land. The example is at Jarlshof, in Shetland, a site which, though much disturbed by later occupation, has been shown to have consisted in the Bronze Age of a group of stone houses enclosed by a dry-stone courtyard wall. The inhabitants grew cereals in small fields and kept cattle and sheep. At one time they had a smith living with them and working at his forge. A remarkable feature of the place is a central tank for the collection of manure which was evidently spread over the fields at intervals. This is very early evidence indeed of the appreciation of the value of manuring as an aid to maintaining the fertility of the soil.

A major improvement in the domestic arrangements of a house of the later

Some of the best-preserved Bronze Age houses are found on Dartmoor.

Bronze Age was the hearth. Cooking-holes lined with stones, usually outside the hut, were gradually replaced by stone hearths inside the building. Some of the best preserved of Bronze Age houses are found on Dartmoor. That is not because Dartmoor was more densely settled than the rest of Britain but because after the poorer climate forced its abandonment, the land continued to be not worth cultivating, so the sites were left undisturbed. As there is little to differentiate between human dwellings and cattle shelters, the sites are generally referred to as hut circles. Over 1,330 of them have been already

Outline of Bronze Age house, Grimspound, Dartmoor.

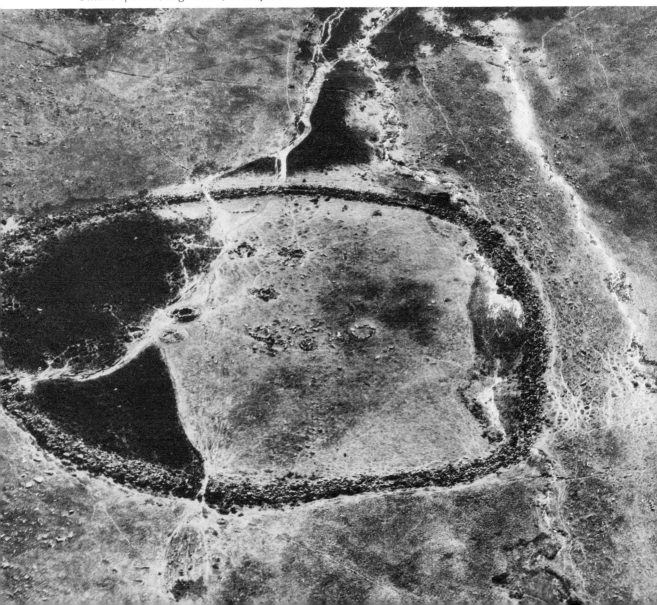

mapped, and there are probably at least 1,500 in all.

Grimspound, the best known of the Bronze Age villages, though not the largest, consists of sixteen huts in a stone-walled enclosure of about four acres. The houses are round, with walls of granite slabs, two or three feet thick in places and backed by banks of turf. Most houses have the entrance on the south-west, but one has a porch or ante-room with the outer door at right angles to the one which gives access to the larger, inner chamber. The floors are eighteen inches or more below the level of the surrounding land, in order to lay bare the underlying bed of granite. The diameters of the huts vary from about six feet to over fifteen feet. Some huts have both a hearth and a cooking-hole, and in some a raised platform of stone along one side may have been used as a sleeping area. A central post-hole indicates that a stout pole supported a beehive roof of thatch. Two large upright stones form doorposts, and there is often a paved approach path and a stone threshold.

At another Bronze Age site, Shearplace Hill, on the downs above Sydling St Nicholas, Dorset, two round huts are situated in a small farmyard around which are paddocks and tracks leading to small fields. One hut is thought to have been a dwelling, the other a cattle shed or byre. The walls of the inhabited hut were of vertical wooden posts and wattle hurdles. An inner circle of posts, taller than the outer ones, supported timbers and rafters for the roof, which was conical in shape and evidently of thatch. At Jarlshof, in Shetland, the early Bronze Age houses are oval but others, erected late in the period, were round and divided by radial partitions. Underground galleries of unknown purpose were also constructed at this time. In the New Forest, however, two square houses with timber frames and ridged roofs were used as burial places, probably for persons who had lived in them, and barrows heaped over their remains.

It may be assumed that if chalk or mud cob was used, as suggested, in the Neolithic period, its use was continued throughout the Bronze Age and, indeed, in every age since, up to the present. If so, it can partly account for the paucity of house sites of the era, for houses built of this material would leave no trace. One archeologist has suggested that the people who created early civilizations around Stonehenge and other sites in Wessex lived in large communal houses somewhat similar to the later Pictish brochs. These tower-like buildings of several storeys and of considerable diameter, were built round a courtyard. On the first-storey inner balcony spectators supposedly watched sports and other spectacles in the courtyard below, while on an outer rampart sentries kept watch. For such edifices chalk cob would be a suitable material.

Within the houses life was increasingly comfortable. The development of metal-working supplied housewives with such accessories as safety-pins and brooches. Buttons, many of them fashioned from jet, also came into common use. Towards the end of the period men shaved with bronze razors, while women employed bronze tweezers for plucking their eyebrows. Hoops of bronze bound domestic wooden buckets and barrels. The introduction of flat-bottomed earthenware vessels by the Beaker people gave housewives a range of kitchen utensils, including jugs, jars, bowls, cups, skimmers and strainers. Wood-turning lathes had also been invented.

Above all, Bronze Age women had mastered the arts of spinning and weaving, but these techniques were adopted only gradually: in the Bronze Age villages of Dartmoor the abundance of stone scrapers indicates that skin garments were more common than woven ones. In other sites, however, loom weights have been frequently found. In Bronze Age burials traces of woven cloth have been noted as covering on the mouths of cinerary urns or as wrappings for burnt bones or for daggers and axes. A skeleton found in a Salisbury Plain barrow is said to have been wrapped in a fabric resembling 'very fine linen'.

With the increase in the cultivation of crops, which bronze implements allowed, people began to enjoy a diet in which cereals were more plentiful and meat less so. The Bronze Age housewife would have spent sizeable chunks of time in baking bread (unleavened) and heating gruel or porridge on her new hearth. But the discovery of particles of grit adhering to the teeth of skeletons suggests that she had not got round to sifting the flour before using it. It is not known whether she had a vegetable garden outside her hut, though white goosefoot is thought to have been used as a vegetable, probably for boiling like cabbage, and the home paddock may well have contained an apple tree or two, of an improved type with crab apples as ancestors.

An awkward fact which has to be fitted into our picture of a Bronze Age farming community is that these were the people who erected Stonehenge, Avebury and a host of other megalithic monuments (though some were started in Neolithic times). It has been calculated that the work involved in constructing Stonehenge in all its phases amounted to little short of 1,500,000 man-days. The official guide-books on Stonehenge and Avebury suggests that to bring the eighty or so stones from the Marlborough Downs, twenty miles away, to the site would have taken 1,000 men several years. Several hundred men would be needed to erect each stone, to say nothing of the sixty-odd blue-stones fetched from the Prescelly Mountains in south-west

Wales. The huge earth pyramid of Silbury Hill, near Avebury, is composed of nearly 50,000,000 basketfuls of soil, each weighing about thirty pounds. And while all these men were thus engaged, they were not growing food. The Bronze Age farmers of Salisbury Plain must have been producing a very large surplus to keep them supplied.

A caste of priest-scientists had to be provided for too. Recent research has shown that they attained an astonishing level of mathematical and astronomical knowledge. Dr Alexander Thom, a distinguished professor of engineering science at Oxford, has established the existence of what is termed the 'megalithic yard', a measurement of 2.72 feet, which was employed in the construction of virtually all the megalithic sites in Britain. The people who erected Stonehenge had advanced knowledge of geometry, including, apparently, certain characteristics of right-angled triangles and the value of *pi* which are normally associated with Pythagoras, more than 1,000 years later. The alignments of stones at Stonehenge and other sites point not only to midsummer and midwinter sunrises and sunsets but reveal a familiarity with a lunar cycle of 18.6 years, known to modern astronomers as the moon's 'minor standstill' and caused by its elliptical orbit. Clearly, then, there were among these Bronze Age people scientists of enormous intelligence and their accumulated knowledge and lore must have been passed on from generation to generation. That implies a school or university and a leisured class able to devote their lives to scientific studies without being bothered about the mundane matters of growing barley and making cheese. In the absence of writing, masses of data would have had to be transmitted orally, and the scholars must have been capable of impressive feats of memory.

Finally there is the evidence of the barrows. The great men buried there, perhaps the equivalent of kings, were richly adorned with golden ornaments as well as articles of bronze. In many tombs have been found beads of amber and jet and also faience beads probably from Egypt. We have already noted that some of the corpses were wrapped in fine cloth.

The manual workers engaged in erecting the megalithic monuments, the priest-scientists and the ruling aristocracy have one common feature—none of them was engaged in producing the necessities of life. We may be sure therefore that our Bronze Age farming ancestors, busily engaged in ploughing their small fields, milking their cows, baking their flat loaves and weaving their woollen and linen cloths, came to know quite well not only the smith, the carpenter, the potter and other specialist craftsmen, but also that sinister figure, familiar to every subsequent era, the taxman.

3. The Iron Age

For peace-loving farmers the first millenium BC was a grim and terrible time. Wave after wave of invading Celtic warriors poured into Britain from Europe, overturning the existing order and making life increasingly precarious. Over the same period the weather continued to deteriorate and the warm, dry Sub-Boreal era was succeeded by the cool and humid Sub-Atlantic period with a climate similar to the present.

The first Celts to arrive in Britain, between BC 800 and 700, were still in the Bronze Age, but the second group, about 500 BC, were equipped with iron weapons and tools. They were followed by yet another invasion in the third century BC and a final one in about BC 75. The arrival of these fierce, blue-eyed, fair-haired horsemen with their iron weapons caused consternation in farming Britain. The bronze weapons of the British chiefs, no matter how skilfully made and wielded, were no match for iron swords and spears. As Sir Winston Churchill caustically commented, 'It cannot be doubted that for smashing skulls, whether long-headed or round, iron is best.' One result of these repeated invasions is that Britain became known to the emerging empire of Rome as a major source of slaves. But adversity is an efficient teacher. It was not long before the survivors of the first onslaughts were equipping themselves with iron weapons to match those of their new adversaries. The travelling bronze-smiths became blacksmiths, and the Iron Age had arrived.

In Britain, iron was abundant and easily obtained. Lumps of iron ore could even be picked up on the surface in the Forest of Dean, and almost unlimited deposits were available in the Weald of Sussex and Kent, in Northamptonshire, North Yorkshire, Wiltshire and elsewhere. Nor was the complicated technique of alloying, involved in making bronze, necessary. Iron therefore became far cheaper and more generally used than bronze had ever been. Soon it was being worked everywhere. Between BC 500 and 300 the inhabitants of the Iron Age village at All Cannings Cross, in Wiltshire, were apparently smelting iron and making tools from it in front of their huts. The ore doubtless came from deposits near Seend, a few miles to the west.

Iron tools lasted longer and were more readily sharpened than bronze, and very soon farmers had iron sickles, axes, bill-hooks, hoes, knives, pruning-hooks and ploughshares. Even wooden spades were fitted with iron tips, and iron was so abundant that unlimited supplies of hand-hammered iron nails became commonplace. In the kitchen the farmer's wife possessed iron pots, pans and utensils as well as knives and, in the latter part of the period, spoons. Roasting was done on iron spits and fire-dogs, while candles or lamps on iron spikes or brackets probably provided light on winter evenings.

Let us look at an example of an Iron Age farm: Little Woodbury, near Salisbury, Wiltshire, is often regarded as typical of the period. Sited on a gentle chalk hill, it comprised a large, round house in an enclosure of between three and six acres and associated with a complex of fields totalling

Iron Age fort at Yarnbury, Wiltshire.

about twenty acres in all. The fields were presumably devoted to the cultivation of crops, for they were too small for feeding the numerous cattle and sheep which the farmer kept. No doubt these grazed in the valley below. The livestock also included some horses and dogs but very few pigs, indicating a probable absence of woodland where they could seek their own living. No provision for housing any of the animals is apparent.

The house itself had a solid timber frame, probably with wattle-and-daub walls. It had two concentric circles of substantial upright posts, around a square of even larger uprights above which an open space at the apex allowed smoke to escape from the central hearth. The roof was no doubt of thatch. The size of the building—50 feet in diameter—indicates that it was

Reconstruction of an Iron Age village circa BC 300.

the home of a well-to-do family or clan. In the courtyard were threshing-floors, granaries mounted on staddle-stones or something similar, frames for drying corn and hay, and pits for storing grain. The threshing-floors were hollows, roughly rectangular, marked by posts which evidently supported a thatched roof and were conveniently situated near other posts which supported the drying frames.

Little Woodbury dates from the second or third century BC. At the time it was built the countryside must have been peaceful, as the only defence was a stock fence to keep out prowling animals—wolves, no doubt. Later, as life became more precarious, a ditch and palisaded bank were constructed. The end of the farm is unknown but can be guessed at.

Throughout all its phases the farmstead would have been well populated, all the clan evidently living in the same house. The men would go out in the morning to cultivate the fields or take the cattle and sheep down to the valley to graze. The women would be cooking, weaving, dyeing, dressing hides, sewing, making butter and curds, and possibly making the household's pottery. The fire on the hearth had to be tended, and the floors swept. Children and dogs were everywhere. It was a busy, bustling and doubtless noisy scene, with many features which a farmer of the early twentieth century would have found familiar.

Some of our ideas of life in Britain in the Iron Age have been turned upside down by recent research. For instance, population estimates keep rising. The latest is just short of 2,000,000 in the years immediately before the Roman annexation, which can be compared with the one to 1,500,000 estimated for the Saxon–Norman population at the time of the Domesday Book (1086 AD). The Domesday population used to be considered somewhere near the optimum that the country, given the agricultural techniques available, could support. Yet, according to Strabo, writing before the Roman invasion, Britain was able to export not only gold, cattle, hides, hunting dogs and slaves, but also grain. To feed such a teeming population and produce a surplus for export implies a flourishing and highly productive agriculture.

New evidence establishes that cultivation was more widely distributed than was once supposed. Far from being confined to the light and easily worked soils of, for instance, the chalk uplands and the shallow heaths of East Anglia, it had spread to the heavy lands of the Midlands, once considered to have been buried in forest. In Northamptonshire, a county which has been intensively studied by archaeologists during the past thirty or forty years, it has been shown that by BC 200 there was one village, hamlet or at least a farmstead per square mile—and this in an area which had been thought of as dense forest, as much of it was in medieval times.

It provokes second thoughts about the impact of the heavy Celtic plough on British farming. This plough, possessing a coulter to slice the soil in front of the ploughshare and a mould-board to turn the furrow, could plough deeper than any of its predecessors and could tackle the stiffest of clay soils. Being so heavy and cumbersome, it was drawn by a team of oxen, in some instances as many as eight animals. Because of the difficulty of turning an eight-ox team with a long plough dragging behind, the natural tendency was to plough as long a furrow as possible before turning. Hence a trend towards long, narrow fields, such as were commonplace in medieval times, and away from the square plots of Bronze Age farmers. The Celtic plough is supposed to have been introduced to Britain by the last wave of Celtic immigrants to invade Britain before the Roman conquest, the Belgae. This warlike tribe came from what is now Belgium and north-eastern France, and the heavy ploughs they brought with them are said, by Pliny, to have been invented in the Alpine provinces of the Empire 'at a comparatively recent period'. Writers of a generation ago confidently asserted that the great Celtic plough enabled settlers to farm land which it had never been possible to plough before. For this purpose, they said, great tracts of primeval forest were cleared and the area under cultivation vastly extended. Certainly this big plough was an important step forward, but whether there were any immense forests to be claimed at that period now seems doubtful.

In the last century before the Roman occupation a vigorous trade developed between south-eastern Britain and the ports of northern Gaul. Wine, glass and other luxuries from the Roman world were imported for the British aristocracy and a British coinage was minted to assist the trade. The export of gold, lead, tin and other metals helped the trading balance, but the awkward fact of that surplus of grain and cattle for export still puzzles archaeologists. How did a peasant community with relatively primitive tools manage to achieve it? We still do not know.

In addition to wheat and barley, oats, rye, beans and perhaps peas were introduced to Britain during this period. The wetter climate probably had much to do with the spread of oats as a field crop; oats are much more moisture-tolerant than wheat or barley. Rye is a 'poor-land' crop, sown usually where wheat or barley will not be successful, and evidence so far available indicates that it was not widely grown. The wider range of crops helped supply Iron Age farmers with coarse grains for feeding livestock, and cattle, sheep and pigs could now be kept in ever-increasing numbers. Horses were certainly used for food as well as riding. Domestic poultry was brought over from the Continent, though at first primarily for cock-fighting, which quickly became popular. Woad, for dyeing and probably tattooing, was most likely grown as a field crop (as it was on quite a large scale down to the nineteenth century).

Apart from ploughing, we know little about the preparation of the soil for a crop. No doubt primitive types of harrow were used and any surface stones removed by hand-picking. Some evidence of the spreading of farmyard manure as fertilizer over the fields has already been quoted for earlier periods, and by the first millenium BC the practice was probably widespread. The quantities of domestic debris, including pottery sherds, found in the fields seem to confirm this.

The Belgae in particular appreciated the merits of marling and chalking. In marling, a layer of light soil such as chalk is spread over the surface of a field of heavy soil in order to render it more friable and to help to release its latent fertility. Liming, or chalking, helps to reduce soil acidity, encourages the release of nitrogen, checks the spread of certain diseases, improves the texture of the soil and supplies calcium, an essential plant nutrient, in the form of calcium carbonate. In their territories the Belgic farmers extracted a fine, white type of chalk from deep pits. Pliny, writing of it in the first century BC, observed that the chalk was dug 'from a considerable depth in the ground, the pits being sunk in most instances as much as a hundred feet.

Ploughs with coulters and mould boards revolutionized farming.

These pits are narrow at the mouth, but the shafts enlarge very considerably in the interior, as is the case in mines. It is in Britain more particularly that this chalk is employed. The good effect is found to last full eighty years.' Some of these pits still survive, as the 'dene-holes' of Kent.

The system of alternate husbandry was almost certainly practised on many Iron Age farms. This means stocking a field as heavily as possible with grazing livestock for a period of years and allowing the animal manure to build up the fertility, then cashing in on the fertility by ploughing the field and sowing a cereal crop. Though again there is no direct evidence, the small size of many of the Iron Age fields and the availability of wattle-hurdles for penning sheep and cattle suggest that our Iron Age ancestors, skilful farmers that they were, would not miss such an obvious and beneficial practice.

At harvest-time the cereal crops were cut by iron sickles. Modern theory tends towards cutting only the ears, leaving the straw in the field. If so, the straw may have been cut at a later stage, for it was needed for bedding for livestock (and humans) in winter, and also for thatch (though in districts where reed was available that would be preferable).

While grain can be threshed by spreading the ears on a flat surface and driving animals to trample on it, the method is wasteful; threshing with flails is more efficient. The wooden arms of flails could not be expected to survive as archaeological evidence, but the traditional eel-skin thongs that bind the two pieces together are virtually imperishable, and it is surprising that none

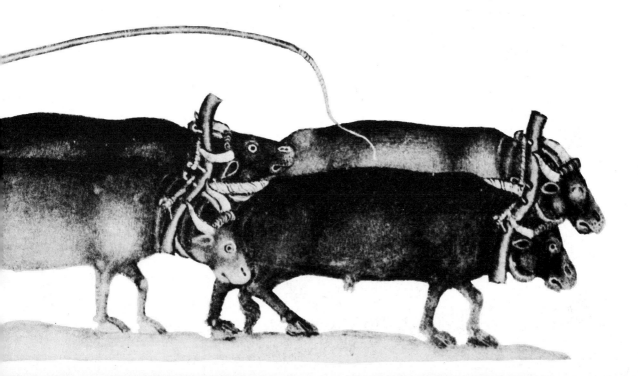

has been found—though perhaps archaeologists do not know what to look for.

As the climate got worse, the need arose to dry much of the grain before storing it. Various methods were employed. Some was dried on racks over a fire built on a stone hearth. Sometimes a handful of straw with ears attached was set alight, the flames being extinguished by careful manipulation before any damage was done to the grain. In some operations the degree of heat was sufficient to kill the germ of the grain so that it would not sprout in store. Much grain was stored in circular pits, which proliferate on Iron Age farm sites. Large pottery jars, barrels and containers slung from rafters or in lofts were also probably used as grain stores. The pits, some of them four or five feet across and eight or nine feet deep, were lined with straw or wickerwork. They normally lasted for four or five years and were afterwards used for dumping rubbish, to the great benefit of archaeologists. When the pits were in use they were efficiently sealed by a clay cap, the effect of which was to retain in the pit the carbon dioxide generated by the stored grain and prevent the multiplication of bacteria which would cause decay. In such a pit even seed grain could safely be kept through a winter in readiness for the spring seed-time.

The Iron Age saw an improvement in the techniques for grinding corn. Saddle querns were gradually replaced by rotary querns or hand-mills, in which an upper circular stone, fitted with a handle, is rotated around a spindle over another stationary round stone. Grain was poured in through a hole in the top of the upper stone, and the flour seeped out at the sides. The flour thus obtained was consumed either as bread or as some type of porridge or gruel. Almost certainly, though so far there is no conclusive evidence, some of the barley was used for brewing beer.

Although pots containing stews simmering on the stone hearth must have been a familiar sight in Iron Age farmsteads, the use of pot-boilers—stones subjected to an intense heat and then dropped into a container to heat it—was common. Bacon was preserved for winter use by both smoking and salting, and salt was a highly valued commodity. Butter was made, but there is some doubt about cheese. Pliny comments that 'the barbarous nations' of the north 'know how to thicken milk and form an acrid sort of liquid with a pleasant flavour, as well as a rich butter'. In other words, they were adept at making curds or yoghurt.

Hides are mentioned as one of the chief exports of Britain in the Iron Age, and the country had a long tradition in the use of hides and leather for a wide range of products. Containers of various kinds, ropes, whips, clothes and footwear are obvious artefacts demanding animal skins. Skins stretched over wooden frames made the familiar coracles, later associated largely with Wales; the larger ships of Rome and doubtless of the Veneti and other seafaring nations had sails of leather. For weaving, the Iron Age housewife possessed a loom frame of solid timber, with loom weights to keep the strands taut. To keep the cloth pressed into place during the weaving process she used long-handled combs, and doubtless she knew the value of teazel-heads for knapping cloth.

To the question, whom did Iron Age farms belong to?, we have to admit, we do not know. We cannot say whether the fields, houses, livestock and crops were individually or communally owned. The farm at Little Woodbury seems to suggest a patriarchal set-up, with a resident well-to-do family, whereas the Lake Villages of Somerset could easily have been communal settlements.

In the last century or so before the coming of the Romans the earliest embryo British towns started to appear. Some, such as Hod Hill (Dorset), Danebury (Hampshire) and Crickley Hill (Gloucestershire), are associated with a complex of small fields outside the encircling earthworks. The inference is that the farming folk carried on working their fields as usual but lived within the safety of the town walls. In some the houses were arranged in regular order, as in streets. The same concept, of going outside a defended group of homesteads to work in the fields, is also found in the Lake Villages.

We have to fit in, too, the fact that there were several social strata, and certainly at the lowest level there were slaves. Perhaps the pattern that best suits the evidence would be the clan system of the Scottish Highlands, or the African extended family where parents, grandparents, uncles, cousins and more distant relatives, numbering perhaps a hundred or more, sometimes live within an enclosing mud wall in a labyrinth of huts, rooms, corridors and courtyards covering the best part of an acre. Each individual has his or her own place in the community, with rights and duties, but has little significance outside it. Loyalty to the clan is everything (and in Africa surpasses loyalty to the new nations created in the present century). The arrangement seems to tally well with Caesar's observation on Celtic life: 'Wives are shared between groups of ten or twelve men, especially between brothers and between fathers and sons; but the offspring of these unions are counted as the children of the man with whom a certain woman has cohabited first.' But it by no means follows that women were an oppressed and inferior class, and the histories of the few women of the period whose names we know, including Queen Boudicca of the Iceni and Cartimandua, queen of the Brigantes (of northern Britain), certainly suggest the contrary.

4. The Roman Era

After the initial landing of the Roman legions in Kent in AD 43, it took the best part of forty years to consolidate the conquest and to extend the Roman frontier to the river Tyne, near which Hadrian's Wall was later to be built. As each new district or tribal area was taken over, however, the impact must have been traumatic. In particular, the imposition of strict Roman administration and organization must have been irksome, and, as always the lower social strata bore the heaviest burden.

When the dust had settled, those peasants who were not requistioned for slave labour were allowed to stay where they were and carry on with their farming as before. The main difference now was that the tax-collector sitting on their doorstep was a Roman, waiting to exact the share of their produce that the Empire demanded. What that share was depended largely on how much trouble the local inhabitants had given the army. For example, in the Cranborne Chase area, where the Durotriges and neighbouring tribes made Vespasian campaign for two summers before they were subdued, it has been estimated that about 60% of the yield went in tax, compared to the 8% or 10% which was the norm in the Roman world.

We have already remarked on the achievements of pre-Roman Britain in producing a surplus of grain and cattle for export, in spite of feeding a large home population. Under Roman rule the population of Britain rose even higher (as high as 3–4,000,000, according to some estimates), yet an even larger surplus was exported. For instance, in one year of the reign of the Emperor Julian (AD 361–2) no fewer than 800 shiploads of grain were sent to the Roman army in Gaul. The farmers of Cranborne Chase and other out-of-favour regions would probably have argued that the produce requisitioned from them was hardly surplus but was badly needed for their own consumption. Doubtless there would have been justification for that complaint, yet at Pitney (Somerset), Hambleden (Buckinghamshire) and other sites there is clear evidence of pigs having been fattened on barley, which would hardly have been likely if the grain was urgently needed for human food.

Apart from the Celtic peasant farms, four types of agricultural holdings

54

can be detected in Roman Britain. In order of importance, they were the private estates of the Emperor, the villa estates belonging to country gentry, the *coloniae*, or groups of farms occupied by retired soldiers, and individual farms also occupied by veterans from the army.

The private estates of the Emperor were administered by an official known as a procurator. The lands of any rebel chieftain or patriotic leader who did not immediately submit to the Roman Army were automatically forfeited to the Emperor, and, though subservient monarchs were often allowed to keep their domains for their lifetime, the same fate usually awaited their estates on their death. The revolt of the Iceni in East Anglia in AD 60 was caused by a ruthless attempt by Roman officials to take over the assets of the royal house after the death of King Prasutagus, husband of Queen Boudicca. Cogidumnus, the king of the Regnenses, who lived in Sussex, sided with the Romans at the time of the invasion and gave them valuable help. In return the Romans made him a client-king and even allowed him to enlarge his kingdom, but the eventual fate of his domain, after his death, was the same; it was absorbed into the imperial estates.

The villa estates are those that we hear most about. The Roman villa was a large country house; the nucleus of an agricultural estate, in fact it was the counterpart of the country estates of the landed gentry of the eighteenth and nineteenth centuries. Run largely by slave labour, it was managed by a *villicus* (bailiff) for an aristocratic owner who probably possessed a town house as well and who spent much time there. The residential quarters of the villa were in a luxurious block of buildings overlooking a courtyard, usually of stone or brick, roofed with red tiles. The house was normally heated by underfloor flues and had piped water and sewers. Hot and cold baths were regarded as essential. On the other sides of the courtyard, or around an outer courtyard, were the living quarters of officials and servants, also stables, cattle-sheds, granaries, store-houses, workshops, communal kitchens for the staff, sheds for other livestock and perhaps buildings for special operations such as weaving and dyeing.

It would, of course, be a mistake to suppose that the gentry who lived on these big rural estates were necessarily immigrants from Italy. The Roman Empire was cosmopolitan. Britons could find themselves in North Africa or Mesopotamia, while Syrians or Dacians (from modern Rumania) might settle in Britain without that sense of being in a foreign land which we would experience. On the whole, however, it is thought that by far the

Overleaf: reconstruction of a Roman villa, painted by Alan Sorrell.

greater proportion of rural landowners were native Britons, descendants of the old royalty and aristocracy. Tribal leaders who took pains to become Romanized, adopting ways and ensuring that their children had a Roman education, were rewarded by a title to estates which probably they had formerly held as trustees for the clan or community. After all, the Roman bureaucracy governed through them, much as the British did in India.

The third type of agricultural unit was the military colony or *colonia*. Veterans, when they had finished their army service, were given grants of land on which they were expected to settle down as farmers. In the *coloniae* the holdings were laid out in units of 200 to 240 acres, or sometimes in half-units. A *colonia* would consist of a considerable series of such holdings, arranged with military precision along straight roads which crossed each other at right angles. One of the earliest of the British *coloniae* was laid out, in the years AD 49–50, on the site of the old capital of the Trinovantes tribe, Camulodunum (Colchester). As it involved the wholesale confiscation of land and the dispossessed peasants had to work the new farms for the harsh veterans, the development was bitterly resented. It is no wonder that when the revolt of the Iceni occurred, the *colonia* of Camulodunum was one of its first targets, the new settlers being obliterated in a bloody massacre.

The *Agri occupatorii* were smaller but somewhat similar units for veterans in places where there was insufficient space for a full *colonia*. The ex-soldiers were given a team of oxen, the basic tools of farming and some seed corn and were then left largely to their own devices. They escaped the strict regimentation of the *colonia* but apparently possessed no special privileges over their peasant neighbours and probably within a few generations were absorbed into the general Romano-British populace.

While it seems that the Roman administration made little effort in the early years to teach native farmers improved methods of agriculture, being interested almost exclusively in the collection of taxes, the native aristocracy, in the process of becoming Romanized, must have picked up a lot of valuable new ideas from their new masters. The first generation of Romano-British estate-owners, and every subsequent generation till the final withdrawal of Roman arms in about AD 410, must have been familiar with, for instance, Virgil's *Georgics*. Virgil was himself a farmer's son, and, though written in limpid Latin verse, *The Georgics* was widely regarded as an agricultural text-book. Many of its observations are, of course, concerned specifically with Mediterranean lands, but others had and still have a general application.

Bearing in mind that a wide gulf existed between the farming practised on a prosperous Roman-type estate and that on a peasant holding, a perusal of

The Georgics gives a fair idea of the state of agricultural knowledge during the centuries when Britain was a province of the Roman Empire. Virgil noted, for example, the value of crop rotation, recommending that wheat is best sown after beans, vetches and lupins; though doubtless he was unaware that these leguminous plants manufacture nitrogen to enrich the soil. He held a summer fallow in high esteem.

> 'That land only
> Answers the greedy farmer's prayers, which twice
> Has felt the sun and twice the winter frosts.'

A two-year fallow is what he seems to have had in mind, which we would regard as extravagant.

The use of farmyard manure and wood ashes to replenish the fertility of the soil was evidently standard practice. So was seed selection. The farmer is urged to take pains to select the biggest seeds every year for sowing. Autumn sowing could begin at the time of the September equinox and continue until prevented by frost or rain. Thereafter as much ploughing as possible should be finished before winter set in.

> 'Your field is best when once made friable;
> This is the work of wind and chilling frost . . .'

Virgil says that after harvest it often pays to burn off the straw, thus anticipating a controversial modern practice. He believed that fire helps to dry the soil and open its pores, which is hardly how a modern farmer would describe the benefits of straw burning.

He describes the making of a plough, using elm for the stock, lime for the yoke and beech for the handles, all the wood being seasoned with heat and smoke. The plough, says Virgil, is equipped with *two* mould-boards, capable of ploughing a double ridge; in other words, it was a double-furrow plough, which on many English farms was regarded as an innovation less than a hundred years ago.

His recommendation that the soil should be well-broken with mattocks is a reminder that plenty of labour, usually slave, was available on the larger farms. For light harrowing he advises dragging osier hurdles over the fields, an operation would be effective though wasteful of hurdle-work. The heavy harrow, or *tribulum* (which gives us our word 'tribulation') was originally used as a threshing implement rather than as a tool for cultivation. It consisted of a flat sledge of wood into which iron spikes had been driven.

The other winter work on the farm which he describes includes the

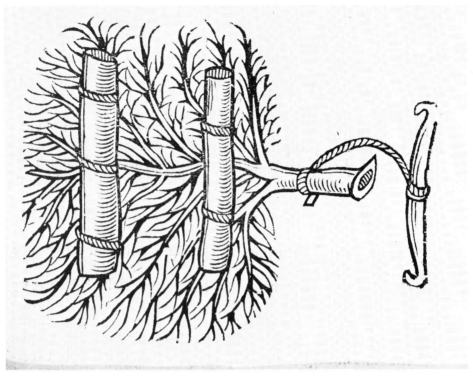

Both osier hurdles and branches were used for harrowing.

sharpening of blunted ploughshares, the branding of cattle, the roasting and grinding of corn, and the laying of live hedges. This last may have been borrowed from the Celts, for in his description of the Gallic Wars Julius Caesar notes with admiration his enemies' method of weaving hedges of living thorn-bushes, through which, he says, it was impossible to see, let alone to penetrate.

On the breeding, rearing and management of livestock the Romans were typically sound. The farmer should select his breeding stock according to the use he intends to make of the progeny, says Virgil. If he wants strong cattle to pull the plough, then he should choose dams and sires with strength and weight. He repeats the admonition for horses and sheep. Pick a foal, he advises, that steps high yet treads lightly on the ground and takes the lead when on the road. With sheep, if wool be your aim, select ewes 'that are both white and soft of fleece'. He advises, though, that rams with dark tongues should be rejected, 'lest the fleeces of your lambs be flecked with grey'—an opinion which a modern flockmaster would regard as decidedly doubtful. He also thinks that chestnut and grey horses are the best, white and dun ones the worst—again a distinction of doubtful validity. Cattle are best for breeding between the ages of four and ten years, he says, after which they should be discarded. (Nowadays, we tend to start earlier and finish earlier.)

Virgil gives useful advice on rearing and training young cattle, and on the humane breaking-in of young horses. Pat the neck of the young colt, he says, and give him 'words of flattering praise'. He also warns against foot-rot and scab in sheep and recommends that as a precaution their pens should be kept well-littered with straw or fern. Sheep should be regularly dipped as a protection against scab, and he gives recipes for several ointments for healing wounds and sores.

He describes a fearful epidemic that apparently occurred among farm livestock within his lifetime—plague, he calls it. Our medieval forefathers would have referred to it as the murrain. It 'brought death to multitudes and heaped the bodies rotting in corruption foul'. On no account attempt to make use of the flesh, fleeces or hides of affected animals, he warns. Bury them deep. And he gives a piece of advice that is now the basis of national policy for dealing with virulent livestock diseases:

'Check the disease by slaughtering before
The dread contagion spreads all unawares
Among your flock.'

Goats featured more prominently in the agricultural economy than they do now, their milk being made into cheese. Virgil recommends that 'whole armfuls of lucerne, with trefoil and salt-sprinkled herbs' be taken to the goat-pens rather than allow the goats free range for grazing. That, basically, is the principle of zero-grazing, now widely adopting for herds of dairy cattle.

He urges his readers to take care of their puppies, feeding them on 'meal and whey', the implication being that many farmers did not bother to feed their dogs but left them to fend for themselves. Dogs were apparently kept for two purposes—to guard the flocks and herds and to hunt wild game.

Of the four books which comprise *The Georgics*, Virgil devotes the second largely to trees and the fourth to bees. On both subjects he is well-informed. He gives detailed instructions for grafting and advises on the types of soil in which various species of trees do best. Evidently it was common practice to take pains over the cultivation of trees—and not only orchard trees—dunging them, digging in gravel and shells around their roots, cultivating the soil between them by ploughing and by work with the 'two-pronged hoe', and supporting young trees with stakes. His bee lore, too, is comprehensive and profound, illustrating the importance attached to bees and honey in the ages before cane sugar was known. Only professional bee-keepers would now have the intimate knowledge of bees which he expects the peasant farmer to possess.

From other literary sources further information is available on agriculture in Britain during the centuries of Roman rule. Palladius, who wrote in the fourth century, notes that stables should have floors of stout planks, to keep the horses' feet dry. They should face south and have a fire in winter. Towards the end of the Roman period horse-shoes probably began to be used; ox-shoes were in use rather earlier. The first horse-shoes were flat soles of iron, with attachments for fastening them. They resembled sandals and were called 'hipposandals'.

Though the evidence is meagre, it is probable that cattle in Britain were improved during the Roman period by the introduction of animals from

Wild cattle at Chillingham, Northumbria are thought to descend from Roman times. Thomas Bewick's engraving was made in 1789.

other parts of the Empire. It is alleged that the wild white cattle of Britain, of which small herds still survive at Chillingham (Northumberland) and elsewhere, are the descendants of white animals introduced by the Romans. It is interesting that in recent years the cattle population of modern Britain has been reinforced by the importation of several breeds of white cattle, notably the Charolais and the Romagnola, from southern France and Italy respectively.

Apparently a hornless breed of sheep, possible ancestors of the now popular Dorset Horn, were also brought in; also sheep with improved white fleeces, which needed to be shorn rather than plucked. Domestic poultry had been introduced shortly before the Roman occupation, though, as already noted, for cock-fighting rather than for meat or eggs. But the contents of rubbish-heaps reveal that it was not long before fowls were being eaten, and Palladius gives instructions for feeding hens, setting their eggs and treating their ailments. Looking after hens, in his opinion, was 'a woman's business', as indeed it was on English farms until after the Second World War. Cats are supposed to have been another Roman introduction, as were fallow deer and pheasants, though the last could have been of little interest to the average farmer.

The prime cereal crop was wheat (mostly of the variety known as spelt), but barley, beans, peas, vetches and oats were also grown. It seems that vetches were often sown with cereals as food for livestock, a practice which remained quite common until about the middle of the present century, a mixture of oats and vetches being known as dredge corn. Lucerne was regarded as an important fodder crop, and flax was cultivated both for its fibre and for its oil-rich seeds. Vineyards were certainly known in Roman Britain. In the first two centuries AD the weather was notably warm and dry, and though it later became wetter it was not necessarily colder. In the year AD 85 the Emperor Domitian decreed that all vineyards outside Italy were to be destroyed, but the edict was repealed in AD 280, having perhaps become a dead letter some time earlier, and certainly thereafter many vines were planted in southern Britain.

Medlars and improved varieties of cherries, pears, apples and plums were probable Roman introductions, as were walnut and chestnut trees. In the making of cheese the use of rennet, from the stomach of calf or lamb, had been discovered.

To Roman farming we owe our land measurement, the acre. The heavy plough introduced by the Belgae needed a team of eight oxen, but many Romano–British farmers preferred the lighter *aratrum*, which required only two. A small team such as this had to stop for a rest more frequently, and this eventually established the length of a furrow at 40 yards. A plot of land 40 yards by 80 yards was considered a good day's work for a two-ox team, and this became the Roman *jugerum* (our acre). The measurements have, however, been adjusted over the centuries, so that the *jugerum* would now be rather less than two-thirds of the statute English acre (now itself being superseded of course by the hectare). Side by side with the *aratrum*, the heavy *carruca*, or eight-ox plough, remained in use on the larger farms.

The introduction of the scythe, a Roman invention, represented a major advance, enabling a mower to cut grass and corn more efficiently, more quickly and nearer the ground. On the larger farms a system of underfloor heating (hypocausts) was used for drying corn in barns and was in common use in houses. The rotary quern was enlarged to become a slave mill, in which the grain was ground between two large, heavy stones. The upper one was turned by slaves pushing on projecting handles. Where slaves were scarce, or after the abolition of slavery, horses or donkeys were harnessed to the mills. The watermill was also a Roman invention, probably dating from the first century AD, though it was apparently not used to any extent in Britain until nearly the end of the Roman period.

South-east Wiltshire provides an interesting illustration of the contrasting economies probably typical of Roman Britain. To the north extends the undulating uplands of Salisbury Plain, characterized by thin, chalk soil. To the south, east and west lies an arc of woodlands, linking up with extensive forest country and eventually with the New Forest. Across the edge of the chalk lands runs the ruler-straight Roman road from Venta Belgarum

Scythes were probably introduced to Britain by the Romans.

(Winchester) to Sorbiodunum (Salisbury). On the heavy clay soil half-a-mile or so within the woodland frontier, the site of a small villa has been excavated. Two miles deeper into the forest country is another, somewhat larger villa. And two miles beyond that, on some of the best land in the district, was situated a very large villa which must have been the centre of a big estate. It is possible that one or both of the others were dependencies of the big one.

On the downland plateau a mile from the edge of the forest was a Celtic village, looking across a shallow valley to the road. It has not yet been excavated, but its graveyard has. Here were found the graves of a peasant people. Some were cremations, but the fact that the inhumations were coffined implies that these were independent peasants, for coffins would not have been wasted on slaves. However, only the minimum number of nails (six) were used per coffin, for iron was evidently too valuable to be permanently buried. The men were buried with their boots on—and slaves would have been unlikely to have boots; the leather had rotted but the hobnails survived. Apparently these villagers lived with violence and oppression; one young man had been decapitated and others had damaged limbs. On the other hand, there were several skeletons of aged persons, who had obviously been provided with enough food to sustain them through a long life. One was crippled by arthritis. All around the settlement are the still visible outlines of the small, rectangular fields which were cultivated by this community of peasant farmers.

From their hilltop these Celtic peasants could gaze down on the broad vale of the Deanbrook and the far more fertile fields of their rich neighbours. There in centrally heated houses the local Romano–British gentry enjoyed a vastly superior standard of living. While the peasants munched their coarse bread and barley bannocks or gulped down their bean broth, the villa aristocrats, having already eaten two meals during the day, would be reclining on their couches for dinner—a three-course or four-course repast starting with hors d'oeuvres such as preparations of oysters, eggs, salads, salted fish and fattened dormice and followed by a main dish of roast or boiled meat smothered in rich sauces. There might be several alternative main dishes, especially if guests were being entertained, for wild game as well as domestic livestock was abundant, and the lady of the house would take pride in serving such exotic dishes as peacocks, sucking pigs, snails fattened on milk, grossly fat pigeon squabs, hares stuffed with chicken livers and herbs, and honey-glazed ham. For dessert there would be pastries, sponge cakes, fruit cakes, baked egg custard, dried or fresh fruit, nuts with honey, and similar delicacies. The appropriate wines, sometimes mixed with honey, were served with each course.

A battalion of slaves were kept busy in the kitchens and outhouses preparing such a meal as this. Apart from imported delicacies, most of the food was produced on the home farm, and such basic tasks as grinding wheat into flour was done on the spot. Outside the immediate precincts of the villa the farm would have been staffed with equal lavishness, for the number of slaves kept not only ensured the maintenance of what the owner regarded as a proper standard of living but also served to reflect his opulence.

We may be certain that, in general, the burden of taxation fell more heavily on the independent peasants of the hill-top than on the wealthy farmers of the valley. Also that they were the community required to supply forced labour for the upkeep of the road. But would there have been no interchange of information about technical farming matters between the two neighbouring cultures?

In a somewhat primitive country in West Africa I came across a parallel state of affairs which may provide the answer. Outside one of the largest cities in that country an international organization had, at the invitation of the Government, set up a model agricultural settlement. Buildings, equipment, implements, livestock and management were all first-class, and Government officials took a pride in escorting visiting dignitaries around the place. Having inspected a number of the peasant holdings not far outside the boundaries of this impressive showpiece, I put to the principal a direct question: 'What impact does this place have on the peasants round about?' The principal was frank. 'None whatever!' he replied. 'They carry on the same as they have always done.' And that probably epitomizes the relationship between the villa estates and the peasant farms of Roman Britain.

The story of the huts on the Wiltshire downs and the villas in the valley has an almost inevitable finale. In both the downland cemetery and at the villa sites, numerous coins have been found. Most of them are of the early fourth century AD, of the Roman Emperor Constantine. But shortly after the middle of the century the series comes to an abrupt end: there is nothing later than the year 360. What happened is reasonably clear. In 367 the fringe nations which encircled Britain—the Picts, Scots and Saxons—launched their concerted attack on the province. While one group broke through Hadrian's Wall, others poured in from the sea on both the east and west coasts. They defeated and killed the Count of the Saxon Shore, who was in charge of the coastal defences, and then for a time Britain was at their mercy. For the best part of a year they ranged at will over the country, looting, killing and destroying. It is not difficult to imagine these wild, bloodthirsty men rampaging along the road between Winchester and Salisbury and fanning out to deal with the villas and villages in the vicinity. Probably they were joined by mutinous slaves on the estates, perhaps by the impoverished peasants of the downland village. It is likely that none of the inhabitants ever returned to their former homes for the history of both types of farm seems to end at that point.

But what fate actually befell the Romano–British population when the 'barbarians' eventually took over? One of the indisputable facts about those chaotic times is that the early Anglo-Saxons did not like towns. They were countrymen-farmers. What seems likely is that in many instances the surviving Romano-British retreated behind the walls of their cities, allowing the invaders to take possession of the countryside. Even then the Anglo-Saxons had little use for the existing farm buildings, the construction of which was so far beyond their capacity that they regarded them as the work of magicians and the abode of ghosts. Shunned and neglected, a farm site quickly became overgrown with nettles and brambles, then with bushes and trees, until it was obliterated by a dense wood. The fields of the farm were a different matter. Coming as they did into a countryside of fields, gardens, orchards and even vineyards, it seems both logical and probable that the Anglo-Saxons took over the cultivations where their predecessors left off, and it is reasonable to surmise that in many instances no real break in continuity in the use of land occurred between Romano-British times and ours.

Pig of primitive type closely resembles pigs of Iron Age and Roman era.

5. Growth of the Manorial System

The Anglo-Saxons who eventually took over the former Roman province of Britannia were both destructive and illiterate. They destroyed the Roman records and kept very few of their own. Their invasion of Britain was no grand military campaign such as that of the Romans, and, far from making themselves masters overnight of the land they coveted, they had to work at it piecemeal, year after year, century after century. The first onslaught occurred in the middle of the fifth century. Three hundred years later Wales, Cornwall, Cumbria and Strathclyd were still Celtic, and Anglo-Saxon England divided into six or seven independent kingdoms.

The countryside that the Saxons encountered had attained a high state of cultivation, as we have seen, and it is fair to conclude that some of the land had been producing farm crops for more than 3,000 years. It has been rightly asserted, too, that a man walking along one of the great Roman roads, or even a rural side-road, in the year 300 would have passed a village, farmstead, villa or human habitation of some sort every few hundred yards. But after the arrival of the Anglo-Saxons much of the country became derelict and depopulated. Forest reclaimed much land formerly under cultivation, becoming perhaps more extensive than it had been since it was first cleared by stone and bronze axes. References to dense woods inhabited by wild beasts and outlaws apply to every part of Britain, and pigs, which can get most of their living from woodlands, superseded cattle and sheep as the most numerous domestic animals. Six hundred years later when the Domesday Book was compiled, the total human population was estimated at 1,750,000—less than half the estimate for Roman times.

About halfway through the Anglo-Saxon period, most of the early village sites seem to have been abandoned. It is true that many of them were probably temporary—the community moved on when the fields began to show signs of exhaustion, as this was quite feasible as long as there was plenty of land. But migration was so pronounced around the beginning of the eighth century that archaeologists have given it a name, the Middle

Medieval 'open fields' can still be seen, as here at Laxton, Notts.

68

Saxon Shuffle. One of these abandoned villages has been excavated at West Stow in Suffolk, and from its imaginative reconstruction we are able to learn something about the lives and habitation of its occupants.

The houses, or log huts, excavated are of two types. The smaller and more numerous ones are grouped around the larger. The walls of the huts are of vertically split logs fastened tightly to a timber frame; the eaves of the thatched roof reach to within a few feet of the ground. Most of the huts were built over shallow pits, and it is suggested that these were originally covered with board floors. The larger rectangular buildings seem to be a prototype of the later hall of the lord of the manor—or thane, as he was called in Saxon times. It is surmised that early Anglo-Saxon halls or farmhouses tended to follow the pattern still familiar on the Continent of housing humans and animals under one roof. The most important livestock was generally housed

Grain was threshed with flails in autumn and winter.

at one end of the farmhouse or hall, while the farmer and his family occupied the other. In the smaller huts humans and animals may well have lived together; it helped to heat the place on a cold winter night. In the course of time a kind of ante-room was interposed between the living quarters and the animal stalls of the hall. Designed as a threshing-floor, where men with flails beat the grain from the ear in autumn and winter, it was called the 'threshold'. Grain was stored in sheaf or loose in a loft above the threshold and thrown down for threshing as required.

The livestock section of the hall had a row of stalls for the oxen along one side of a floor, probably of beaten earth, where the animals were fed. On the other side of the threshold the main room had the hearth in its centre, immediately below a hole in the roof through which the smoke escaped. On the far side was the store-house or buttery, perhaps partitioned off, and in better-class houses there was probably a retiring chamber for the women. Later in the period other refinements, such as a kitchen, a dairy and a malthouse, may have been added, but usually as separate buildings or perhaps lean-tos.

As West Stow belongs to an early phase of the Anglo-Saxon settlement it seems to have been established on a communal basis. Later each hut or homestead was set apart from the others and enclosed by a fence or hedge. The enclosure also included a rickyard, garden plots, outbuildings and perhaps an orchard. A thane's hall was surrounded by a stronger stockade.

During the dark centuries of turmoil that characterized the establishment of the Anglo-Saxon kingdoms, two events of maximum importance occurred which had a profound influence on the fabric of life in Britain. One was the conversion of the Anglo-Saxons to Christianity; the other, the invasion by Northmen or Vikings.

The break-up of the Roman Empire had left the Church the chief custodian of civilization. The majesty, the authority and, more particularly, the administrative and organizational genius of Rome were bequeathed to the Church. It was Pope Gregory I, one of the greatest of all the Church's organizers, who sent Augustine, Paulinus and other missionaries to bring the English kingdoms into the Catholic fold. The process by which this was achieved is veiled, but the organized pattern of village life which we find in subsequent centuries and which became the manorial system, bears Gregory's hallmark. Instead of impermanent settlements scattered haphazardly over the countryside, we suddenly find well-ordered villages, most of which have lasted to the present day. In the village community every person has his or her appointed place in a fairly rigid class-system. The village fields are arranged and farmed according to a similarly rigid programme. And in almost every instance feudal villages coincide with an ecclesiastical parish.

One can appreciate the appeal which such organization would have had to an Anglo-Saxon monarch striving to maintain authority over an unstable, heterogeneous kingdom and always in difficulties over collecting taxes and other dues. What suited the Church suited him—and it suited the Church to have ordered communities, each centred around a church, and a priest to whom the peasants could pay their tithes. What the peasants thought about the changes we shall never know. Quite possibly they viewed them with the same simmering resentment that the Iron Age Celts felt when the invading Romans began to organize them.

The second traumatic experience of the Anglo-Saxon period occurred in the 830s when the Danes started their raids on eastern and southern England. For the next 200 years or so they were a constant menace and for one brief period, in the year 878, they controlled the whole country except for a few islets in the Somerset marshes, where the West Saxon king, Alfred, was holding out. Eventually they were driven back but they settled permanently in the north-eastern half of the country, where the subsequent rural development proceeded on slightly different lines from that of the other half. The final act of the drama was of course the conquest, in 1066, of the entire realm by Vikings who had settled and lived in Normandy for two or three generations.

So we arrive at that monumental survey of England, the Domesday Book, ordered by William the Conqueror in 1086 to provide a complete record of the assets of his new kingdom. In other words, a comprehensive record of his *own* assets, for, according to William's theory, prevalent throughout feudal times, the entire kingdom belonged to him personally, and even the greatest lord held property solely by virtue of giving allegiance to the king. He could be and was dispossessed if he failed to toe the line. In turn the great barons demanded similar allegiance from their underlings, and the chain reached, with similar links, right down to the meanest serf.

The Domesday Book gives us an insight, unparalleled in any other country of that period, into the details of the social structure of England under the feudal system. It has indeed a double value for, as an aside to their main task, the commissioners who compiled it made comparisons with the previous reign, that of Edward the Confessor. For hundreds of English villages we are thus supplied with two detailed pictures, with a twenty-year gap between them.

The Domesday Book makes it quite clear that the new system, described in detail, did not differ greatly from the existing one. And though the Norman occupation was traumatic because it substituted a harsh alien aristocracy, speaking a different language from the native one, it did tighten up a system which had been operating pretty slackly. By committing everything to writing, the Domesday Book obviated too the chances of wriggling out of dues and obligations. Of the Domesday Book the chronicler states, 'It was so investigated that there was not one hide of land in England that he did not know who owned it, and what it was worth, and then set down in his record.'

The England of the Domesday Book is recognizable. Most of the places mentioned bear much the same names as they do at present. In very many instances individual farms or manors are identifiable, and from the Domesday base-line we can trace their history to the present day. For some it is even possible to work out an unbroken chain of owners. Let us look at some of the entries. Here is one for Broad Chalke, a large village in South Wiltshire, which Domesday calls *Chelche*:

> 'The Church itself holds Chelche. In the time of King Edward it paid gold for seventy-seven hides [see definitions of terms below]. There is land for sixty-six ploughs. Of this land there are in demesne ten hides, and therein are ten ploughs and twenty serfs. There are eighty-six villeins and fifty borders and ten coliberts having fifty ploughs. There are five mills paying sixty-five shillings, and twelve acres of meadow. The pasture is three leagues long and one league broad, and there is much woodland.
>
> Of the same land Girrard holds three hides. He who held them, in the time of King Edward, could not be separated from the Church. There are two ploughs. It is worth three pounds.
>
> The demesne of the Abbess is worth sixty-seven pounds.
>
> Of the same land Richard Poingient holds seven-and-a-half hides of the King. Of these Aileus held two hides, in the time of King Edward, and the men of the Church held the others, rendering services such as are due from villeins. The Abbess claims them. Richard has there five ploughs. And it is worth seven pounds.'

For Great Bardfield, in Essex, the entry runs:

> 'Half-hundred of Frossewella-Birdefelda was held by Wisgar for one manor and four hides; now it is held by Richard in demesne. Then twenty-four villeins, now twenty. Then and afterwards seven bordars, now twenty-two. Always eight serfs. Always four teams in demensne. Then and afterwards twenty-one teams (of the homagers), now nine. Wood for eight hundred swine; thirty-two acres of meadow; always two mills. Then four horses, now five. Then twenty-eight beasts, now forty-one. Then sixty

swine, now one hundred and seven. Then one hundred sheep, now two hundred. It has always been worth sixteen pounds. . . .'

For Rothwell, in Lincolnshire, which is in lands settled by Danes, some of the terms used are therefore different:

'In Rodowelle is one bovate of land rateable to gelt, and one sokeman there has one ox.' (This entry relates to property of the Bishop of Bayeux.)

'In Rodowelle Rolf has thirteen bovates and a half and the third of another bovate of land rateable to gelt. There is land for twice as many oxen. Durand has there one carucate—in demesne—and three sokemen with two bovates and a half of this land, and six villeins and one border with one carucate. There are eighteen acres of meadows. The annual value in King Edward's time was forty shillings; it is now thirty shillings.

In Rodowelle Grinchil and William have four carucates and one bovate of land rateable to gelt; the land is eight carucates. . . .'

There follow details of the holdings of three other named persons in the same parish.

So the tally goes on, for village after village, county after county. The picture we gain is of a highly organized society. Every person in it has his or her allotted place, from which escape is virtually impossible. And one thing that the Domesday Book makes clear is that the feudal system did not originate with the Normans. It was in operation long before they arrived. Yet it seems poles removed from the free adventurers who hired themselves to the Romano-British kinglets after the Roman legions departed, 600 years earlier. Do we detect here the organization of England initiated by Pope Gregory and his emissaries? It seems the likeliest explanation.

The terms used in the Domesday Book require explanation. A *hide* is a unit of assessment. The king on his peripatetic progresses around his realm expected to collect his dues in kind, so if an estate were assessed at, say, a hundred hides he knew approximately how much food he could expect to find there and therefore how long he could stay. Innumerable attempts have been made to reduce the measurement to something meaningful to us. One such attempt defines a hide as the amount of land needed to maintain a free family and its dependants for a year. Another, the amount of land a man and his family could cultivate annually, which is much the same thing. Yet contemporary documents quote examples of families managing on half-a-hide or even a quarter-of-a-hide. In Wessex at the time of the Domesday Book it seems to have been well-established that there a hide was equal to four yardlands of 30 acres each, which tallies quite well with the other definitions. Another subdivision of the hide is eight ox-gangs, the derivation being that as a hide is the amount of land that an eight-ox team can plough in a year, therefore one ox-gang is an eighth of that.

A *carucate* may be regarded as a synonym of a hide and was used primarily in the eastern districts of England settled by the Danes. The word is obviously linked with the *carruca*, the heavy eight-ox plough first introduced by the Belgae. A synonym for the yardland, or one-fourth of a hide or carucate, is a *virgate*. A *bovate* is synonymous with the ox-gang. A *demesne* was a manor or estate. A *league* varied considerably according to district but generally was about three miles. The Domesday Book also differentiates between meadows and pastures. *Pastures* were a parish's common land, where all free householders had grazing rights for their livestock. *Meadows* were areas, usually enclosed, of better grassland which were mown for hay and afterwards grazed, though perhaps by only one person's stock. They were valued highly.

Turning to the several classes mentioned in the assessments: A *villein* was technically a free man, usually holding a virgate or bovate for which, as a tenant, he paid rent either in cash or in service or in both. In the Danish districts he was known as a *sokeman*. A *bordar* was a step lower in the social scale; probably the equivalent of a cottager. He would have a toft or close behind his hut and the right to pasture a limited number of livestock on the common and to turn a few pigs to forage in the woods, but much of his time was spent working for the lord of the demesne. In all probability these tasks would be regarded as his obligations, for which he received no cash payment, but he would at least be fed.

Harvesting grain, as depicted in the fourteenth-century Luttrell Psalter.

Coliberts were ostensibly freed slaves. From the tenth century onwards it became fashionable for estate-owners to provide in their wills for the freedom of their slaves. In practice most of these men remained on the estate or in the parish, where they were subject to numerous duties and obligations, so that they were little better off.

Serfs were in effect slaves, tied to the land and bought and sold with it, though they possessed certain basic rights. By the time of the Domesday Book they were not an abundant class, but most manors had a few, though the general tendency was to get rid of them. The motives for doing so were not entirely altruistic, nor even out of a desire to obtain merit in the life to come. According to Wulfstan, Archbishop of York in the early eleventh century, a master was expected to supply each serf with two loaves of bread a day in addition to two good meals—an expensive obligation. The Church, too, encouraged the emancipation of serfs, partly because even the humblest free man was required to pay his dues to the church, whereas a serf was not.

A *ceorl* was a wide-embracing term covering any free peasant. A *geneat* was a completely free peasant, presumably free from birth. A *gebur* was a freedman now occupying a farm. A *cotsetla* occupied a position between a gebur and a serf.

Let us now look in more detail at one of the villages described in the Domesday Book. Broad Chalke (Chelche) will fill the bill admirably, not least because its lands have been occupied from the earliest times. The church referred to was represented by the Abbess of Wilton, one of the great landowners of the district. The £67 mentioned is a very large sum. The taxation assessment is for 66 ploughs, which, at the standard Wessex rate of 120 acres per plough, indicates a total of 7,920 acres for the parish. Its assessment in the reign of King Edward was 77 hides, or 9,240 acres, but whether it was considered over-assessed or whether it had lost some acres to a neighbour is not known. The Abbey has 1,200 acres in demesne, which implies that it retained the land in hand and cultivated it, with the aid of ten ploughs and twenty serfs. The fifty ploughs belonging to the 86 villeins, 50 bordars and 10 coliberts would be theoretically capable of cultivating about 6,000 acres.

It seems that Girrard holds three hides, or 360 acres, as a tenant of the Abbess, though now, with only two ploughs, he is cultivating only about 240 acres. As a direct tenant of the king, Richard Poingient, evidently a Norman, holds 900 acres. As he has five ploughs, he is presumably cultivating about 600 of those acres. Apparently there is some dispute about the ultimate ownership of part of the land, though the Abbess must have been ill-advised if she presumed to argue about it with King William.

76

The great wood would cover some 1,920 acres and probably extended over the southern hills into Cranborne Chase. (The several manors into which this parish was subdivided would eventually become villages, hamlets or large farms. Among them are contemporary Knighton, Stoke Farthing—Stoke Verdun in early days—and Gerardston or Gurston, which evidently took its name from the Girrard of Domesday.)

The holdings of all the farmers, from the Abbess down to the humblest colibert, consisted of one-acre strips in the two or three great fields into which the arable land of the parish was divided. This was the famous 'open fields' system of agriculture. For one of the early lessons learned by the Anglo-Saxon settlers was that land can be overcropped. They had found that if they kept growing crops on the same land year after year, yields diminished, so they divided the cultivated land round the settlement into two or three great fields, so that every two or three years one of them could be rested. Under the 'three-course system', which was by now standard in many districts, one of these vast fields was devoted to wheat, and another to barley, while the third lay fallow. And by a simple rotation of crops, each field had a fallow, every third year. (As late as the fourteenth century, however, the manor of Stoke Verdun was being run on a two-course system. During the fallow year the land was not entirely idle, for cattle and sheep grazed there on the grass which sprang up naturally.)

The strips into which the great fields were divided were long and narrow. According to a later ordinance (of the thirteenth century), they were 40 statute rods long, a rod being the equivalent of $5\frac{1}{2}$ yards. This produces a measurement of 220 yards, which was a furlong, or 'furrow-long', and which is supposed to represent the distance an eight-ox team could be expected to pull a plough without stopping for a rest. The strips were, under ideal conditions, four rods in width, or 22 yards, a measurement which became the English chain. An area 220 yards by 22 yards is 4,840 square yards, or one acre, which was regarded as a good day's ploughing for the team. These calculations should be regarded only as a kind of average; they must have varied considerably according to the stiffness of the soil, local custom and other factors. Again in theory, the strips held by each farmer were scattered about the great fields so that no two of them were contiguous. That way each farmer had his fair share of the best land and of the poorer stuff. In practice it must have been difficult to avoid allocating a big farmer, such as the Abbess of Wilton, strips adjoining each other. In Broadchalke, however, the strips are known to have been allotted on the runrig system, that is, by ballot each year.

A fairer division of land could hardly have been devised and it all worked passably well for a good many centuries; but it had one serious defect. It was too rigid. In the year when one of the great fields was devoted to wheat, every farmer had to sow with wheat every strip he held in that field. No exception was made except by general agreement. In later centuries, when horizons were expanding and farmers were becoming interested in new methods and crops the system proved a straightjacket; whatever improvements the more progressive farmers proposed were sure to be vetoed on the grounds that they did not conform with ancient custom.

Broad Chalke possessed only twelve acres of good meadow, which presumably was fertile grassland on either side of the pleasant little river Ebble, or Chalke. Between the arable fields and the woods lay an area of indeterminate size, uncultivated and regarded as 'common land'. Here, as in the arable fields, the rights of each villager were strictly defined. The number of livestock he was allowed to keep there was rigidly regulated, as were the rights of *estovers* (the gathering of wood), *turbary* (the cutting of turf), *denbera* or *pannage* (pigs foraging in woodlands), *house-bote* and *hay-bote* (the taking of wood for specific purposes, such as the building of houses and the making of ploughs), and the rights to gather bracken, heather, furze, peat, clay, nuts, berries and even building stone and mineral ores.

Just how the rights were defined and allocated is not known but those few which survive to the present day suggest that there were many variations. At Cricklade, in north Wiltshire, for instance, every householder was entitled to turn out nine head of cattle to graze in a certain meadow from August to February and thirty sheep from September to February. In the New Forest common rights were in some instances attached not to individuals, families or even holdings but to certain chimneys and hearthstones, which could not be destroyed or rebuilt without the rights being forfeited. Common rights in Epping Forest were preserved in the nineteenth century by the determined action of a labourer, Thomas Willingale, who in 1866 successfully maintained his ancient right as a commoner to lop the hornbeam trees.

The system that prevailed at Broad Chalke was probably the one which survived in much of Wiltshire till the end of the eighteenth century, when it was described by Thomas Davis, who compiled the first full survey of the county's farming for the recently-formed Board of Agriculture in 1811. According to general practice, he says, each parish had a common herd of cows and a common flock of sheep. Beginning early in May the cows spent the summer in the charge of an appointed cow-herd. All day long they fed on the open downs, which were common land, returning to the village in the evenings, except in the heat of summer, when the procedure was reversed. After harvest they grazed with the sheep on the stubble-fields until about Martinmas (November 11th), when the herd broke up and the cows were returned to their individual owners, who kept them in straw-yards throughout the winter.

The sheep also ran in a common flock, under the control of a common shepherd, and grazed the unfenced downs in summer. When they had access to the ploughland, after harvest and before seedtime, they were evidently penned in folds, for the value of sheep dung on arable land was recognized. When the sheep required hay, with the advent of winter, 'every commoner finds his own fold and his own hay, but the common shepherd feeds and folds the whole'. Davis comments, however, that in his day the system had proved unsatisfactory because of the 'neglect or partiality' of the shepherd.

From earlier sources we glean further details of the life of the shepherd and

Wattle sheep-pens, shown here in the fourteenth century, are still in use.

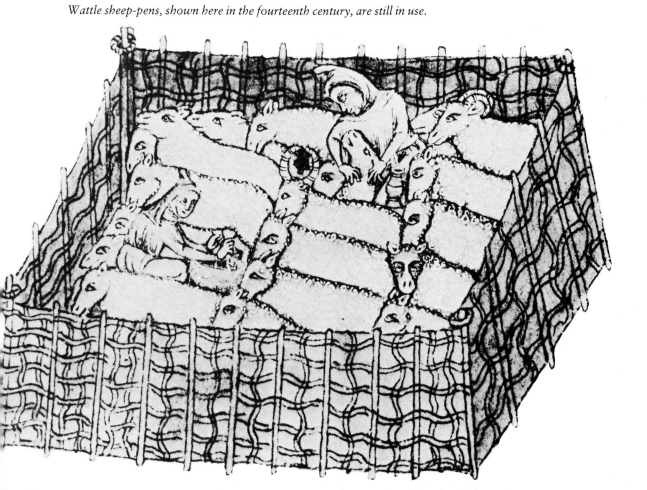

his flock. In Saxon and early Norman times he was probably one of the lower-class peasants whose tiny holdings were inadequate to provide a living, or he may even have been a serf. He led the sheep out to pasture every morning, stood guard over them all day (with fierce dogs to ward off wolves) and brought them back to sheds in the village each evening. He milked the ewes twice a day and made butter and cheese. In the dark, hungry days of winter, when wolves were a menace, someone had to stay on guard in the sheepfold all night, and in this task the shepherd was assisted by other peasants or serfs, by rote. The shepherd enjoyed a number of perquisites. He was entitled to a lamb and a fleece annually, all the milk from the entire flock for seven nights after Midsummer, and a bowl of whey every evening during the summer. He also possessed the right to pen the sheep on his own land for twelve nights at midwinter (evidently the twelve nights of the winter holiday).

The oxherd was distinct from the cowherd. His was a night-shift. The oxen worked in the fields all day, drawing ploughs or carts, and when they had finished their stint they were handed over to the oxherd, who took them to pasture and had the duty of standing guard over them all night. In the early morning he brought them back to their stalls and saw that they were fed and watered before the ploughman called for them. In winter the oxen remained in the stalls all night, but the oxherd still had to be with them. Caedmon, the first known English poet, who died about 680, was an oxherd;

Medieval cattle were kept primarily for draught purposes and for meat.

80

he was first inspired to compose his poems by a vision that came to him when settling down for the night in the ox-stalls.

Unlike the shepherd, the cowherd did not make butter and cheese; that was the duty of the cheese-maker, who was female. The cheeses she made were for the lord's household, but she was allowed to keep for herself the buttermilk or whey, after the shepherd had had his ration. She also made butter from the curds strained from the cheese, a practice still followed by some farmhouse cheese-makers today. As for the cowherd, his perquisites included the milk from each old cow for seven days after calving and from each heifer for fourteen days after calving. The cows were milked twice a day for most of the year but three times a day in May.

In most parishes the swineherd was a fairly important person, commensurate with the importance of pigs in the Anglo-Saxon economy. The change in pig-keeping practice reflects the development of village life during the Saxon and early Norman period. At first the pigs were probably half-wild, finding their own living in the forests where wild boars mated with the sows. But as forests came under the control of the community, the pigs' foraging expeditions were proscribed, and the animals had to spend more and more time in their sties. The swineherd seems, like the shepherd, cowherd and oxherd, to have had charge of all the animals in the village. In some places a class of tributary swineherds grew up, the lord of the manor or perhaps all the village farmers supplying the swineherd with a herd of pigs on a share-cropping basis. The swineherd looked after them and kept a proportion of the young pigs as payment. He also killed and dressed the pigs and converted them into ham and bacon, and, in return for this service for his neighbours, he was allowed to keep the 'chitterlings'. In Saxon times the pigs were allowed in the woods from August 29 till the New Year, but later the period was gradually restricted until it became only six or eight weeks in October and November.

Modern pig farmers know that one criterion by which their animals' carcases is assessed is the thickness of back fat (a measurement which can now be made on living pigs electronically). Surprisingly, the same criterion was applied at the time of Alfred the Great, and lords of the manor adjusted their tolls for all pigs foraging in the woods in accordance with thickness of the back fat. The lord claimed a third of the pigs which had put on back fat to the thickness of three fingers, through feeding on beech-nuts and acorns; he claimed a quarter of those with back fat of two fingers' thickness, and a fifth of those with back fat thickness of a thumb.

The Domesday Book records goats on many manors, and these, too, were kept on a common basis, with a goat-herd in charge. Evidently they were milked, and the kids reared for table. A coarse cloth was woven from their hair. For some reason, however, goats became less popular as the centuries passed.

The general lack of controlled breeding of all livestock probably meant that horses of the period were small. The old Celtic custom of turning horses loose where the mares could mate with any stallion they happened to find was widely practised, and their progeny were rounded up as required. King Athelstan (895–939) imported some breeding horses from Spain, but any benefits they conferred were doubtless limited to a few top studs. The Norse and Danish invaders made greater use of horses than did the Saxons. One of their sports was the staging of fights between stallions.

Few farm horses are mentioned in the Domesday Book, but as England settled down under Norman rule they became more plentiful and so available for wider employment. Writing in about 1174, William Fitz-Stephen noted that every Friday a sale of horses was held at Smithfield (London). While one part of the field, he said, was reserved for 'sumpter horses, costly chargers and horses fit for esquires', in another could be found 'the mares fit for the plough, dray and cart, some big with foal, and others with their young colts closely following.' They shared their side of the field with 'swine with long flanks, cows with full udders, oxen of bulk immense, and woolly flocks'.

Geese were kept as a common flock on the commons, and were watched over by a goose-herd or a goose-girl. Domestic hens, on the other hand, were confined in poultry yards adjoining almost every peasant house. Looking after them fell to the lot of the housewife, except at the manor house and the larger farms, where a dairymaid had to fit it in with her other duties. According to one contemporary author a hen should lay 115 eggs a year, while another puts the total at 180—not far from the quota to be expected from free-range hens today. Ducks do not feature in contemporary tallies of poultry but by the late thirteenth century many manors were keeping peacocks, swans and pigeons. The peacocks and swans were fattened in coops, while the pigeons had special dovecotes, some of which still survive. The pigeons living there often numbered thousands, and, as they were supposed to feed without molestation on the parish fields, they must have been a sore trial to the peasant farmers, who were obliged to watch impotently their harvest disappearing into the maws of greedy birds.

Bees were much more important in the rural economy than they are now, being virtually the only source of sweetness in the villagers' diet as well as, doubtless of greater significance from the villagers' point of view, an essential ingredient of mead. The village beeward was sometimes a serf, sometimes a tenant farmer who hired the hives from the lord of the manor in return for a share of the honey. Perhaps of equal importance to the honey, by medieval standards, was the beeswax, which was needed for church candles. This usage was explained in an ancient Welsh code of laws which asserted that 'the origin of bees is from Paradise . . . God conferred blessing upon them, and therefore the mass cannot be sung without the wax.'

The most numerous workers in the village, were, of course, the plough-men, of whom, as we have seen, there were sixty-five on the Abbess's land in Broad Chalke. They would include many free farmers but also some men of lower castes, right down to the level of serfs, and even the free farmers had certain duties to perform to the lord of the manor—in this instance, the Abbess. So it seems likely that we can take the ploughman's lament from *Piers the Plowman*, set down by William Langland in the fourteenth century, as being true for earlier ages:

> 'O, my lord, I labour hard; I go out at daybreak in order to drive the oxen to the field, and I yoke them to the plough. There is not so stark a winter that I dare stay at home, for fear of my lord, but having yoked the oxen and fastened the share and coulter to the plough every day I have to plough a full acre or more . . . I have a certain boy driving the oxen with a goad who is also hoarse from cold and shouting . . . I have to fill the stalls of the oxen with hay, and water them and carry out their litter . . . Indeed it is a great toil . . .'

To this, as to his other complaints, Piers the Plowman adds as a refrain, 'because I am not free.' The restriction on his freedom is the greatest hardship he has to bear, and we may be sure that generations of similarly oppressed Anglo-Saxons felt the same.

For lighter work, horses began to replace oxen on medieval farms.

83

Weaving was women's work, as was dyeing cloth, milking cows, making cheese, cooking, and tending poultry and children.

The ploughmen and the stockmen who had charge of the various classes of livestock by no means exhausted the number of specialists whose services were required in the Anglo-Saxon village. There were smiths, carpenters, builders, wheelwrights, thatchers and probably masons, while indoors women worked at weaving, dyeing, making herbal medicaments, grinding corn, making bread, gardening, brewing, cooking and tending poultry, as well as rearing children. The peasant farmer's wife must have been as busy as farmers' wives have been in every age, though the higher her social class the more underlings she had to help her.

As the taming of the forest proceeded, the woodward, who had charge of all the wood growing there, both timber and underwood, assumed increasing importance. It was he who allocated to individual farmers the wood needed for fencing, building and fuel. He also ensured that they turned loose in the forest only the number of animals for which they had a customary right. In many villages a hayward was responsible for the upkeep of hedges and fences. (Each of the peasants was required to do a stint at hedging, but the hayward had to ensure that they did it.) Above all was set the reeve, the man in ultimate authority. He is not to be confused with the bailiff, who was appointed to look after the lord's interests and was directly responsible only to the lord. Theoretically the reeve was the champion of the villagers, against the lord if necessary. He was chosen from among their numbers, though whether by any democratic process seems doubtful. His duty was to see that the affairs of the village ran smoothly and that everything was ordered fairly and according to custom. Every detail, from the maintenance of farm implements to the allocation of individual duties, from checking the supplies of bacon and ham to the control of vermin, came under his supervision. A conscientious reeve must have had an almost impossible task.

Although the great arable fields of the Anglo-Saxon village were devoted to a few major crops, notably wheat, barley, oats and beans, many minor ones were also cultivated, mostly on private plots. In the gardens were cabbages, leeks, lettuce, peas, parsnips, onions, turnips, garlic and several herbs. The art of growing the vine had survived from Roman times, and vineyards were quite widely tended by the Anglo-Saxons. Flax was well-known and valued both for fibre and seed (which produces linseed oil). Woad and madder were cultivated, their roots used for dyeing. Anglo-Saxon village communities were, indeed, so nearly self-sufficient that for many of them the only commodity they had to import was salt.

The hard labour of the fields, about which the Anglo-Saxon peasant so consistently complained, was punctuated by a series of holidays, or holy days, many of which had been pagan festivals long before the Church appropriated them. The festival of the winter solstice became, under ecclesiastical direction, the feast of the birthday of Christ, and those in modern times who deplore the merging of Christmas and the New Year to form one long, extended holiday should take note that in Anglo-Saxon and medieval times, and even beyond, the Christmas celebrations traditionally lasted for twelve days. They culminated in the Twelfth Night celebrations, some of which survive. After that followed yet another festival—Plough Monday—when the plough was fetched from the shed where it had spent all Christmas and was ceremonially blessed by the priest. One hardly knows whether to commend the villagers for making the start of a new season's work a matter for celebration or to admire their ingenuity at making the festival an excuse for yet another day's holiday.

Candlemas Day, February 1st, was derived directly from Imbolc, a Celtic lambing festival. Shrove Tuesday, or Pancake Day, which marked the beginning of the arduous season of Lent, required time off for merry-making, processions and such sport as hurling matches and street football. Village feasts marked the festival of Easter and the now obscure one of Hock-tide at the following weekend. May Day was entirely pagan but had too strong a hold on people to be shaken off by the disapproval of priests. Unashamedly a

fertility festival, one of its prime features involved young men and girls spending the night in the woods, for obvious purposes.

Rogationtide (the beating of the bounds), Ascensiontide and Whitsuntide afforded welcome breaks from labour during the long summer days, and the Church did its best to Christianize the old summer solstice celebrations by appropriating Midsummer Day to St John the Baptist. The old Celtic quarter-day of Lugnasad (August 1st) became Lammastide, the feast of the first-fruits. Harvest Home was a natural occasion for rejoicing, and many old customs associated with it are still remembered. Michaelmas saw the disposal by sale of surplus livestock born during the year, while Martinmas (November 11th) is associated with the slaughter of the remainder of the surplus stock, as there would not be enough food to see them through the winter. The old Celtic Samhain, when the veil between the visible world and the realm of ghosts and spirits wore very thin, became the Christian festivals of All Souls and All Saints, more popularly known as Hallowe'en. Needless to say, the celebrations followed much the same programme as they had always done. And so the circling year arrived at Christmas once again. As well as these major festivals, the Church sprinkled the calendar with numerous saints' days, so, by and large, the villagers of Anglo-Saxon and early

Blessing the crops at Sneaton Castle near Whitby, May 1947. An annual event in medieval times, the custom is probably rooted in pre-christian fertility cults.

medieval times fared not too badly for holidays, even if they did not have every weekend off.

It is worth remembering that, owing to the inordinate length of time the Anglo-Saxons needed to push their way across Britain, much of the country still remained Celtic for several centuries after the first Anglo-Saxons settled in the east. By the time the newcomers eventually penetrated deep into the west they had become Christians, and their wars with the Celts had become wars between Christian states, whose traditions were beginning to merge. Therefore, in at least one-third of the country, the old Celtic way of life still prevailed.

The chief difference between the Anglo-Saxons and the Celts was that the latter, due to the hillier countryside and the damper climate, followed a primarily pastoral economy. Cattle and sheep were more abundant than arable fields, and cattle were often used as currency. The practice of transhumance took the flocks and herds in summer to the mountains and hills, or in Somerset to the lowlying flood-plains that were under water in winter, where their attendants lived in simple temporary shelters or 'bothies'. Otherwise agricultural practice did not differ greatly from that of Anglo-Saxon villages. The best and most level lands were cultivated, some by the heavy eight-ox ploughs, some by lighter implements. Pigs were abundant but of indifferent quality. Horses, as in Anglo-Saxon communities, were turned loose in the forest to breed. Cats, relative newcomers, were highly valued; any hardy individual misguided enough to kill a cat in a royal barn had to pile up grain (his own of course), around the cat suspended from a beam by its tail, with the nose just touching the floor, until the very tip of the tail was covered.

Game of many kinds was extremely plentiful in the Celtic west, and hunting it seems to have been entirely unrestricted, for almost everyone, even serfs, were allowed to carry a hawk.

The prevailing atmosphere of both Anglo-Saxon England and Celtic Wales around the beginning of the present millenium seems to have been casual and kaleidoscopic. Laws existed but were applied haphazardly. Local custom was far stronger than any legal code. Peasant farmers went about their daily life, ploughed their land, harvested their crops, manipulated their livestock and complained about everything, much as their ancestors had always done. The framework of the feudal system had evolved but the rigid regimentation which characterized that system in the early Middle Ages lay ahead.

6. *Rise of the Independent Farmer*

Although the feudal or manorial systems was still functioning efficiently in the early Middle Ages, some of the factors which were eventually to destroy it were already at work. These included the principle of primogeniture, which gave rise to a class of landless younger sons; the increasing population, owing to peace in England; the opening of new horizons, largely due to the Crusades; the growth of England's trading interests; and the continued worsening of the climate. Finally there occurred the Black Death, a devastating visitation of bubonic plague in 1340 and succeeding years. The horrific mortality certainly relieved the pressures on land, which had become chronic, but it also created a situation in which the survivors were no longer prepared to remain on their native manors, being often able to migrate to wheverever the best terms were offered.

Saxon custom was for a man's property to be equally divided among his children at his death. That shrewd king, William I, spotted its weakness. The entire realm was bound to him by the bonds of service and many a lord held a manor on condition that, when required, he would supply a stated number of soldiers to serve the king. What would happen if, after several generations, an estate became so divided that none of the segments into which it had been split was large enough to support a single soldier? Primogeniture was an obvious solution to the problem. Let the eldest son inherit the estate intact. The change was introduced gradually, but by the time of Henry II it had become recognized as the custom.

What, then was to happen to the younger sons? They became warriors, and if under Henry I and Henry II's reigns there was no fighting in England, there was plenty on the Continent. What could be more natural than for unemployed younger sons, equipped with martial skill and training, to offer their services overseas, either to the king in his numerous wars or as mercenaries? With these ambitious young knights went squires and attendants—village lads with whom they had grown up—many of them younger sons too, who lacked an inheritance.

Simultaneously, trade with the Continent was steadily increasing. Merchants bringing cargoes of luxuries for barons and bishops were becoming rich themselves. A new middle class was coming into being, and the younger scions of the nobility were not adverse to marrying into it. The old, strictly-regulated feudal system of rights and obligations according to class and custom was beginning to crack and split under the new pressures.

Another upheaval was due, ironically, to the Church. After the Norman invasion, swarms of clerics had followed the army into England and soon they replaced Anglo-Saxons in key positions, from abbacies and bishoprics down to parish level. The first of the Continental monastic orders to gain a foothold was the Cluniacs, who established scores of monasteries and priories, most of them small, during the first century of Norman rule. While the monks of Cluny were other-worldly, spending their time praising God in perpetual choirs, the Cistercian monks who followed them in the twelfth century were a very different lot. Their outlook on life was puritanical. All luxuries and wealth were forbidden to them. They collected no tithes or other dues and would accept no gifts of manors to provide them with an income. They denied themselves warm clothing, cloaks, bed-clothes, even combs, and had to spend their hours growing their food, studying the Scriptures and praying. Inspired by such ascetic motives the Cistercians sought the wildest and loneliest places for their settlements. By clear streams in desolate valleys they established the great abbeys of Fountains, Rievaulx and Kirkstall. Their impact on the rural scene should have been entirely

Rievaulx Abbey, Yorkshire, one of the great Cistercian monasteries.

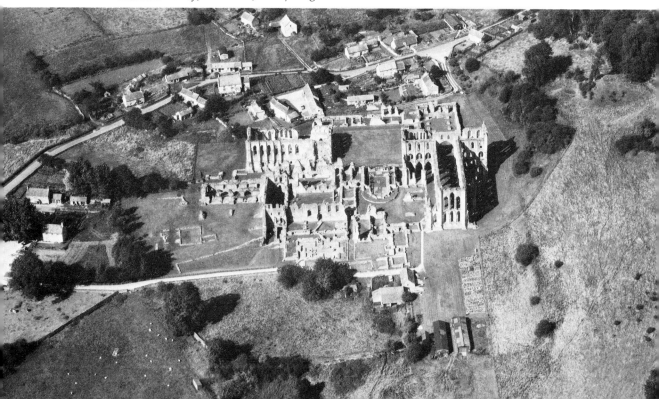

beneficent, and in many instances it was, but as the order became popular, wealthy landowners began to give properties which were not wildernesses, and which the Cistercians deemed it their duty to *make* into wildernesses. They accordingly depopulated villages, pulling down houses and even churches and evicting the tenants. Modern researchers have identified thirteen villages in Yorkshire alone which were demolished by the Cistercian abbeys and a further fifty or so which may well have been. Work in other counties, including Leicestershire and Oxfordshire, has established similar evidence of destruction.

A further development was their establishment of *granges*. As the Cistercian establishments acquired more and more land, some of their properties were at considerable distances from the mother abbeys. The authorities were in a dilemma, for they were forbidden to draw rents from tenants. They solved the problem by creating what were in effect large farms on their distant properties and staffing them with lay brothers. These were usually penniless labourers, who did not aspire to become monks. Night and morning they said brief prayers in the abbey church, but for most of the time they were kept hard at work. In order that their minds should not be distracted they were allowed no books and were kept deliberately illiterate. Many flourishing manors ended their career as granges, their former inhabitants either dispersed or perhaps, in some instances, remaining to till the accustomed fields as lay brothers for the monks.

What agricultural product were wildernesses best suited to? The answer, early arrived at, was wool. In consequence, the great Cistercian abbeys, and many other religious houses that followed their example, became sheepmasters. Immense flocks of sheep, cared for by the lay brothers, grazed over their extensive lands, and, as the wealth of medieval England became more and more bound up in the wool trade, the abbeys accumulated enormous riches.

But while the monasteries were consolidating large tracts of land for sheep-grazing and ousting whole communities in order to pursue that wealth-producing enterprise, the worsening climate was steadily making more and more land untenable. The rain-sodden upland fields no longer produced worthwhile crops, forcing cultivation steadily downhill. In the dales of Yorkshire, for instance, traces of medieval fields are to be seen far higher up the hillsides than the cultivated fields of today. Nor were lowland regions immune. Heavy, sticky clays in particular became almost permanently waterlogged, resulting in entire villages being abandoned. In Norfolk and Lincolnshire there seems to have been a widespread movement from the heavier to the lighter soils.

Yet, in spite of every adversity, the population of England increased. Having fallen drastically during the Dark Ages, it had climbed by slow and painful stages, to an estimated 1,750,000 at the time of the Norman Conquest, but during the next 280 years it more than doubled itself, and estimates of it in 1340, on the eve of the Black Death, range between 3,700,000 and 4,600,000. A population of around 4,000,000 was somewhere near the maximum that the country could be expected to support. Even Roman Britain, with all its efficiency, had done no better. As already noted, in Roman times lowland Britain was intensively cultivated, with farms and villages every few hundred yards along the highways and byways and with large areas of former fenland tamed and growing crops. In medieval England the fens had long ago lapsed into their former amphibious state, and now the climate was driving farming communities from the hills and from the more difficult lowland soils.

Inevitably the pressures on the available land grew steadily worse. The commons and woods which surrounded most villages were obvious targets for sacrifice. Many manors carved new open fields out of their commons and wastes. As a result, new restrictions had to be imposed on the use of the common land that remained, and many of the local by-laws regulating the number of animals and the other rights enjoyed by individual persons or holdings on the commons date from this period. The stage was being set for the wholesale enclosures of a later age, and these early attempts met with the same resistance as those of the eighteenth and nineteenth centuries. Peasants clung tenaciously to their customary rights, even to the extent of engaging in violence. In 1306 villagers of Potter Hanworth, in Lincolnshire, accused of stealing fruit and pulling up cultivated plants on fourteen acres of recently enclosed land, retorted that they were only maintaining their traditional rights on the common.

Lords of the manors were not the only class engaged in land enclosure. Almost everyone was at it. The records of the time are crowded with details of lawsuits about illegal enclosures. In 1269 in the Forest of Gillingham (Dorset) it was stated that 'Peter de la Babent occupied anew at Gillingham one acre of land of the Lord King and built upon it a house and enclosed the rest with a ditch and a hedge'—no doubt without permission. In 1273 a new and vigorous king, Edward I, ordered a survey of all the enclosures and encroachments which had been made in Windsor Forest during the reign of his predecessor and was astonished at the length of the list. He confiscated all the unauthorised ones.

A tiny example of enclosure, witnessed in my own Wiltshire village in the

1920s, must have been typical of what went on in previous centuries. The local thatcher, living in a cottage by the village green, began to store his spar-gads (the hazel rods from which he fashioned the spars to peg his thatch) on a section of the green. After doing so for several years he decided to put a cover over them, a roof of thatch. Then he erected a fence around them, to keep passing cows from tossing them about. No one interfered with him or raised any objection, so he extended the fence to include a little garden plot. 'That is how all the houses on the south side of The Green began,' my father told me. 'Householders on the other side of The Green enclosed bits of land and, when they found they could get away with it, took a little more and a little more and eventually built sheds on it and then replaced the sheds by cottages. But it was all once common land.'

There used to be a commonly held tradition that if a squatter could build on common land a house with a chimney and light a fire on the hearth within twenty-four hours he was entitled to keep it and live in it and also retain as much land as he could fence in within the same twenty-four hours. Probably many squatters got away with it in medieval times, as some did in the New Forest as recently as the nineteenth century. Those who tried it and failed were probably not deterred from having a second attempt.

A surviving item of evidence of the land pressure in medieval times is provided by the hillside terraces known as *lynchets*. Usually following the contours of steep scarps, they were evidently deliberately made. Though it is difficult to date them, some are prehistoric but others were created in medieval times. One can imagine land-hungry farmers, having claimed for the plough every acre of other land within their borders, undertaking the onerous task of carving level strip-fields on the hill slopes.

The ever-increasing population seemed likely to produce a major disaster, and how things would have worked out if the Black Death had not intervened, with devastating severity, is difficult to visualize. Famine and revolution seem possibilities. Under the circumstances, the epidemic served to give society a breathing-space, though at a tragic cost. More than any other single factor, it caused the collapse of the feudal system. Contracts of fealty and hierarchic obligations went by the board. Even the old methods of agriculture, such as the shared cultivation of open fields which had characterized farm life for so many generations, were largely abandoned.

The Black Death was bubonic plague (*Pasturella pestis*), associated in many instances with pneumonic plague, and in some instances with septicaemic plague. Its vectors were fleas, carried by black rats. For some reason, perhaps prolonged drought, in the decade preceding the appearance of the

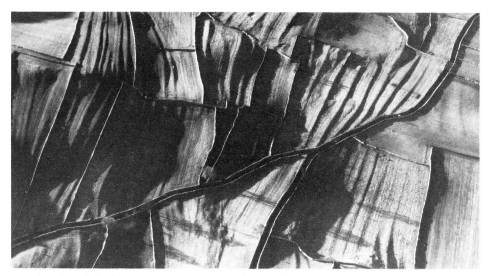

Strip lynchets, hillside terraces at Linton, North Yorkshire.

epidemic in Europe a massive migration of rats south-westwards from their home in Central Asia seems to have occurred. By the end of 1346 the plague was raging in the Near East where, since the First Crusade, an abundant maritime trade with the ports of western Europe had existed. By midsummer 1348 the Black Death had spread across much of southern and central Europe.

The first case recorded in Britain occurred in the port of Melcombe Regis, now incorporated into Weymouth, in June 1348. The epidemic swept quickly across the country, reaching the north by the middle of 1349. By the end of that year nearly half the population of England was dead. Nor did the plague end when that first tidal wave had passed. It flared up time and again, culminating in its last devastating outbreak in 1665. Throughout the later Middle Ages it was endemic in England, always a hazard to be reckoned with.

For England as a whole the prevailing order of life was turned upside-down. Instead of the intense pressure on land through over-population, land everywhere was going derelict for lack of labourers to cultivate it. As the plague passed its peak and began to subside, the survivors realized that crops had to be sown and harvested and livestock fed and cared for if famine were not to be piled on top of pestilence. But who would do the work, and on what terms?

Consider the likely course of events in a typical village. With half the farmers dead, the obvious course was for the survivors to share the vacant land. They agreed that, while they were about it, it would be more convenient and economical to apportion the land so that each farmed a block instead of cultivating one-acre strips in the open field. So each acquired a farm consisting of fields adjacent to a farmstead and was able to put a hedge or fence around his land. The nucleated farmstead that we know today had arrived, and with it a modern workforce, the wage earner.

The largest farm in the village was of course the lord's demesne. If the lord himself had been a victim of the plague, his family's inclination would probably be to carry on as before, but where were the workers? The free farmers (the villeins) were no longer prepared to put in so many days a week working on the lord's land; they preferred to substitute a cash payment in lieu of the ancient duties. Always in the past there had been serfs or labourers or low-class cottars from whom work could be demanded, but where were they now? Some had succumbed to the plague and most of the survivors had decamped, having found that they need only trek for a few miles along country lanes to discover another stricken manor where they could work for a negotiated wage and no questions asked. The manor therefore acquired a labour force on very different terms from the old.

Some stewards, however, were so disheartened by adversity or resentful at having to bargain with upstart inferiors that they refused to accept the new order of things. They preferred the easier option of dividing out the lord's demesne among the village farmers. Thus, the lord's family ceased to be farmers and became instead country landowners, living on the rents; and the vagrant serfs and labourers found employment with newly created independent farmers. But the steward had another option and he was more likely to be aware of it if he lived near one of the sheep-keeping abbeys. If finding sufficient labour on conventional terms was impossible, why not give up cultivation entirely and turn the whole demesne into a sheep-walk? This obvious solution occurred to a good many landowners and their representatives.

It is the development of these alternative arrangements, initiated in the aftermath of the Black Death, that forms the central theme of agrarian history throughout the rest of the Middle Ages, and is indeed the background to modern farming. The turmoil that accompanied the changes occasioned by the Black Death is illustrated by contemporary chronicles. Henry Knighton, a canon of Leicester Abbey, lived through the pestilence and afterwards wrote down his impressions of the disaster. Having quoted figures illustrating a catastrophic fall in the prices of farm livestock, for the reason that 'men seemed to have lost their interest in wealth or in wordly goods', he continues:

> Sheep and cattle were left to wander through the fields and among the standing crops since there was no one to drive them off or collect them; for want of people to look after them they died in untold numbers in the hedgerows and ditches all over the country. So few servants and labourers were left that nobody knew where to turn for help . . . The following autumn it was not possible to get a harvester except by paying eightpence a day with food included. Because of this, many crops were left to rot in the fields. However, in the year of the pestilence, these crops were so abundant that no-one cared whether they were wasted or not.

Like all change, that from a feudal hierarchy to an independent labour force did not evolve smoothly. Not surprisingly, the powerful, who had most to lose by the breakdown of the old order, tried to shore it up. In 1351 Parliament passed the Statute of Labourers, which sought to re-establish the ancient feudal customs of the rural manors and to fix wages at their pre-pestilence levels. During the next sixteen years, 9,000 cases of breach of contract came before the court of Common Pleas under this Statute, but far more recalcitrant labourers must have avoided ever being caught. They could, after all, rely on their own two feet. In 1376, after the Statute had been in force for fifteen years, a petition to the Commons complained, 'As soon as their masters accuse them of bad service, or wish to pay them for their labours according to the form of the statutes, they take flight and suddenly leave their employment and district, going from county to county, hundred to hundred, and vill to vill, in places strange and unknown to their masters.'

Commentators have remarked on the contrast between the general fatalism and acquiescence of the English peasant in the thirteenth century and the independence and cockiness of his descendants in the fourteenth. It is worth remembering that in the intervening years English village lads in very large numbers had gone adventuring on the Continent, as mentioned earlier. They had, moreover, been forged into an extremely formidable fighting force through their mastery of the longbow as a weapon of war, and now they had, after a period of unparalleled horror, options as to where and how they might work. Attempts to re-establish the *status quo* were met by forceful resistance. Resentment came to the boil in the terrible Peasants' Revolt of 1381. For a few months in summer the rebels were in control. London was sacked; the Archbishop of Canterbury was beheaded on Tower Hill; foreigners and money-lenders were murdered; the manor rolls which recorded the duties owed by peasants to their feudal masters were everywhere burned. When the rebellion subsided and some of the ringleaders had been punished, order was to some extent restored by the granting of a general amnesty, but dissatisfaction continued to smoulder, fuelled by further attempts to reimpose ancient shackles.

Meantime the creation of new sheep-walks went on unchecked, its pace varying according to the comparative profitability of wool and corn. When corn prices were high there was an incentive to cultivate land and produce grain for sale; when wool was in the ascendant, fields were abandoned to the sheep. Recent research has suggested that by the end of the reign of Elizabeth

Cheviots gathered for shearing in Sutherland, a scene which is little changed since medieval times.

I, at least 1,000 English villages—and perhaps twice that number—had been deliberately made derelict and their inhabitants evicted to make more space for grazing sheep. In the 1480s a Warwickshire priest, John Rous, testified that to his own knowledge 58 villages, which he could name, had been depopulated within twelve miles of Warwick. As Sir Thomas More remarked, it was an age when 'sheep ate men'.

The natural consequence was an increase in the number of vagrants wandering the highways and lanes of England. For some time after the Black Death the problem remained manageable, in that land and work were still available for anyone who wanted them, but, as the population began to build up again, it became intractable. The anxiety it caused to the authorities is reflected in the increasing severity of the penalties. In the fifteenth century, laws were enacted to enable local justices to put vagrants in the stocks; by the middle of the sixteenth century the common penalty was whipping at the cart tail; a little later it was increased to death.

Meantime, attempts were made to tackle the problem at its source. Acts of Parliament were passed in 1489, 1515 and 1536 to prevent the demolition of villages and the conversion of ploughland into pasture. The latter two enactments contained provisions for the restoration to agriculture of land that had been laid down to grass, but they had only limited effect. It is estimated that by the early fifteenth century at least 10,000 vagrants were afoot in England, and by the reign of Elizabeth the number is thought to have doubled, maybe trebled.

Enclosures of common land went on at a rapid pace and continued to cause great resentment. In the reign of Edward VI, Robert Kett's rising in East Anglia (1549) captured the city of Norwich and presented a list of demands to the local gentry. While they were waiting on a heath outside the town for a response his men slaughtered and cooked 20,000 sheep, in revenge for the filching of land for sheep pasture. One of the demands was the abolition of all the old feudal dues by which farmers performed certain services in return for land tenure. Emancipation was not finally achieved until the reign of Elizabeth, who set free all Crown tenants from their feudal obligations, though in return for exorbitant cash payments.

Throughout the fifteenth and sixteenth centuries there was also a growing trend away from the old subsistence economy, whereby each manor did its best to feed itself and produced little surplus, to a commercial economy, in which farmers produced goods for profit. The new-rich merchants, who in the 1540s bought the former monastic estates, regarded their purchases as a good investment and expected a satisfactory return on it. Almost everyone, down to the lowliest peasant, was imbued by the same motives. It was during this period, too, that the word 'farm' came to acquire its modern meaning. Originally it was applied to the rent paid, either in cash or in services, for land. Now it meant that the land itself—not an indefinite area but a unit of fields, house and buildings adequate to provide a family living. A new class of farmer also played an increasingly prominent role in the countryside. He was the franklin, who owned the land he farmed and who was firmly on the ladder which led upwards to the status of a country gentleman.

The Great Barn at Great Coxwell, Faringdon, is a fine example of a medieval barn, most of which were ecclesiastical.

7. The Farm in Tudor Times

In Broad Chalke, the descendants of Girrard (whom we met at the time of the Domesday Book) would, 500 years later, be enjoying a vastly improved style of living from that of their ancestor. True, they would not be franklins, or freeholders, for at the dissolution of the monasteries all the estates of the Abbess of Wilton had passed to the Herbert family, who, as Earls of Pembroke, still own most of them today. On the other hand, the Girrard of 1550, if he were still farming the three hides (about 360 acres) cultivated by the family at the time of Domesday, would be a prosperous farmer who would ride horseback to Salisbury market to haggle with merchants for the sale of his corn, wool and other produce. The feudal services by which earlier Girrards had held their land would have been commuted to a cash rent and the farm would now comprise a block of enclosed fields round a substantial farmstead.

Let us look more closely at some of the changes which have taken place. Wheat, oats, barley and rye continued as the dominant field crops. In some districts there was a tendency to mix seed. Rye and wheat, for instance, produced a mixture known as *maslin*, which was thought to keep bread moist longer than pure wheaten flour. A mixture of oats, peas and vetches, used for feeding livestock, was known as *bullimong* or *dredge corn* (a term used for the very same mixture on my father's farm in Wiltshire in the 1920s).

Harvest yields, after falling off in the years following the Black Death, had improved considerably. For the estates of Merton College, Oxford, in the 1330s they were 10 bushels per acre for wheat, 16 to 32 for barley, 10 to 16 for oats, and 10 to 13½ for peas and beans. In the reign of Elizabeth I an estimate puts wheat and rye at 16 to 20 bushels per acre, barley at 36 bushels, and oats at 32 to 40 bushels, with the average somewhat higher in the South and lower in the North.

Methods of seed selection were designed to effect this improvement. One was to set children to pick out the largest grains from a scattering on the barn floor. Another was to cast a shovelful of grain over the floor; those grains which fell to the floor first would be the heaviest and the best. The development of recognized cereal varieties was beginning; already in the sixteenth century we hear of *flaxen* wheat, *white* wheat, *pole-eared* wheat and others. The trend was even more pronounced with peas, which were said to have pronounced local varieties, suited to local soils and climates. *Hampshire Kids* were reckoned excellent on land newly dressed with chalk, *Cotswold* peas for gravel soils, *Red Shanks* for recently reclaimed land, *Hotspurs* and *White Hastings* for early cropping. Peas and beans were normally allowed to ripen for harvest, but towards the end of the period housewives started to pick them before they ripened and to cook them as green vegetables.

Of the two new crops which appeared on English farms, buckwheat was introduced in the sixteenth century from north Germany or Russia. In most districts it was never a real rival to established cereals, but as a poor-land crop it caught on in the breckland region of East Anglia and in similar districts with light, sandy soils. Norfolk's speciality of fat poultry, particularly turkeys, may have its origin in buckwheat, an excellent poultry food.

Hops, the second new crop, was introduced as an aid to brewing. Before this time the English drank ale, which lacks the tang and flavour of beer. But beer soon became so popular that a writer at the end of the century commented that 'few farmers have not (hop) gardens of their own'.

Of minor crops, woad and madder were still cultivated for dyeing, madder was never a popular crop for it took three years to come to harvest, but in the second half of the sixteenth century woad was in great demand by cloth-manufacturers and was grown on the most fertile lands of central and southern England. During the same century coleseed was introduced from Holland, where it had long been grown for its oil. It was on a par with oilseed rape, which is today enjoying a revived popularity. Farmers were also aware of its value as sheep food and as green manure.

Flax and hemp were widely grown for their fibres, flax seed was used in linseed oil and for feeding livestock. As one who was required to grow his quota of flax during World War II, I can appreciate that it would not have been a popular crop because of its uneven ripening, its vulnerability to bad weather, its attraction for birds and its demands on labour. The fact that in Elizabeth I's reign everyone farming 60 acres of land was compelled to grow at least a quarter of an acre of flax suggests that it was no more popular then. Hemp is of course cannabis, and there are hints that its properties were not unknown. Hemp leaves were chewed to produce abortion; also put in a pain-killing cake given to women in labour (and to the husband); also used to soothe crying babies and quieten restless horses; and as a substitute for tobacco.

Of the rarer crops, saffron was grown in Essex and East Anglia, for dyeing, medicines and confectionery; teazels in Somerset, for wool-combing; and carrots as a field crop in East Anglia.

One major and important consequence of the change from acre strips in the open fields to nucleated or enclosed farms was that farmers were not forced to observe conventional 'three-course' or 'two-course' rotation. Replenishing soil fertility by spreading animal manure had never been adequate in feudal times, largely because so few animals were kept through the winter and the lord of the manor had first call on what manure there was for his home paddocks. The open fields got only what the animals dropped while grazing there and, in districts where wood was scarce, some of the dung was collected and mixed with clay for fuel, as in primitive parts of Africa and India today. However, the value of manuring was generally recognized, and medieval farmers certainly made use of what they could obtain, including sludge from fish-ponds, the rushes that had been used to carpet floors, bracken spread over the surface of lanes in autumn and well-trodden during the winter, ashes, malt dust, entrails from butchers, and droppings from pigeon lofts. But there was never enough of any of these commodities.

As already noted, when sheep were kept on arable land in winter they were usually penned in hurdle folds, to make the most economical use of what food there was on the land, and also to concentrate the deposits of dung. In some districts it seems to have occurred to farmers quite early on that grassland on which sheep and cattle were regularly grazed attained a high state of fertility. In parts of northern England it became the practice when land was claimed for the plough to crop it for only a limited number of years, say from two to seven, and then allow it to lapse into grass again. This system of alternate husbandry was preached as a new idea in the late 1930s by Professor Sir R. G. Stapledon and others and adopted by the Government as official policy shortly before the outbreak of World War Two. On it the tremendous productivity of the soil of England during the war years and afterwards was based. Yet it was well known and quite widely practised as early as the reign of Henry VIII. Writing in about 1539, Fitzherbert recommends to any farmers fortunate enough to have enclosed lands that

> if any of this three closes that he hath for his corn be worn or wear bare, then he may break and plough up his close that he had for his leys, or the close that he had for his common pasture, or both, and sow them with corn and let the other lie for a time, and so shall he have always rest ground, the which will bear much corn with little dung.

Fallow land is now seldom seen on English farms but medieval and Tudor farmers set great store by it, and until within living memory farmers could be found who would maintain that opening up the soil by ploughing and harrowing during the fallow year would do as much good, by letting the sun and air into the soil, as a coat of manure. Modern science does not at present confirm this but is cautiously coming round to the idea that there may be something in the contention. In the sixteenth century, ploughing the fallow field three times during summer was normal—once in April, once in June and once in July or August.

Over the centuries local types of plough had evolved. Some had two wheels, some one wheel and the lightest and commonest of all no wheels. Wheeled ploughs allowed the depth of the furrow to be readily adjusted. One type of double-wheeled plough, the Kentish or turnwrest plough, enabled the ploughman to reverse at the end of the furrow without turning the plough, an improvement now universally adopted. The early turnwrest ploughs were, however, very heavy and cumbersome. All types of plough were constructed of timber, with iron coulters and shares and sometimes with iron plates covering the mould-boards.

By the sixteenth century, too, the pros and cons of horses and oxen as draught animals were being widely discussed. For the heavier ploughs on heavy soils oxen were still preferred, but with light ploughs on easily worked soils horses got along much faster. An acre a day had been thought reasonable for ploughs in early medieval times, but by the sixteenth century a light plough drawn by two horses could tackle two or even three acres a day of light soil.

During the fallow year open fields were normally cross-ploughed in summer, to break up the furrows and reduce the soil to as fine a tilth as possible. Refining was done by harrows; the simplest form was a thorn-bush dragged over the ground. Even after timber-framed harrows with iron or wooden tines at the corner became common, thorny branches were often interwoven between the timbers. Wattle hurdles with spikes inserted at

Turnwrest or Kentish plough.

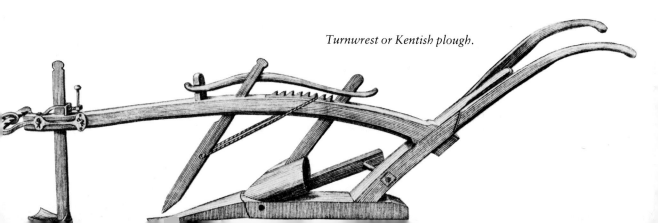

Wheeled ploughs allowed the depth of furrow to be adjusted.

intervals were also used for harrowing. Clods of heavy soil which defied the efforts of ploughs and harrows were broken to pieces by mattocks as in earlier ages.

Seed was usually sown broadcast by hand from a seed-lip suspended at waist-level by a strap over the sower's shoulder. Scattered over rough-ploughed land it was then buried by harrows. Seed was also sprinkled along furrows and buried by the plough. When labour was plentiful (and boys and girls could be employed for the purpose) corn was hand-weeded in May and June. Boys and girls were also employed to keep the birds off newly sown or sprouting crops, though on many manors there were prohibitions against interfering with the lord's pigeons. Beans were often planted individually, with a dibbing-stick.

At harvest, wheat was still cut by sickle, usually fairly near the ear or at least halfway up the stalk, to leave a length of stiff straw for thatching. Barley, oats and grass were mown by scythe, beans cut either by hook or

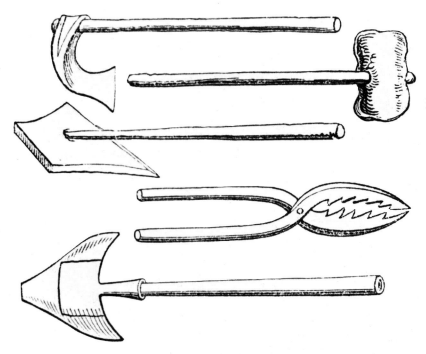

Husbandry implements from Gervase Markham's Farewell to Husbandry, *1620: '1. hack for breaking clods after ploughing; 2. clotting beetle for breaking clods for harrowing; 3. clotted beetle for wet clods; 4. weeding nippers; 5. paring shovel for clearing ground and weeding.'*

scythe. In the harvest-field the work of each harvester was carefully defined. A reaping band comprised five men or women, who apparently shared the work equally and who were expected to harvest two acres a day. Later, when scythes were in more general use, they were wielded by men, while their wives followed, gathering up the fallen stalks into sheaves and binding them with straw bonds. After the sheaves had been dried in stooks or hiles, they were collected by carts or waggons and taken to the farmstead to be made into ricks. The least skilled, and hence the lowest-paid workers, were those who, with pitchforks, pitched the sheaves on to the cart and from the cart to the rick. Of a higher grade were those who could be trusted to fashion a load of sheaves so that they would not fall off on the way to the rick. In the rickyard the farmer himself or the most skilled man on the farm undertook the task of building the rick. Four or five hundred years later, in the 1930s, the same divisions of labour were recognized. I myself started as the boy who led the horses, then became the pitcher of sheaves, then the loader on the

Sowing oats broadcast, a time-honoured though inefficient method.

For centuries boys and girls were employed to scare birds off crops.

waggons (where I learned to build the load according to a pattern known as 'swan-back' which ensured that the load would never fall off, even when jolting over the roughest ground), and then, finally, the rick-builder. As a matter of fact, I became quite an expert rick-builder and am sorry the skill is no longer required.

In the medieval village economy, the hayward, as we have seen, was responsible for supervising the hay harvest for the entire manor—organizing the labour force to cut, turn, toss the hay, make it into cocks or pooks and deciding when it was ready to go into ricks. He was also known as the 'lurard'; and in the course of time, became the man who organized both haymakers and harvesters, often, by the eighteenth and nineteenth centuries, as independent gangs who went from farm to farm, undertaking the work on contract. He survived in Essex and East Anglia until the present century as the Lord of the Harvest, 'Lord' being evidently a corruption of 'lurard'. The term is found in the New Testament and also in nineteenth century hymn-books, where a hymn with the chorus,

'The Lord of the Harvest shall soon appear,
His horn and his voice we shall quickly hear . . .'

was quite popular.

After the sheaves had been removed from the fields the ground was raked by men with hand-rakes, so that nothing was wasted. But the practice of gleaning or leasing gradually became more general, reserved for women and particularly for poor widows, who gathered the loose ears to secure a quota of grain for milling and bread-making in winter. The master farmhand who made the ricks was expected to be equally proficient with the flail, threshing the sheaves on the barn floor in winter when bad weather prevented outdoor work.

Milling also became a specialist task. Some 5,000 mills are mentioned in the Domesday Book, all of which would have been watermills or, where water was unavailable, mills operated by oxen or horses. Windmills are thought to have been introduced from the East at the time of the Crusades, the first types probably being fixed post-mills, though, later, revolving post-mills were developed. Throughout the Middle Ages each manor had possessed a mill, the property of the lord of the manor who insisted that everyone have their corn ground there in return for a toll. This arrangement was vigorously resented and caused endless friction between lords and tenants, who preferred to use querns or handmills and so keep all their grain for themselves. (The Abbot of St Albans, Cirencester, had all the querns on his estates confiscated, smashed and made into paving-stones for his parlour.)

As the medieval centuries passed, more and more landlords let out their mills to tenant millers, who retained a portion of the grain as payment. By the very nature of his job the miller had ample scope for cheating and in general his fellow-villagers were convinced that he made the most of his opportunities:

'Miller-dee, miller-dee, dusty poll,
How many sacks of flour hast thou stole?
In goes a bushel; out comes a peck!
Hang old miller-dee up by his neck!'

At the beginning of the medieval period oxen were kept primarily for draught purposes. Cows, when they *were* milked, were milked only in summer, there being insufficient fodder to keep them producing during the winter. In the century or so following the Black Death they seem to have deteriorated in size, doubtless through lack of attention to breeding, and by the middle of the fifteenth century they were only about a third of the size of a modern Friesian cow. Authorities believe that the total quantity of milk given by the average medieval cow during the summer milking period could not have been more than 120 to 150 gallons as compared with 2,000 gallons per lactation produced by a modern cow. But by the sixteenth century improvements were noticeable, visitors from overseas commenting on the beauty and excellence of English cattle.

Local types, which were later to evolve into breeds, were beginning to develop. Most important of these were the red cattle of Somerset, Devon and Gloucestershire, with deep bodies and short horns, noted chiefly for milk though North Devon had a similar type valued as draught animals; Lincolnshire cattle, white with black markings, which were large, deep-bodied and short-horned and were valued for draught purposes and for beef; Suffolk duns, whose milk was considered excellent for cheese-making; black longhorns from Yorkshire and the north Midlands—square-bodied and short-legged, with long white horns tipped with black; the deep-red cattle of Sussex and Kent, esteemed as good for draught and beef; and a red type in north-western England. Black Welsh cattle also came in considerable numbers into the English markets, and there was a big trade in imported Irish cattle, chiefly to south-western England.

From early times sheep were the pampered darlings of the farm. Contrary to common practice today, most were housed in winter, though taken out for an airing to sheep-folds on sunny, windless days. They were fed on hay,

Above: medieval manuscript depicts peasant cutting grain with serrated sickle. *Overleaf:* the Blackwell Ox, 1779, outstanding example of early Shorthorn breed.

Top: Thomas Coke, Earl of Leicester, inspecting improved Southdown sheep at Holkham Hall, c.1808. *Above:* the Durham Ox, 1802, displayed its 27cwt to admiring crowds at shows and fairs for six years.

Above: eighteenth-century painting by George Morland; higglers preparing
for market. *Overleaf:* Stubbs's portrayal of reapers binding sheaves as the
landowner watches from his horse, typifies romantic ideas of
eighteenth-century hierarchical country life.

Warwick, a magnificent Shire horse, one of the founders of the breed, c.1831.

pea-haulm and straw and had their houses cleaned out and freshly littered once a fortnight. They were milked by the shepherd himself, who delivered it to a dairymaid for making into cheese or butter, though milking ceased after September 8th. Among the perquisites of the shepherd were a stock of candles for his lantern, so that he could move about among his ewes in the sheep-house at lambing-time. The lambing season was from January to the end of March for housed sheep and in April for those kept outdoors round the year on grass. In Wiltshire, Hampshire and neighbouring counties, there existed as early as the sixteenth century, if not before, a type of sheep, evidently the ancestors of the modern Dorset Horn, which would lamb in November—a propensity which began to have a commercial value when sheep came to be valued for their meat.

Ewes were still commonly milked in the sixteenth century. Thomas Tusser, writing in 1573, stated that he weaned his lambs on May 1st and thereafter milked the ewes till August 1st. Five ewes, he reckons, would give the same quantity of milk as one cow—a vast improvement on early medieval standards, where one cow produced as much as ten ewes.

By the end of the sixteenth century fleeces were averaging four to six pounds, twice that of the fourteenth century. The best wool was produced by short-woolled types of sheep and some of the finest of these were found in the border counties of Wales, from Gloucestershire to Shropshire and including the Welsh county of Radnorshire. The wool from Leominster, in Herefordshire, had a nationwide reputation. The sheep were evidently the ancestors of the modern Ryeland and several Welsh border breeds. Somewhat similar were the downland sheep of Dorset, Wiltshire, Hampshire, Sussex and East Anglia. All these local types were rather small, white-faced animals with light fleeces—not more than about two pounds in weight—whose value was derived from the quality of their wool. The Midlands and Lincolnshire possessed a group of coarse, long-woolled sheep, suitable for grazing on heavy, wet soils. They produced much heavier fleeces than the shortwools but of a less valuable quality. A pocket of similar sheep had established itself on Romney Marsh.

Finally, there was a wide range of mountain sheep, whose chief recommendation was that they could thrive in difficult climates. They were mostly small, with light fleeces, though some of their wool was quite fine. Some of them had white faces, some black, and most were horned. As in modern times, many mountain-bred sheep were sent to lowland farms for fattening. From these medieval types are descended the present breeds of the northern Dales, Scotland and Wales and the moorland breeds of Devon.

The numbers of sheep in medieval and Tudor England were prodigious. Not long before the Black Death, Winchester Cathedral Priory was running 20,000 sheep on its estates, Canterbury Priory had 13,700 sheep, and the abbey of Crowland 10,960. The monastic houses of Yorkshire are estimated to have shorn nearly 200,000 adult sheep per year, and modern authorities consider that these ecclesiastical flocks constituted no more than half the total population. An informed estimate of the sheep population of Britain in the early fourteenth century is around 12,000,000. It was probably about the same in Tudor times.

Since the twelfth century, horses had been used for farm work, but first they were often harnessed with oxen, and seem to have been of nondescript type. In the early sixteenth century, however, Henry VIII, appalled by the wretchedly low quality of English horses, decreed that all owners of enclosed lands of a mile or more in circumference should keep at least two mares of 13 hands for breeding and that they should be mated with stallions of not less than 14 hands. This was followed in 1541 by an Act which prohibited stallions of less than 15 hands from being turned loose in the forests or on commons, while mares obviously incapable of bearing a good-sized foal were to be killed and buried. The northern counties were exempt from these rules; the last thing Henry wanted to do was to provide good horses for Scottish raiders. Though it is doubtful whether these regulations were widely observed, standards gradually did improve, and by Elizabeth's reign specialization was beginning to occur, for we hear of heavy horses being bred in Suffolk (the ancestors of the Suffolk Punch), Lincolnshire, Yorkshire and elsewhere.

Poultry, like horses, had become established farm livestock by the twelfth century. The manor house kept a flock in an enclosed yard, while almost every peasant and cottager had a few hens running about around the house, and probably inside it as well. Chaucer, at the end of the fourteenth century, gives a graphic description of the widow's cock, Chauntecleer: his crowing was 'merrier than the merye organ', and anyone who was ever kept a cock with hens will appreciate the description of the cock's behaviour when foraging in the backyard:

'He chukketh, when he hath a corn i-founde
  And to him rennen than his wives alle.'

Chaucer notes that the cock and his seven hens were all yellow, and, in the reign of Elizabeth I, Leonard Mascall observed that yellow (or gold) was still the most popular colour.

Towards the end of the sixteenth century a specialist poultry industry was developing in Norfolk, and buckwheat, as mentioned above, was introduced there as a poultry food. In addition to chicken, the Norfolk poultry-keepers bred and reared geese, ducks and turkeys. Turkeys were imported from Mexico in the 1530s and by the 1590s were quite plentiful in Norfolk. Ducks were not included in lists of domestic poultry until the end of the fourteenth century but, after that, became common. Large numbers of geese continued to roam the commons and to go stubbling after harvest, but goslings were often fattened on special foods such as malt and milk. As times became more prosperous there was a demand for goose down for feather beds and pillows, while goose grease was popular as a base for sundry ointments and medicines.

Swans and peacocks were widely fattened for the table. Swans were the more popular, for an Elizabethan commentator regarded the peacock as a 'strange bird to feede and to governe, for they hardly bee so familiar with any person as other birds will', while another writer objected, 'He hath an horrible voice.'

Throughout the Middle Ages the manorial dovecote had been well populated with pigeons and one of the grievances listed by Robert Ket, who led a peasants' revolt in Norfolk in 1549, was the damage done to crops by the pigeons from demesne dovecotes. The birds were not allowed to depend entirely on what they could forage, however, for there are records of peas and lentils being grown for feeding pigeons. In the Fens ruffs, godwits and perhaps other species of wading birds were fattened in coops and, when ready for eating, were killed by cutting their heads off with scissors.

From the thirteenth century onwards many lords had been granted permission to enclose land for rabbit warrens—a novelty at first but soon an unmitigated nuisance to the neighbouring peasants, whose crops the rabbits ate. Hedges could keep cattle and other livestock from straying into rabbit warrens, but before the days of wire-netting nothing could prevent the rabbits from getting out. However, many warrens were established on poor, sandy soil that was useful for little else. The rabbits were valued for their fur as well as for their meat, and black ones were particularly favoured.

Goats were still being kept at the end of the period, but usually only in the hill districts of the north and west, where cattle would not thrive. As they were easy to feed and were said to give three times as much milk as a sheep, their comparative scarcity is surprising.

In addition to crops and livestock, changes naturally occurred in the role and status of the various village officers. The rise of the franklin has already been mentioned. The bailiff and the reeve maintained their respective positions until the fifteenth century when the bailiff was superseded. As he was often overseer to a number of manors, he paid infrequent visits to each, and the reeve soon stepped into his shoes. Originally appointed as the representative of the peasants in their dealings with the lord of the manor, the reeve gradually switched sides, for in the absence of the bailiff he had charge of all the lord's livestock and, as ever, he who pays the piper calls the tune. The villagers naturally regarded him as a turncoat and detested him accordingly.

Another new character whom we have also met was the lurard, who seems in East Anglia to have been a hayward with special duties in relation to haymaking. Traditionally, the hayward, whose duty also was to see that hedges were kept in good repair, had his strips of land in the open fields, but it seems that he was normally allotted strips nearest the hedge, so that if, through his neglect, cattle or other livestock strayed into the corn, his would be the first to suffer damage. A messor was probably another sort of hayward with special duties at harvest. A suggestion that, whereas in small manors a hayward would look after haymaking and harvest, in larger ones the duties would be divided between the hayward, the lurard and the messor, may well be correct. In some manors where a messor existed he was entitled to three meals a day in return for watching over the lord's fields all night during the ripening and harvest period.

Another offshoot of the hayward's office was that of the pinder. As the wasteland and commons shrank and straying animals consequently caused more problems, the village pound became a feature of most parishes. Here straying livestock were confined and released only on payment of a fine, and the man who rounded up the strays, shut them in and collected the fines was the pinder. He usually had a small farm of his own and was paid in kind, normally in sheaves of corn, for his services.

The establishment of rabbit warrens naturally created a new job, that of warrener, a servant of the lord of the manor. And with the increasing use of horses on the farm there also appears the carter, as distinct from the ploughman, who worked with oxen.

The ploughman had replaced the former oxherd and seems to have possessed a wider range of skills, for he had to be able to make or repair ploughs and to sow, harvest and thresh corn. Piers, the plowman of Langland's poem, could also mend metal tools and utensils, weave cloth and stitch clothes. He was evidently a small farmer, for he possessed a few cattle and a horse. Chaucer's ploughman was brother to the village priest.

By Tudor times most pigs had ceased to run wild in the woods.

Distinct from the ploughman was the cowherd, who apparently had charge of only the milking cows and their calves. He too slept with his charges, outdoors in summer and in the cow-house in winter. Sometimes he and his wife made cheese but this work more often fell to the dairyman or dairymaid. Other aspects of the dairymaid's work have already been noted; she usually had charge of the farm poultry and sometimes of litters of piglets. Chaucer introduces a 'poure wydow' who with her two daughters makes a living from doing dairy work and keeping her own pigs and poultry.

A statute of 1495 laid down the hours of work to be expected from farm workers. In the summer, between the equinoxes, they started work at 5 am and continued to 7 or 9 pm, according to the work on hand. During that period they were allowed half-an-hour for breakfast and an hour-and-a-half for dinner at midday, when they also took a nap. Supper was taken in the evening, after the day's work was over. By an earlier Act, working for hire (though not for oneself) was forbidden on Holy Days and for a half-day preceding each Holy Day. As Holy Days were frequent in the medieval Church calendar, averaging about one a week, the labourers probably enjoyed as much leisure time as their twentieth-century descendants with their Saturday afternoons and Sundays off.

Three o'clock in the morning was the normal time for work to begin in the farmhouse. That was the hour at which the maidservants were required to rise and get busy. Four o'clock in summer and five in winter were the very latest times for them to bestir. One of the first tasks of the day was to sweep and dust the house, but this ought not to be done 'as long as any honest man is within the precynct of the house, for the dust doth putryfy the ayre, making it dence.' That implies that the man was up and out-of-doors even earlier than the law required. And when the houses were simple and there was less to do indoors, the women were expected to do more outside. Besides helping at haymaking and harvest they took a share in sowing, weeding the cornfields, pulling yealms (thatch bundles) for thatching and bird-scaring.

One of the chief innovations of the era was the feather-bed, a luxury which William Harrison, writing in 1587, deplored:

> 'We ourselves have lain full oft upon straw pallets, on rough mats covered only with a sheet, under coverlets made of dagswain or hopharlots, and a good round log under our heads instead of a bolster or pillow. If it were so that our fathers or the goodman of the house had within seven years after his marriage purchased a mattress or flock bed, and thereto a sack of chaff to rest his head upon, he thought himself to be as well lodged as the lord of the town, that peradventure lay seldom in a bed of down or

whole feathers, so well were they contented . . . Pillows were thought meet only for women in childbed. As for servants, if they had any sheet above them, it was well, for seldom had they any under their bodies to keep them from the pricking straws that ran oft through the canvas of the pallet and rased their hardened hides.'

Another novelty noted by Harrison was the replacement of wooden vessels by pewter and of wooden spoons by those of silver or tin. In the old days, he said, one would scarcely find four pieces of pewter in a good farmer's house, whereas now he has 'a fair garnish of pewter on his cupboard, with so much more in odd vessels going about the house, three or four feather beds, so many coverlets and carpets of tapestry, a silver salt, a bow for wine, and a dozen spoons to finish up the suit.' The 'carpets' were probably not for the floor, as rushes and herbs continued to be the common floor covering. They were cleared out either quarterly or half-yearly.

On the whole, farmers and their families fared reasonably well. Back in the thirteenth century a farmer would have had bread made from his own wheat, and beer made from his own barley; plenty of milk, cheese, eggs and herbs; and at times honey. Almost all wild birds and animals were thought good for the pot, small birds such as larks, wheatears and robins were regarded as delicacies, and few peasants could resist helping themselves to one of the lord's deer when they thought they could do so undetected. Before the Reformation freshwater fish, bred in fish-ponds, were much more plentiful than they are today.

By Tudor times farmers and their families were feeding even better. The stock-pot was probably kept simmering all the time, for from it the housewife ladled out a breakfast of 'pottage', sometimes mixed with oatmeal. Dinner around midday was a minor meal, of not more than 'three dishes well dressed', but all the farm hands came in to share it, unless working in distant fields. The main meal of the day, supper, was served in mid-evening and was substantial, though doubtless based on the stock-pot again. The farm hands, however, expected a joint of roast meat twice a week—on Thursdays and Sundays.

For drink, the farmer's family had beer or ale, mead or one of the derivatives from spiced mead or ale, such as metheglin or pyment. Fortunately for their health, no one normally drank water. The *Northumberland Household Book*, from the early part of the sixteenth century, notes that Lord Percy, aged ten, had for his breakfast half a loaf of bread and four pints of beer. His parents, incidentally, had 'two small loaves, half a chine of mutton or else half a chine of boiled beef, and one quart of wine and a quart of beer'. For Coventry in the year 1520 the records show that, comparing the population with the annual consumption of ale, everybody, including children, drank a quart a day (which doubtless implies that the men drank a good deal more).

The time-honoured adage that a farmer leaves his gardening to God is not only true but understandable, for the busiest seasons on the farm almost invariably coincide with the busiest seasons in the garden, and naturally the farm has priority. The fact is, though, that the average farmer leaves his gardening to his wife. That was as true in the Middle Ages as it is today, and we have already noted how the Tudor farm wife fitted in gardening with all her other chores.

It is not surprising, therefore, to find an interest in flowers developing alongside that in vegetables and fruit. For both flowers and vegetables, however, the farmer's wife had probably to thank the monasteries, abbeys, nunneries and other religious establishments, which were chiefly responsible for keeping alive the art of gardening through the Dark Ages. Writing in 1530, William Turner, Dean of Wells mentions the following plants cultivated in his time:

> Vegetables and Herbs: artichoke; asparagus; kidney bean; borage; cabbage; caraway; carrot; chervil; chicory; coriander; cress; dill; endive; fennel; gourd; hemp; hop; colewort (or kale); lentil; lettuce; liquorice; madder; marjoram; orache (used as spinach); parsnip; pea; purslane; radish; savory; betony; camomile; sorrel; walnut; watercress; woad.
>
> Fruits:—medlar; mulberry; peach; quince.
>
> Flowers:—alexanders; anise; archangel; asarabacca; burberry; bramble; white bryony; Butcher's broom; catmint; greater celandine; centaury; chickweed; cinquefoil; clary; cockle; comfrey; crowfoot; cuckoo pint; daffodil; daisy; elecampane; feverfew; galingale; germander; gith (a kind of larkspur); hart's tongue tern; black hellebore (Christmas rose); hollyhock; white horehound; henbane; house-leek; wild hyacinth (bluebell); white iris; yellow iris; lavender; marigold; mugwort; black nightshade; orpine; pellitory; penny royal; periwinkle; pimpernel; plantain, pomegranate; poppy; rocket; Solomon's seal; tansy; teasel; vervain; waterlily; wormwood; yarrow.

It is, of course, highly probable that, while the rose, violet, peony, daffodil and some others were appreciated for their beauty, many of the others were valued for their medicinal properties, alleged or real.

Wild strawberries and raspberries were apparently first transplanted into gardens for cultivation in the second half of the thirteenth century, and

116

lavender about the same time. About the year 1440 John Gardener wrote a treatise on the plants known to him in the gardens of Eltham Palace, and to the above list he was able to add avens (or Geum), bugle, calamint, campion, cowslip, gentian, gromwell (Lithospermum), mouse-ear, primrose, St John's-wort, scabious, spearwort, stitchwort, tutsan, valerian, wallwort, wood sanicle, woodruff, wood sage, wood sorrel (shamrock). Most of these are wild plants which gardeners were now choosing to transplant into gardens.

By the sixteenth century gourds, pumpkins (known as 'pompions), globe artichokes, turnips, spinach and shallots had been added to the vegetable catalogue, while the orchard might hold greengages, damsons, red currants, apricots and filberts, as well as many different varieties of apples, pears and plums. Thomas Tusser is well informed as to what should be grown in a farmer's garden, with the housewife and her maidservants as gardeners, but his interests are strongly utilitarian and the flowers he mentions are for growing in 'windows and pots'. The housewife was advised 'either to be present herself or to teach her maids to know herbs from weeds', when weeding was to be done. We can imagine, however, that many a housewife took pleasure in the roses, lilies, gillyflowers and daffydowndillies in her flower borders and did the weeding there herself.

Domestic records of the time demonstrate clearly that, compared with the austerities and anxieties of the preceding centuries, rural life was becoming much more spacious and relaxed. On the English farm, which previously had had to concentrate almost exclusively on the grim struggle for survival, time and space could now be found for such refinements as gardens. There was money to spare for furnishings that were not entirely utilitarian, such as curtains and window-glass. Above all, a steady growth in literacy was eroding the isolation of life on the farm. With forefinger slowly following the lines of printed books, the ploughman and the shepherd now read for themselves the Scriptures, the classics of Greece and Rome, the accounts of voyagers to new lands overseas and even treatises on husbandry. As they read, new and limitless horizons beyond the confines of their native parish would become their heritage.

8. The Threshold of Modern Times

During the seventeenth century the population of England and Wales rose from 4,000,000 to about 5,500,000. This was a greater total than the country had ever had to support, yet, owing to increasing efficiency, the farmers managed it easily. At times, even as early as 1620, there were temporary gluts. The price of wheat, for example, fell from 48s. 8d. per quarter in 1617 to 30s. 4d per quarter in 1620, rising quickly again to 58s. 8d. per quarter in 1622. The period of the Commonwealth was one of high prices, but by the end of the century they were much the same as at the beginning. Four-fifths of the population were still living in villages and gaining at least part of their livelihood from the land. Contemporary estimate of livestock in Britain at the end of the century shows 4,500,000 cattle, 12,000,000 sheep and 2,000,000 pigs.

Bad weather and severe winters were frequent. The Thames in London was frozen over in 1607, 1608, 1614, 1615, 1629, 1634, 1649, 1658, 1662, 1664, 1667, 1683 (when the ice was eleven inches thick), 1684, 1685, 1688, 1689, and 1695—though, by contrast, in 1661–2 the weather was so unseasonably mild that prayers were said and a fast proclaimed for colder weather. The century was also notable for renewed outbreaks of bubonic plague and of smallpox. In 1674, one-eighth of London's population died of smallpox. Epidemics affecting livestock were correspondingly severe. Great mortality among sheep was recorded in 1615; in 1620 nearly 20,000 sheep died on Eskdale Moor during thirteen days of snow; in 1648, according to the diarist John Evelyn, 'cattle died everywhere of a murrain'; a 'great rot in sheep' occurred in 1663 and again in 1673; in the latter year Orders in Sessions were made to compel farmers to bury the bodies of animals which had died of disease, 'whereby the air is likely to become corrupt from the infinite numbers of sheep and other great cattle being suffered by their owners to remain dead above ground'.

With the invention of printing, farmers had begun to learn from books as well as by old lore, and, following the setting up of Caxton's press in Westminster in 1476, books of all kinds had begun to proliferate, including some on husbandry and agriculture. Fitzherbert published his *Boke of*

118

Common-Good:

OR, THE

IMPROVEMENT

OF

Commons, Forrefts, and Chafes,

BY

INCLOSURE.

WHEREIN

The Advantage of the Poor,

THE

Common Plenty of All,

AND

The Increafe and Prefervation of TIMBER,

With other things of common concernment,
Are Confidered.

By S. T.

LONDON,
Printed for *Francis Tyton*, and are to be fold at his
fhop at the fign of the three Daggers neer the
Middle-Temple gate, 1652.

Husbondrye in 1523, John Gerard his celebrated *Herball* in 1597, Thomas Tusser his equally famous *Five Hundred Points of Good Husbandry* in 1573. In the following century Gervase Markham contributed *Cheape and Good Husbandry* (1615) and several other books; Walter Blith *The English Improver Improved* (1652); Samuel Hartlib *The Compleat Husbandman* (1659); while other authors dealt with more specialized subjects including orchards, 'the country housewife's garden', ploughing techniques, and bees. In addition monographs of agriculture in several counties were prepared, and general pictures of the English rural scene were supplied by such authors as William Camden, Daniel Defoe and the antiquarian, John Aubrey.

Travellers from other countries, too, began to set down their impressions of England in writing. Those who penetrated beyond London were attracted by the verdure of the woods and fields. Observed Estienne Perlin, a Frenchman who visited England in 1558, 'The country is well wooded and shady, for the fields are all enclosed with hedges, oak trees and several others sorts of trees, to such an extent that in travelling you think you are in a continuous wood.'

Yet writer after writer, both native and foreign, displayed an unfortunate misunderstanding of the foundations on which the natural wealth of English farming was built. Grass is the crop that England grows best. Over much of the country it is the natural herbage which will, of its own accord, cover any land left open and derelict. Given efficient management, grass can give a higher return per acre than any grain crop. Yet for these observers agriculture meant ploughing fields, sowing seed and reaping a harvest, and they felt that any farmer who neglected to do so was bone idle. Thus Walter Blith (1652), taking note of the rich grazing pastures of the Midlands, observes that the Midland grazier

> will not plough any old pasture land at all, upon any terms, or for any time
> . . . He will not have it ploughed, come what will. 'What,' saith he, 'destroy
> my old pasture, my sheepwalks, and beggar my land!' All the world will
> not persuade him to do that . . . 'No,' saith he, 'I can raise a constant profit
> by wool and lamb, my fat beef and mutton, at an easy quiet way unto
> myself and family, without much vexing and turmoiling . . .'

Less censorious but still making the same error, Paul Hentzner, visiting this country from Germany in 1598, remarked, 'The soil is fruitful and abounds with cattle, which inclines the people rather to feeding than to ploughing, so that near a third part of the land is left uncultivated for grazing.' An Elizabethan surveyor of forests in Northamptonshire was more forthright in his opinion of the local peasants. 'So long as they may be permitted to live in such idleness upon their stock of cattle, they will bend themselves to no kind of labour,' he wrote.

Grassland farmers, however, in the time of the Tudors and Stuarts, as well as in the twentieth century, knew the value of their stock-in-trade. When, in the sixteenth and more particularly the seventeenth centuries, farmers began to exert themselves seriously to effect improvements in their industry, one of the first projects to which they gave their attention was the improvement of grass.

One of the chief problems of farming in a northern climate has always been to grow enough food in six months to feed livestock for twelve. For many centuries the quantity of food for humans and animals, grown in a summer, was thought to be determined by an inscrutable God. The only thing a farmer could do was, after taking stock of provisions after harvest, kill off surplus livestock so as to adjust the number of mouths to the available food supplies. The concept of increasing grazing times, which farmers now began to grasp, was decidedly novel.

In most districts cattle and sheep could not be turned out to graze before late April or May, while after harvest they usually returned to their winter quarters and routine by October or November. A month or two of earlier grazing in spring and a similar margin in autumn would make a world of difference. Who deserves the credit for changing this routine by the invention of floating meadows, or water-meadows, has been a matter for some speculation, but it now seems fairly certain that the principle was devised in Herefordshire, where, after several decades of experiments, Rowland Vaughan devised an excellent system of 'wetshod waterworks' in the Golden Valley in 1589.

These earliest water-meadows were arranged on what became known as the 'catchwork' system. A small stream was dammed and equipped with hatches so that the water could be diverted along a new channel parallel with the old but higher up the hillside. In winter, when the stream was in flood, it was dammed at its lower end so that the water had to brim over its banks and find its way to the old channel by trickling over the meadow. The grassland thus became covered by a shawl of gently-flowing water an inch or so deep. The system was further improved by installing a grid of cross channels designed to ensure that the water was distributed evenly.

Floating meadows were irrigation against frost rather than drought. In hard weather, when the rest of the countryside was snow-covered and in the grip of iron frost, a water-meadow was a green oasis—a hot-bed where the grass continued to grow unchecked. In flood-time, too, the stream brought down much sediment to deposit on the meadows and enrich them. The value of floating meadows soon became up to ten times that of unimproved pasture. More important still, the system extended the grazing season. The hatches were finally closed early in March, making the meadows available for grazing two or three weeks later, which was at least a month earlier than unimproved pastures could produce a worthwhile bite of grass.

The invention came at a time when farmers were ready to receive new ideas, and within the next forty years it was so widely adopted that floating meadows utilized the waters of every suitable stream in Herefordshire and was quickly adopted by farmers in neighbouring counties. Manipulating the hatches to allow water into the meadows became known as 'drowning' and the men responsible for it 'drowners'—highly-skilled, they were allegedly web-footed. So successful was the system that it gave rise to an ironical proverb—'A good husband (farmer) is he that doth drown.'

A drowner with his tools on the river Ebble in Wiltshire, 1948.

The system employed in the valleys of the chalk streams was more elaborate than that devised by Rowland Vaughan for the Golden Valley and was certainly more expensive to install, though it suited the chalk country style of farming admirably. Known as the 'ridge-and-furrow' system, it involved laying out a meadow in a series of ridges at right angles to the course of the stream or water-channel. One ditch, known as the carrier, was dug along the crest of each ridge; another, the drain, at its foot. The distance from the crest of each ridge to the crest of the next was ten or twelve yards. The entire surface of the meadow was thus occupied by a series of gentle corrugations. When the hatches controlling the intake of water were opened, the water poured in at the level of the ridge crest and, quickly overflowing the ditches, flowed down the slopes into the drains which, at the end of the meadow, diverted it back to the main stream.

Plan of a water meadow made for the Duke of Bedford.

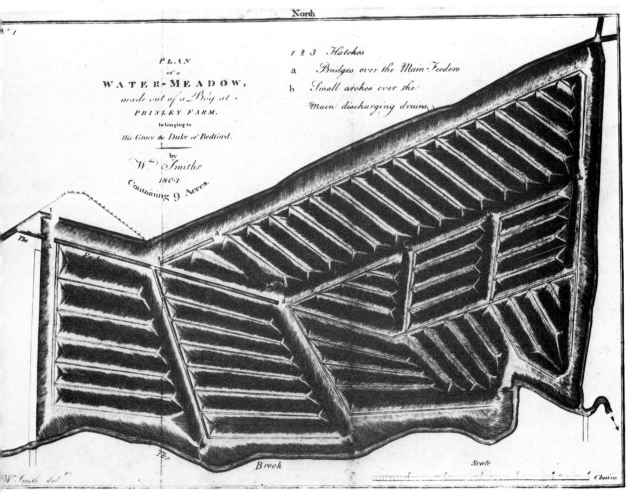

It sounds somewhat complicated, but the management 'customs' which it demanded were even more so. By the end of the seventeenth century floating meadows were in operation throughout the chalk country and in some parts of the Midlands. The valley of a chalk stream, where they were at their best, would be laid out in irrigated meadows from its source to its mouth, each section belonging to a different owner. Under such an intensive system an individual farmer could not be allowed unlimited use of the water, so systems of rationing were devised whereby each farmer drowned his meadows between stipulated dates and then had to close the hatches. One can imagine that the arrangement would prove a fruitful source of friction, and doubtless disputes did arise, but on the whole it seems to have worked pretty well for more than 200 years. Much of the land so irrigated was by this time in private hands, but the system also worked in parishes still using the old open-field system.

Floating meadows fitted perfectly into the sheep-and-corn pattern of farming evolving in the chalk country. Here they were planned entirely for the sheep, and the water levels delicately adjusted. From a lambing in early February the lambs were just the right age to take full advantage of a floating meadow in which the fresh, lush grass was six or eight inches high in the third week of March. The daily growth of the lambs on this rich pasture was almost visible. The farm benefited in another way. The sheep and lambs were admitted to the meadows for a few hours, until their stomachs were full; then, when they were ready to lie down, they were hurried away to the arable fields where they dropped their dung and urine, vastly improving the fertility of the soil in these fields.

In some counties, notably Dorset, the meadows were given two further irrigations. One was for five or six weeks from the middle of May, which produced a heavy hay crop, mown by scythe and estimated to yield as much as $2\frac{1}{2}$ tons per acre. The second was in August and was designed to yield a further period of grazing for mid-September.

Floating meadows served their beneficent purpose for as long as farming remained prosperous and labour plentiful and cheap, but the system eventually foundered in the great agricultural depression which began in 1875. It failed to revive after World War Two for two reasons: corrugations and ditches made it almost impossible to mechanize, and most of the skilled drowners had died off without passing on their expertise. The demise of the floating meadows is nevertheless to be regretted, for the idea was a sound one and, with the sophisticated machinery now available, could well be worth reviving.

Another system of husbandry practised to increase soil fertility was the 'up-and-down' system. Pioneered from the mid-sixteenth century and widely practised in the seventeenth, it will be instantly recognizable by modern farmers under its modern names of 'alternate husbandry' and 'ley farming'. But there were reasons why it was not as productive and efficient as is present-day ley farming.

The underlying theory has already been described. Medieval farmers, even Bronze Age farmers, were aware that animal droppings helped to replenish soil fertility, and under the open-field system livestock were penned or allowed to roam over the arable fields whenever possible, such as at intervals during the fallow year or on the stubbles after harvest. It had also been observed that land newly-reclaimed from the forest yielded its best crops in the years after it was first ploughed. We have noted Fitzherbert's recommendation in 1539 that any farmer who had an enclosed field which was 'wearing bear' should plough it up and sow it with corn, 'the which will bear much corn with little dung'. Indeed, he visualized a farm with three such fields, on which he could ring the changes between pasture and arable, 'so shall he always have rest ground'. The argument was sound, and by the middle of the seventeenth century it had been widely adopted, especially in the Midlands. But when it came to returning the land to grass after a period of years under the plough, the sixteenth- and seventeenth-century farmer was faced with a formidable difficulty. He had no seed of productive new grass varieties to sow, such as are available to us. All he could do was to let the land lie fallow after harvest and wait for a new growth of grass to spring up naturally, or at most to scatter hayseed over the soil.

Some modern writers have assumed that the turf turned under by the plough stayed alive through three to twelve years of tillage and so was ready to send up new growth when conditions were right. This seems to me impossible, except where couch-grass and other rhizomatous grasses were concerned, and even they would be hard-pressed to contend with frequent and thorough cultivations. In any case, it was the rotted turf which supplied the nutrients on which the subsequent corn crops fed. No, it was one thing to plough up a pasture and cash in on its accumulated fertility, but quite another to create a new pasture: it would take years for the new sward to become anywhere near as good as the old, as farmers subsequently learned by experience. They summed up that experience by coining a new proverb: 'To break a pasture makes a man; to make a pasture breaks a man.'

A farmer-scientist, W. S. Mansfield, commenting on the situation in 1946, after the official ploughing-up policy for agriculture in wartime had reached its zenith, declared, 'There is no doubt that up to fifty years ago the making of a permanent pasture was a dark and difficult adventure, and one not to be undertaken lightly. At best it was a slow and expensive business, and even in the most favoured districts the results were uncertain. In the absence of a proper supply of grass seed, of wild white clover seed and of phosphates, who would undertake the putting down of a field to grass with any degree of confidence? Yet this is what our great-grandfathers had to do; small wonder that they regarded it with dismay, and that their justifiable fears and trepidations should have outlived them.'

Nor was Fitzherbert correct in his belief that the fresh young herbage that springs up naturally on land left uncultivated is sweeter, better and more productive than old pastures, contaminated with 'corrupt weeds and filth'. When sowing new leys in the 1940s and 1950s I used to include a herb strip, in which I sowed the seeds of chicory, ribwort, plantain, yarrow, dandelion and other herbs, and it was instructive to watch the grazing cows return to those strips time and again in the course of the day. The explanation was that the deep roots of the herbs were tapping mineral resources in the soil which the cows instinctively knew that their bodies needed. Old, long-established pastures contain similar herbs which serve the same purpose. Modern grassland farmers, with their reliance on pure stands of perennial ryegrass, have a few more lessons to relearn.

Probably the earliest experiences of sowing new pastures were gained by patching bare places in old ones. The seed would have been obtained by threshing grass cut for hay, and a primitive method of doing this, still practised on some farms at the end of the nineteenth century, was to beat handfuls of ripe grass-heads against a horizontal hurdle and allow the seed to fall through the interstices of the wattle-work on to a sheet spread below.

Meantime on the Continent the Dutch were, at the end of the sixteenth century, already cultivating specially sown clover leys, and within the first two decades of the seventeenth century clover seed was being sold in Norfolk. By the 1660s it was available at most markets in England. But another 'artificial grass' was introduced and accepted before Dutch clovers. This was sainfoin, a leguminous plant native to England but apparently first exploited by the Dutch, though English farmers considered it a French grass ('saint-foin', sacred hay). It was being widely grown on the Cotswolds (where it was suited to the stony, limestone soil) by the middle of the century and spread quickly across the Midlands, East Anglia and the chalk country. Once established, it provided an excellent hay-cut with aftermath grazing for at least five years, and was much liked by sheep. That other excellent legume, lucerne, also enjoyed an early vogue in the seventeenth century, particularly on the North Downs, but failed to achieve the popularity of sainfoin because, being a native of a warmer climate, it would not produce seed satisfactorily in England.

Of greater importance were the experiments with varieties of clover. Here again the initiative came from Holland, where productive clover leys were well established. Norfolk farmers were importing clover seed as early as 1720, and in the 1640s Sir Richard Weston, a Surrey landowner, was pioneering a clover-flax-turnip rotation and was himself selling Flemish clover seed. He also introduced the practice, later almost universally adopted and still frequently followed, of sowing clover seed under a nurse crop of barley or oats.

Of the two chief species of clover, of course, red clover is used primarily for one-year leys for cutting for hay, while white clover is better suited to long-term leys, for grazing, and the distinction was soon widely understood. Clovers, like other leguminous crops, have the power of 'fixing' nitrogen in the soil, thus greatly increasing its fertility, and this property was well appreciated by Andrew Yarranton who in the 1660s published an excellent treatise on the use of clover in improving soils. Sir Richard Weston also grew hop clover or trefoil as food for sheep.

Although stands of pure clover were at first grown in many districts, farmers soon realized that clover was best used in association with grass. A parallel development in growing and selecting the best grass seeds therefore occurred. Again the Dutch were pioneers, but the idea quickly caught on in England. Experiments were made with various species of grass, including annual meadow grass in Suffolk, but it was soon recognized that the best and most productive species was rye-grass, especially the perennial variety then known as 'evergreen'. It happens that rye-grass, like most other commercially useful grasses and also wild white and red clovers, are indigenous to England, so, although most of the early supplies of seed were imported, English farmers were soon making their own selections and growing their own. By 1675 the Kentish wild white clover, soon to become famous, was being cultivated and harvested for seed in Romney Marsh and other parts of Kent.

Back in early medieval times turnips had been kitchen garden crops but the realization that they were valuable food for cattle and sheep was slow in coming. In spite of Sir Richard Weston's pioneering efforts in the 1640s they did not come into general use as a farm crop until the 1670s (though perhaps a decade earlier in Suffolk). From that time onwards, however, they were

Frontispiece of Complete Country Housewife *shows women's chores.*

grown almost everywhere. Adolphus Speed, writing in 1659, was enthusiastic about them, recommending turnips for cattle, horses, poultry, pigs and rabbits. For horses they had to be sliced, for poultry boiled, and even the water in which they were boiled was useful for helping to fatten pigs. The farmers of Suffolk grew them mainly for cattle rations in winter. Immediately after harvest, fields which were destined for fallowing were ploughed and quickly sown with turnip seed. The early varieties being very hardy were mostly left in the ground during the winter, and pulled as required. When the crop spread to the chalk and limestone soils, however, it was grown primarily for sheep, which were penned on it in hurdle folds which were shifted daily. Here the less hardy but more productive white turnip seems to have been evolved.

No doubt farmers soon discovered that turnips tend to be indigestible, as well as tainting milk. The ideal compromise is to feed cows with hay or good straw, a practice which was early adopted by Suffolk dairy farmers. More advanced was the technique, also advocated by Speed, of mixing them with cattle 'cake'. Here again, the originators were the Dutch who had conceived the notion of buying English rape seed after the oil had been expressed and using it as the basis of a dry feed for their cattle. Mixed with grain and pressed into slabs, it formed an exceptionally valuable winter food for the production of both milk and meat. Linseed, after the oil had been extracted, was just as good.

Rape was also sown for green fodder for feeding sheep and cattle. Sown from May onwards, it could yield crops of from ten to fifteen tons per acre of green matter for controlled grazing in autumn and had a better feeding value than turnips. Rape for seed was sown a little later, usually in August, and harvested in the following summer, the farmers taking a chance of it being killed by frosts, which sometimes happened. The oil—colza oil—extracted from the seed was used for lighting, lubrication and in the manufacture of soap; and it was not long before oil mills for its extraction were established in England, and oil-seed cake became a local product.

Oddly enough, turnips were not the first root crop to migrate from the kitchen garden to the farm as a food for livestock. In the 1590s Gerard referred to carrots being 'sowen in the fieldes' in the sandy soils of Suffolk. Apparently they were grown particularly for feeding the magnificent Suffolk Punch horses, which were being developed locally and which maintained their splendid physique on a diet of carrots, hay and oat-straw. Increasing quantities of carrots were also sent to London for the horses there, and experiments were made in putting carrots into rations for pigs and poultry. Before the end of the century the crop was being grown wherever suitable sandy soils were found throughout England.

For some unexplained reason parsnips were never developed as a field crop for livestock, though potatoes, introduced from America probably by Sir Walter Raleigh in 1586, were, by the end of the seventeenth century, being grown extensively in Lancashire. At first they were intended as a food for young cattle, and their use as a household vegetable only developed later.

The alert and questing minds of progressive seventeenth-century farmers were geared to experimenting with anything which enabled them to keep more livestock or offer a profit. Some tried Jerusalem artichokes, which are easy to grow and make excellent pig food, but for some reason these remained a market garden crop. In the Midlands spurrey, now regarded as a weed, was grown on sandy soils for grazing by sheep in winter. The national acreage of woad increased considerably, and two other dyeing plants, namely madder and weld (or dyer's weed), were grown on a lesser scale. Weld was a new introduction in the seventeenth century and great things were promised for it, but it failed to catch on, except locally in Kent. Around Pontefract, in Yorkshire, and over the county border in Nottinghamshire, liquorice became established as a field crop, the basic material for the celebrated Pontefract cakes.

One of the new crops which attracted a great deal of attention and a large number of adherents was tobacco. First cultivated in England in the 1570s, it quickly became established and by the middle of the seventeenth century was being grown extensively in the Vale of Evesham, the Vale of Pickering and a dozen other districts. Attempts by Stuart monarchs to restrict its acreage, with a view to protecting their interests in American and West Indian plantations, were ineffective, though in the end English growers lost their markets to the more competitive product of Virginia.

Wheat varieties were multiplying. Dozens were now available, though little is known about them save the names, and many of those were probably synonyms. Nearly all were for autumn sowing, but there was one variety, grown in the North, which could be sown in March.

Varieties of barley were less numerous. Most of them were of the two-rowed type, though six-rowed barleys were grown on some of the poorest land. There were also a naked barley, which shed easily from the ear, and a rath-ripe barley for which it was claimed that it needed only two months from sowing to harvest.

Most oats were of either black or white varieties, but there was one so-called red variety which was quite popular in the North, where it was used for porridge. In the South and Midlands oats were grown mainly for horses, though also for pigs, cattle and poultry. All were varieties for spring sowing.

Of rye, which was quite extensively grown, there were two main varieties, one for autumn sowing and one for spring. Lentils were cultivated in certain districts, apparently both for feeding green, for Blith commented that they made 'excellent sweet fodder' for young cattle, and for threshing when ripe, for in Lancashire they were grown for pigeon food. Hemp seems to have become less popular, in spite of the fact that in the second half of the century the Royal Society, seeing possibilities in its export trade, tried to encourage its cultivation. However, big acreages of it were grown in the Fen country around Wisbech. Hemp was not greatly liked by those who had to work with it, for they claimed it gave them headaches or caused rashes; but it was useful for quietening restive horses and squalling babies, as noted previously, and some countryfolk smoked it instead of tobacco, with the natural result that they became stupefied.

Farming was now increasingly a capitalist enterprise and was making good profits. Land became more and more attractive as an investment for surplus money accumulated by merchants and tradesmen. As the demand began to exceed the supply, landowners began to investigate the possibilities of creating more land. They found them in the amphibious realm of fens and marshes which then covered large regions of England.

The most extensive of such areas were the Fens of Cambridgeshire, Lincolnshire, the Marshland division of Norfolk, and parts of the adjacent counties. Here in a dead flat countryside the Midland rivers lost their way while still many miles from the sea. Staggering this way and that, they changed their course every winter, creating new meres and new islets while destroying old ones and constituting a paradise for water-birds and fish. The territory thus in perpetual dispute between land and water extended some seventy miles from north to south, thirty or forty from east to west.

Roman engineers, with the conscripted labour of the Iceni and other British tribes, drained considerable areas of the Fens for cultivation, as we have already noted, but in the anarchy of the succeeding centuries the rivers won them all back again. Nor were the medieval inhabitants of the Fens averse to this state of affairs. The great abbeys of Ely, Peterborough, Ramsey, Thorney and Crowland derived at least part of their wealth from fish and waterfowl, and many a peasant supplemented an inadequate living from a few waterlogged acres by what he could catch among the reeds. Indeed, the reeds themselves provided a welcome income when cut for thatch, and in that woodless country they were also used for fuel. Nowhere in England were the peasants more jealous of their common rights, which they maintained with a fierce independence arising partly from the fact that, their amphibious home being so unhealthy and unattractive, they were used to being left to their own devices by absentee lords. Malaria and other diseases associated with marshland were so prevalent that Daniel Defoe, on a visit in the mid-seventeenth century, was told that many Fen-men, choosing upland brides, lost as many as fifteen wives through illness, and one claimed to be living with his twenty-fifth.

Spirited opposition therefore attended most early attempts at drainage, though from time to time small local schemes were carried out with general assent. When, however, in the 1620s the great capitalist onslaught on the marshes began, the indignant Fen-men, operating under the name Fen Tigers, blew up the sluices.

Land successfully reclaimed proved to be so fertile and the financial rewards therefore so great that the 'adventurers' persisted. One of the chief of that farsighted group was the first Duke (and fifth Earl) of Bedford, who inherited his father's treasure-chest in 1641. His family, the Russells, had acquired the Fenland property of the monks of Thorney at the time of the Dissolution, and later an Elizabeth member of the clan, on military service in the Netherlands, had been impressed by how the Dutch tackled similar aquatic wastes. In due course his descendant brought over Dutch engineers to advise on the projected drainage of a large section of the Fens, and one of the greatest of them, Cornelius Verymuyden, took charge of the scheme, creating as a main artery the straight canal, twenty-one miles long, still known as the Old Bedford River. Twenty years later the New Bedford River was cut on a parallel course, the land between the two channels being reserved as a 'wash' or flood basin into which floods could be diverted instead of spreading freely over the surrounding fields.

The work went on through the reign of Charles I, the Commonwealth and under Charles II. Charles I was indeed so impressed by the promise of the project that he insisted on taking it over, hoping for a big profit for himself, but as these were early days he had to cope with the violent hostility of the commoners without reaping any commensurate reward. Oliver Cromwell favoured the venture, and Charles II, employing more circumspection than his father, invested heavily in it.

Opposition eventually died away as a new generation of Fen-men found they could make a better living by working on the reclaimed land than ever their fathers did by the precarious devices of fishing and snaring wildfowl.

The reclaimed soils—some silt and some peat—were so rich that yields of wheat previously unheard-of could be grown without manuring. The land would in fact produce anything, and small farmers could, by growing vegetables and other market garden produce, derive a good living from a few acres, often cultivated by their wives while they themselves earned high wages on the big farms.

It is difficult to estimate the total amount of land made available in the Fens by these 'adventurers'. The acreages quoted are staggering: 16,000 acres around Spalding in one scheme; 70,000 acres in the Lindsey Levels in another; 21,500 acres in Holland Fen. When the final reclamation was

The Old and New Bedford Rivers, canals begun as a drainage system by Cornelius Verymuyden in the Norfolk fens.

completed, the province of good agricultural land added to England could have been little less than 1,000,000 acres.

Similar though lesser reclamation projects were initiated in other parts of the country. Much of the marshland in the coastal districts of Kent and Sussex, e.g. Romney Marsh, Sheppey and the Pevensey Levels had been drained sufficiently in earlier times to create good grazing meadows, but in the second half of the seventeenth century the plough began to make their accumulated fertility available for corn crops. In the central Somerset plain, as subject to flooding as the Fens of the east Midlands, the drainage engineers were content to straighten out the meandering river courses with a view to improving the grass, a crop for which the soil and climate are admirably suited. Limited drainage schemes were also undertaken in the Lancashire and Cheshire plains and in the Holderness district of Yorkshire.

Problems were later encountered, especially in the Fens. One of the main ones was the steady shrinkage of peat soils, amounting to twelve feet or so in a century. The land level around the mouths of the Fenland rivers, where they entered The Wash, was slightly higher than in the central basin, which was below sea level, so there was always a drainage problem, which the peat shrinkage aggravated. In due course it became necessary to pump the drainage water from the field channels into the main drains, from the main drains into the rivers and eventually from the rivers into the sea (which last operation can be accomplished only when the tide is ebbing). Nowadays the work is done by a system of pumping stations, culminating in gigantic ones at the river mouths, but before the invention of steam power, windmills tried to do the work, not with entire success. All this, however, lay in the future for the seventeeth-century 'adventurers', who were immensely satisfied with their imaginative joint-stock venture.

The principle of up-and-down husbandry, or the rotation of grassland with arable cropping, one of the main innovations of this invigorating century, was practised chiefly on lands that had been enclosed and were under individual ownership. It was also introduced by common consent, in some instances, on open-field lands where the old strip system still prevailed. Where opinion was divided—some of the farmers being eager to try the new system, others insisting on the old—it sometimes proved possible to re-arrange the fields so that both schools of thought could be satisfied. Paradoxically a form of leasehold became common whereby a penalty of £5 per acre was imposed for ploughing up old grassland—a clause which, incidentally, was still to be found in many tenancy agreements until the middle of the twentieth century. But its purpose in the seventeenth century

134

was not to discourage farmers from using the plough on old grass but rather to ensure that the landowner received his share of the increased production.

Up-and-down farming allowed more efficient use to be made of farmyard manure. The old method of spreading manure over grassland in autumn resulted in much of its nutrient value being lost to the air, but burying it by the plough ensured that it was properly incorporated in the soil, to the benefit of the following crop. Some farmers installed drainage systems to take the effluent from livestock buildings to underground tanks, from which it could be pumped over the fields, and numerous experiments were made with virtually every substance which promised to have manurial value: sea sand, fish offal, wheat chaff, rags, street refuse, soot, the ash from soap-boiling, coal dust, malt dust, pulverized shells and brine from salt-works were among the less obvious materials tested. But the success of most manures, of course, depended on the types of soil to which they were applied.

Blith also describes two other futuristic ideas with which seventeenth-century farmers were experimenting but which have had to wait till the late

Eighteenth-century plan of a dung pit.

twentieth century for their fulfilment. For the first he recommends that 'you shall take the slimie thick water which commeth from dung-hills, or for want thereof, water in which Cow-dung hath been steeped, and therein you shall steep your seed-corn; that is to say, if it be barley you shall steep it for the space of thirty-six hours or thereabouts . . . and the seed thus steeped you shall sow it according to good Husbandry, and there is no doubt of wonderful increase.' The principle is that of pre-sowing germination, which seed-merchants have recently been rediscovering. The second idea Blith describes as follows: 'There be others which take the Seed-corn, and steeping it in good store of Cow-dung and water, stir all together for an hour in the morning and an hour at night, and then being settled, drain the water from the seed and the dung, and the next morning sow the corn and the dung both together on the land, being sure not to scant the land of seed, and no doubt the increase will be wonderfull.' Here we have a concept which has been applied in two ways in the present century. First combine-drills were devised to deposit fertilizer alongside the seed, so that its nutrients should be readily available when the seed started to sprout. More recently seed merchants have introduced pelleted seed, chiefly for vegetable and salad crops, with a coating of fertilizer around each seed.

While the farmers of Stuart times were thus exercising their ingenuity over seeds and sowing they seem to have paid little attention to harvesting. Or perhaps it was simply because they could not think of a way to improve that highly satisfactory tool, the scythe. Indeed, there *is* no way, and it was not until inventors dismissed the scythe from their mind and began to think about scissors that they made progress.

Builders of farmhouses in past centuries usually had in mind the possibility of war or raids. The houses were therefore either so flimsy that they could easily be rebuilt or, if more substantial, were strong enough to stand a short siege. A surrounding moat was often a feature of the better farmsteads. Now that times were more settled, more attention could be paid to convenience, permanence and even comfort.

The substantial seventeenth-century house often has gardens and grounds arranged in neat squares, with the orchard occupying one square. An interesting feature of many houses, typical of the new age, is the door midway along one side, which had now become the front. This represents a distinct break with the old type of long house, in which the door was at one end and led into the great hall. Now the number of rooms multiplied and the hall became little more than an ante-room in which visitors were received. The downstairs rooms were matched by others on the floor above, these being devoted more and more to bedrooms, though some were regarded as storage space for farm produce. An innovation increasingly adopted as the century progressed was the central chimney stack, designed so that the main rooms on either side of it could each have a fireplace. As timber became scarcer brick was increasingly used, though stone was naturally favoured where it was readily available. The kitchen, buttery, milkhouse and parlour were all separate rooms, even in the houses of modest yeomen and tenant farmers.

A farm would have been well staffed both with male and female workers, some of the latter engaged in semi-domestic duties such as dairy and poultry work. Most slept and ate in the farm-house, though in some instances the unmarried men slept in lofts over the stables or byres. The married men of course had cottages of their own. In a typical farmhouse the big bedroom at the head of the stairs was occupied by the farmer and his wife, the bedrooms on one side by daughters and maidservants, those on the other by sons and menservants, so that, theoretically at least, no one could pass from one wing to the other or creep downstairs without the master and mistress knowing.

The farm housewife was as busy as in Tudor days but as her husband prospered she made sure that some of his money was used to make the house more comfortable. The windows were now not only frequently glazed but also were fitted with curtains. There were chairs instead of forms and benches, and cushions on some of them. The best bed was stuffed with feathers; the pillows with down. The utensils on the table were pewter.

The probate inventory of the property of William Symes, of Chetnole, Dorset, dated 26 February 1671, illustrates the standard of living. He is described as a yeoman—the word 'farmer' was not yet in common use. No mention is made of house or land, so it may be assumed that both were rented, in which case the term 'yeoman' seems to have been rather loosely applied.

	£.	s.	d.
His wearing apparrell	3.	10.	0.
in money	3.	1.	4.

In his Lodging Chamber
One ffeather Bed; one Bolester;
two pillowes; one Coulead; two
Blanketts; one Bedsted;
one Chest; 3 Coffers; a
little Table board; 2 Boxes .... 3. 17. 0.

137

In a little roome annexd his Lodging Chamber
a little Bedstead; one
ffeatherbed; a Coulead;
two Blanketts; two pillowes
& one bolster . . . . .1.   0. 0.

In the Middle Chamber
One standing Bedstead; one
ffeatherbed; one Rugg; two
Blanketts; one ffeather Bolster;
two pillowes; one Trucklebedsteed;
one dust Bed; one Coulead; two
Blanketts; one ffeather Bolster;
2 pillowes; one Presse; one
Coffer . . . . .5.   5. 0.

In annother Chamber annexd the Middle Chamber
Twoo grinterres . . . .   5. 0.

In the Chamber at the East end of the dwellinghouse
of Cheeses 7 . . . . .1.   2. 0.

In the Hall
One Cupbourd; one Tableboord;
one little tableboord; one
fforme; 2 Joynd stooles; 2
Chaires; one Chest . . . . .1.   5. 0.

In the roome annexed the Hall
One Bedsteed; one dust Bed;
6 Barrells . . . .   10. 0.

In the Buttery
Twoo Silting Trowses; 4 Barrells . . . .   10. 0.

In the Milkehowse
one butter Barrell with aboute
5 or 6 doz of Butter in it . . . . .1.   0. 0.

In the Kitching
One Tableboard and fforme; one
Ambry; 3 Chaires; one paire of
Andierrs; 2 Spitts; one dripping
pan; fender; one firepan and
tongs; one Churne; 2 Bruing Tubbs;
one Long Trindle; 7 other
trindles; 3 Tubbs; Butter barrells
and a Salting Tubb; 7 Brasspans;
4 kettles; one Skillet of Brass;

pots; 2 paire of hanging Crookes
and Griddier; 2 paire of pothookes;
one Skimmer; 17 peawter platters;
3 flagons; one pewter dish; 4
Candlesticks & a pistle & morter;
4 sides of Bacon; a brest of beefe ....11. 5. 0.
5 pailes; one gun; one Iron
barr; 3 Irone wedges; 1 peckake
& 2 matterks .... 13. 0.
7 paire of Sheetes; 3 paire of
pillowties; 3 table Cloths; 2 doze
of Tablenapkins; 12 Silver Spoons ....5. 10. 0.

Out goods

11 Cowes	38. 10. 0.
2 yearelings	2. 10. 0.
2 horse beast	8. 10. 0.
2 hoggs	1. 10. 0.
one silver Bole & furnace pan	4. 0. 0.
the plow tackling & wood & sacks	2. 10. 0.
a little Stack of wheate & hay	4. 10. 0.
in Lumber	10. 0.
	95. 0. 0.

As the beds were evidently made at the time of the inspection one gathers that the household consisted of Mr Symes, probably his wife, three other persons (perhaps children) who slept upstairs, and possibly a servant who slept on the dust bed in 'the roome annexd the Hall'. The presence of a Mrs Symes can be deduced from the numerous items of particular interest to a housewife. We note the featherbeds, pillows, bolsters and blankets, the kitchen utensils, the silver spoons, the table-napkins, the table-cloths, the brass pans and the 'seven paire of sheetes'. As Professor W. G. Hoskins, the agricultural historian remarks, 'Left to themselves, men would probably effect few changes in their domestic surroundings. It was their wives, from the sixteenth century onwards, who saw improvements in other people's houses and agitated at home for something better. The money was there, but it was they who made sure where some of it was spent . . . If it were not for women, one sometimes feels that a great number of men would still be content to live in a cave.'

There is however no real demarcation line between between the affairs of the household and those of the farm. The 'twoo grinterres', which are compartments or containers for threshed corn, are upstairs next to a bedroom. The kitchen contains not only the necessary equipment for cooking, brewing and salting butter—and the household treasures such as the silver spoons, table-napkins and sheets—but also the farmer's gun, pick-axe, mattocks and iron bar and wedges. The presence of the butter barrels, buttery and salting tubs, as well as of eleven cows and two yearlings, indicates that this was a dairy farm, as one would expect in that district. The eleven cows represent a rather larger than average herd. For eleven herds in the same district in the 1670s the average number of dairy cattle per herd was 7.4.

From similar seventeenth-century inventories it seems that there was little difference in the standard of living of men who classified themselves as yeomen, husbandmen and gentlemen. In 1679 Thomas Griggs of Chetnole, who styled himself a 'husbandman', left an estate worth £183. 4. 0, his household goods being very similar to those of William Symes. His livestock consisted of nine cows, two calves, two hogs and a mare. William Harris, of Leigh, however, who is recorded as a 'gentleman' when he died in 1684, left an estate valued at only £102. 4. 1. His household goods were rather more diverse and included a warming pan, more than sixty pewter utensils (among them 'three pewter Chamber potts'), four table-cloths, a clock, a carpet, a pair of curtains, various items of silver, six gold rings and some books. Evidently, though, he engaged in dairying, having all the equipment for making both butter and cheese. His livestock comprised five cows, two heifers, four steers, five young bullocks, one pig and one old mare. He also owned a plough.

An interesting feature of these inventories is the number of craftsmen who were also farmers, usually in a small way. Robert Bailey, a tanner, had two cows, two heifers, three horses and a field of growing corn. His estate was worth £167. Benjamin Miller, a baker, had two cows, a bay mare and one hog, as well as hay worth £6. He owned his own house, valued at £60, and left £276, though £20 are recorded as 'desperate debts'. John Evered, a blacksmith, had seven cows, a steer, a yearling, a pig and a substantial quantity of corn, hay and hemp. Widows evidently carried on farming after the death of their husbands; we find Elizabeth Symes, who died in 1693, leaving three cows, five two-year-old heifers, two yearling bullocks, two hogs, hay worth £10 and cheese worth £5.

It was good to be alive in the seventeenth century. The windows had been thrown open in Elizabethan times to the sunlight and air of the Renaissance. Across the Western ocean a new world had been discovered. English seamen had successfully challenged the menacing colossus of Spain. Books from the new printing presses were promoting the wider dissemination of knowledge and Shakespeare had worked miracles with the English language. English farms, always strongholds of conservatism, were not immediately transformed by the ferment, but they were not immune to it. The leaven took time to work, but work it did. The countryside was poised for the tremendous advances that lay ahead.

Time past and time present: dairy shorthorns going to pasture in front of sixteenth-century barn and fourteenth-century church, Astwick, Bedfordshire.

9. The Agricultural Revolution

The key to the dramatic agricultural developments of the eighteenth century is political. In the reigns of Charles II, James II, William and Mary, and Anne political power became polarized on two great parties: the Tories dominated by High Anglican landowners and the Whigs ruled by dissenting merchants and financiers.

The Tories, who were in the ascendant during the last years of Queen Anne, would gladly have welcomed her half-brother James as her successor if he had consented to become a Protestant, but this he would not do. So, on the death of Anne, the Crown, following the 1689 Act of Parliament, passed to the House of Hanover, whose head, now George I, spoke not a word of English and who knew nothing of English ways and customs. Working under these disabilities and being not particularly interested in his new kingdom, George naturally left the management of affairs to his ministers. Because the Tories had been intriguing to prevent his accession, the first administration of his reign was Whig, and thereafter from 1714 to 1761, the Whig party played its cards so astutely that the Tories were kept out of office.

Resentful and disgruntled, they retired to their country estates, forming Jacobite clubs at which they toasted James, 'the king over the water'. From time to time opportunities occurred to substitute deeds for words. The first, in 1715, happened so soon after the arrival of George I that they were caught unprepared. The rebellion against the House of Hanover that erupted in that year was confined to Scotland and some of the northern counties and was suppressed without great difficulty. Thirty years later an altogether more formidable challenge came in the invasion led by James's son, Bonnie Prince Charlie. A Scottish army, with the popular and glamorous prince at its head, marched unopposed from Edinburgh to Derby. Since most of England's small army was overseas, fighting in The Netherlands against the French, all that was needed for success was a general rising of the old Jacobite and Tory gentry. It did not happen. For a generation the Tory landowners, excluded

Romantic and somewhat exaggerated scenes of English farm life depicted by eighteenth-century artists.

from office, had exercised their fertile minds and expended their energies on their estates. They took pride in their achievements and were full of what they further intended to do. When it came to the crunch, they were unwilling to risk everything on the hazards of a civil war. So the opportunity slipped past and was gone forever.

Another sixteen years were to pass before they could leave their rural retreats and again assume control of the affairs of state. By then there was a new king, George III, who, unlike his two predecessors, was no foreigner. English born and bred, he aspired, after a few fairly disastrous sorties into politics, to be above all else an English country gentleman. With him the Tory country landowners could readily identify, and throughout his long reign (which ended in 1820) the dominance of the squire in the countryside was complete.

The stage was now set for a vast expansion of the enclosure movement, without which the agricultural revolution would hardly have been possible. Only politics could make enclosures legal, and now the country had in power politicians who were interested in doing so. There had been hardly a decade from Norman times onwards when some enclosures were not being made, as we have seen. Even when the feudal system was at its height, and strip cultivation of the open fields was the norm, each little farmstead and even cottage had its own 'close', enclosed by a hedge or fence. Throughout the Middle Ages opportunists had helped themselves to slices of waste or forest, and in the bleak centuries following the Black Death, big landowners, including abbeys and other ecclesiastical establishments, had enclosed vast areas of land as sheep-walks—sometimes evicting whole communities of peasants in the process. On enclosed land it was possible to build up fertility, introduce a proper rotation of arable crops and adopt the beneficial practice of alternate husbandry, to say nothing of the advantage of having all one's land within a ring fence rather than scattered in acre strips all over the parish.

The people who resisted the enclosures were, naturally enough, those who were going to be dispossessed by them. A peasant could make a living on a few acres of land if he had common rights (grazing, etc.) over a much larger area. Take away those subsidiary rights and he lost his livelihood. At the opening of the eighteenth century something like half the arable land in England was still being farmed under the old open-field system, though most of it was situated in the corn-growing counties of the East, the east Midlands and South.

It is true that the old open-field system offered more flexibility than was at one time thought possible. Groups of farmers did at times agree on improvements. For instance, on the Oxfordshire manor of Taston, near Woodstock, in 1700, twenty-two tenant farmers, with the approval of the lord of the manor, the Earl of Litchfield, agreed to sow a section of one of the open fields with sainfoin. Each farmer contracted to sow the strips he held in that field. When the crop was established it was to be grazed according to the traditional common rights, which allocated grazing for two cows for every yardland (about thirty acres) held on the manor. However, no grazing was permitted until each farmer had cut his own strip (or strips) for hay. After October 13th sheep were also allowed to graze on the sainfoin, at the rate of six sheep and ten lambs per yardland. Grazing had to cease on January 2nd. In order to provide water for the grazing stock all the participants had to assist in digging a pond. Ploughing up the sainfoin before there was general agreement about terminating the ley was punished by a fine of £10. And three fieldsmen were appointed to see that everyone did his share and complied with the rules.

It worked, but what a cumbersome arrangement. How much simpler for each farmer to have permanent occupation of an area of land to farm as seemed to him best. The advantage was so obvious that by the sixteenth and seventeenth centuries much enclosure by private agreement was going on. For some reason, enclosure by agreement came first to pastoral regions, to the grasslands of the north and west. Most of the open fields in Northumberland had been enclosed by the early eighteenth century. Most of the land in the Vale of York had likewise been enclosed 'before the time of the Parliamentary enclosures'. In the late sixteenth century a witness testified to a Somerset tribunal that, to her knowledge, people had been enclosing land and turning arable land into pasture for the past fifty years 'at their will and pleasure without denial of anyone'.

Until the early eighteenth century, land enclosed by general consent of the owners and tenants was registered by agreement with the Court of Chancery. But as the rural and predominantly Tory landowners began to devote their attention more wholeheartedly to their estates they realized the potentialities of private Acts of Parliament. In the House of Commons a man with plenty of friends in politics could bypass troublesome local opposition. The procedure for getting a private member's enclosure bill through Parliament was soon resolved in detail. To set the ball rolling it needed only one owner to petition for an enclosure. After 1774 he had to give notice of his intention by fastening a notice to the church door for three Sundays in August or September, but before that date he was not compelled to give any notice at all, and in some instances the arrival of the commissioners to apportion the land was the first intimation to some of the farmers concerned that anything was afoot. In any case, any landowner contemplating an enclosure took care to have all the necessary legal documents prepared and the stages of the bill carefully mapped out before he consulted any of his lesser neighbours.

In Parliament, after brief first and second readings, each bill was passed to a committee under the control of a Member, who could appoint to that committee any other Members he thought fit to choose. Under the principle, 'you scratch my back and I'll scratch yours', the committees were naturally loaded with interested parties who took little notice of any cries of protest from peasants in the distant fields. So most of the Enclosure bills sailed through Parliament with a minimum of opposition. Only when two distinguished landowners fell out was a bill sent back to its instigators for further consideration, and it usually managed to get through at the second attempt.

From 1702 to 1762, 246 private Enclosure Acts, concerned with about 400,000 acres, were passed by Parliament. But in 1761, when the Tories returned to power after their long exile, the flood-gates were opened: more than 3,000,000 acres were enclosed by 2,000 or so Acts passed between 1761 and 1801. From 1802 to 1844, just short of 2,000 more Acts dealt with a further 2,500,000 acres. The torrent culminated in a General Enclosure Act in 1845.

Examination of typical Enclosure Acts suggests that the provisions were reasonably fair.

> The open common fields, commons, marshes, etc., were to be divided among the several persons according to their respective Rights and Interests, due regard being paid to Quality, Quantity and Situation, and the allotments being placed as near the Homesteads, etc., as is consistent with general convenience.
>
> All houses erected 20 years or more before the Act, and the sites of all such houses, to be considered as ancient messuages entitled to right of common, with the exception of houses built on encroachments, the owners of which are to have whatever allotment the Commissioners think fair and reasonable.

The poor were taken care of by retaining an area of common land for their communal use, as in times past. If thought advisable, the trustees (normally the Vestry Meeting of the parish) could enclose a part of it and let it to a tenant farmer, using the rent for the benefit of the poor. In some instances, however, this procedure does not seem to have been adopted. Many parishes have small blocks of land, now fields, named 'Poor Folks' or 'Poor Patch', often in the remotest part of the parish, which seems to have been enclosed and rented off without any attempt at commonage.

Getting a private member's bill through Parliament was naturally an expensive business. In one instance the payment to the Commissioners was put at £2 a day, plus an unspecified sum to the surveyors. In another the Commissioners received a lump payment of £210. These of course were official payments and take no account of private expenditure incurred by the initiators of enclosure bills in such matters as legal services and concealed bribes. The legitimate expenses naturally had to be borne by the estate, and so a section of common land was usually set aside for sale, the proceeds being used for that purpose. Who would buy such land? Why, the principal landowners, of course. They were permitted to mortgage their land at up to £3 an acre to raise the money, and it has been suggested that this £3 an acre was probably about the average a man would have to pay for his title to land acquired under an Enclosure Act. While the major landowners and larger farmers might have little difficulty in borrowing the necessary cash, for many cottagers and small farmers it was impossible. There are instances of them selling their allotment of land to their wealthier neighbours simply in order to pay the legal expenses.

These smallholders now retreat into a minor role; instead of peasant farmers they become wage-earning labourers. At least, some of them do. But large numbers migrated to the new industrial towns where they were welcomed by factory owners who saw them only as a reservoir of cheap labour. Their descendants were to become the means by which nemesis eventually fell on the country squires and farming in general. For when, after the Reform Acts, the franchise was extended to the working classes, the latter had no sympathy with their aristocratic rulers nor any understanding of rural affairs. A deep chasm had opened between town and country, and the town had the votes.

But that development lay in the future. For the present the eighteenth-century enclosers triumphantly took stock of their new possessions and set about moulding them into attractive estates and farms. The open fields with their baulks and furrows, and the furzy commons with their multiplicity of peasant rights and customs, were erased from the scene. The fashion was to regard the rural landscape as a bare canvas, on which a gifted landscape artist, such as 'Capability' Brown could produce a work of genius. Brown got his name through his habit, when called in to advise on the laying-out of an estate, of cocking his head and observing, 'Yes, I see great capability of improvement here.' He and his fellow practitioners were in great demand.

The nucleus of the country estate such as Brown laid out was, of course, the 'big house', which had its parallel in the villa of late Roman times, and many of these country mansions now assumed the proportions and grandeur of palaces. We have only to look at Wentworth Woodhouse, in Yorkshire (built about 1734–40), Blenheim Palace, Oxfordshire (1705–20), Petworth House, Sussex (*c.* 1690), Ashridge Park, Hertfordshire (1808–17), Dodington Hall, Gloucestershire (1797) and many others to appreciate the scale and splendour of the architecture. The interiors, equally imposing, were exquisitely designed and furnished, and replete with art treasures.

The immediate setting of a great house comprised gardens and a park. At the beginning of the period the rural gentry had little time for wild, untamed

Magnificent mansions and pleasure parks such as Whiteknights Park, Berkshire (now the Institute of Agricultural History, Reading University) typify the eighteenth-century preoccupation with nature as an adornment of country life.

nature. Formality prevailed. The original design for Wilton House, Wilt-shire, in 1633, shows a series of rectangular plots on either side of a broad central avenue leading in a dead straight line to the exact centre of the front of the house. The pergolas, the trees, the pools, the flowerbeds are all arranged with mathematical precision. Gardeners of the age were skilful at coaxing trees by expert pruning to throw out branches at the correct height and angle to transform an avenue into a symmetrically arched cloister.

In the eighteenth century the vogue switched from straight lines to curves and circles. Contemporary pictures of some of the great houses built in the sixteenth and seventeenth centuries strike us as bleak and austere, with no trees to break the severe lines of their environment, but in the second half of the eighteenth century a better appreciation of sylvan surroundings had developed. Guests at country houses were invited to walk round the grounds after lunch, and their leisurely perambulations would be frequently enlivened by the discovery of new and unheralded delights. Visitors to the Stourhead estate in south-west Wiltshire, once the home of the Colt Hoare family but now the property of the National Trust, may savour the same pleasures. A stroll around the lake, by paths that lead over lawns and through clearings amid stands of majestic trees, offers a succession of vistas in which the focal point is either a Palladian summer house or, from the far side of the lake, the house itself. The summer house was an important feature of the amenities of the home park, for here, as they rested from the exertions which had brought them thus far, the guests partook of afternoon tea—a platoon of servants having preceded them.

Naturally there was competition between estate-owners to go one better than the neighbours. Exotic trees and shrubs were planted, imitation ruins were a valued feature, caves and grottoes enjoyed a vogue. The rural landscape was something to be 'improved' and its owners were completely ruthless and single-minded in their approach. A stream was a godsend, for it could be dammed to create an ornamental lake, preferable with an associated waterfall. Inconveniently situated houses were demolished.

Whole villages shared the same fate. In Yorkshire the village of Hinders-kelfe disappeared in 1693 to clear a space for the monster palace of Castle Howard. At Everleigh, on the borders of Wiltshire and Hampshire, Francis Dugdale Astley transferred the village to a new site in the first decade of the nineteenth century. When he inherited the estate 'he found the main village clustered around the church and inn, hard by his front door', an arrangement which evidently did not suit his second wife, whom he married in 1805. So all the buildings within a radius of several hundred yards of the Manor

149

House, including the ancient hostelry of the *Rose and Crown* and the Church, were pulled down and re-erected elsewhere, and the area was enclosed as a park. The main turnpike road was diverted around the park boundary. He had to obtain a special dispensation from the Bishop of Salisbury to dismantle the old fourteenth-century church and build a new one.

Perhaps the most remarkable instance of the wholesale clearance of an old settlement to make room for a new park is provided by Milton Abbas, where Lord Milton demolished not a village but a town of more than a hundred houses, with church, grammar school, four inns, a brewery, a market place and a number of shops. Three feet of soil were heaped over the market place and main street, but the grassy humps and hollows that mark the site of other streets and buildings are still visible along either side of the little valley between Milton Abbey House and the ornamental lake. The new village which Lord Milton built for the dispossessed townsfolk, a mile or so away, is now one of the showpieces of Dorset.

Lord Milton surrounded his new park with a wall five and a quarter miles in circumference, but in neighbouring Wiltshire William Beckford, a highly eccentric genius, went one better by erecting a twelve-foot-high wall many miles long around his estate. His motive was to keep out horsemen and hounds, after his meditations had been disturbed by the irruption of a pack when he was walking in the park. His reaction to the disturbance was unusual, for most landowners were keen supporters of fox-hunting. Indeed, most of them put a high value on their estates as game preserves. Over much of England the fox had taken the place of deer as the animal of the chase, but the popularity of the pheasant and partridge was in the ascendant.

Landscape planning did not end at the park perimeter; it was applied to the whole estate. New woods were planted, old ones reshaped, and clumps of beeches were placed like beacons on the highest hills. At Amesbury a local landowner is said to have adorned his estate with a pattern of round tree-clumps, representing the battle plan of the Battle of Trafalgar. Each clump is said to have marked the relative position of a ship of the British or French fleets. It is impossible now to check the truth of the tradition, for some of the clumps have been destroyed by a new by-pass of the A303, but the survivors are still visible from the road. Shelter belts of tall beeches marked the boundaries of many estates.

Outside the limits of the parks the field pattern was now very different from that of the pre-enclosure countryside. The land was divided into square or rectangular fields of varying size, usually between ten and twenty acres;

the boundaries planted with 'quickset' hedges of hawthorn. Ownership of a hedge was often indicated by a ditch on the far side, which protected it from browsing cattle, and the relative positions of hedge and ditch have since been used to decide ownership of hedges. New lanes on a grid pattern, in contrast to the old meandering ones of medieval times, served the fields.

The houses of the wealthier farmers were in many respects miniatures of the great house of the estate, especially when they were occupied by well-to-do tenant farmers. The estate-owners, on the whole, looked after their farmers, provided they behaved themselves. In the eighteenth century only about 5% of the populace was entitled to vote, but farmers possessed of an adequate income were among them, and landowners with political aspirations took good care of their voters. Moreover, much of the money for the lavish expenditure on their property came from rents. Many fine examples of Queen Anne and Georgian farm-houses and farmsteads still serve as the headquarters of modern farms.

As the eighteenth century progressed, more and more landowners developed a home farm of their own. The prosperity of many of their tenants convinced them that there must be money in the business. Besides, having become sold on the idea of 'improvements', and having effected all they could on their houses and parks, they turned naturally to their farms as the next target. The great landowners were thus in the forefront of the changes in farming practice that caused the Agricultural Revolution of the eighteenth century to match the Industrial Revolution. They were among the great pioneers.

Even King George III joined in. Disillusioned with politics, he left the affairs of state to his ministers and turned his attention to Windsor Great Park, which was a wilderness of bog, bracken, brambles and ancient trees. Having drained and levelled a considerable section of it, he created there two model farms, one of which he called Norfolk Farm, after the Norfolk style of farming popularized by Viscount Townshend and described below, the other Flemish Farm, planned on the lines of a model farm in Flanders. Here he experimented happily with all the innovations that the age was producing, though he was disappointed that, right to the end, profit eluded him. He had other farms, notably at Richmond and Kensington Gardens, and performed a valuable service to posterity by importing a nucleus flock of Spanish merino sheep. Although eventually they proved to have little future in England the royal flock flourished long enough to provide foundation stock for Australia, where they became ancestors of the millions of Corriedales and Polwarths which have contributed so much to the prosperity of that continent. The King even wrote articles on agriculture and his ideas on controversial farming topics appeared under the pseudonym 'Ralph Robinson' for a popular periodical, *Annals of Agriculture*, edited and published by his friend Arthur Young.

The personal enterprise and ingenuity that characterized the century are epitomized by the efforts of two outstanding landowners, both with estates in Norfolk. One was the second Viscount Townshend, who, on his retirement from politics in 1730, undertook the improvement of his lands at Raynham. He is generally credited with the introduction of the Norfolk 'four-course rotation' of crops, on which the agriculture of the future was to be based. Its essence is the alternation of a straw crop with a root or seeds crop. Typically, its four-year programme consists of: first year, roots; second year, barley; third year, seeds; fourth year, wheat.

The roots used by Townshend were turnips, which earned him the nickname, 'Turnip Townshend'. They were eaten by sheep folded on them in much of England, though on heavy soils the turnips were fed to stock in yards, and the dung returned to the fields later. The barley crop, which cashed in on all this fertility, was undersown with red clover and rye-grass, but sometimes red clover alone and sometimes sainfoin and trefoil with clover and grass. The next year the seeds would yield a cut of hay, then the land was grazed before ploughing in autumn. Alternatively, farmyard manure was sometimes spread over it after haymaking. Either way, the soil was in good heart to produce a fine wheat crop in the fourth year.

Turnips had been grown in England, as already noted, as a field crop in the previous century, but their enthusiastic adoption by Townshend did much to get the new programme for arable farming widely established. He talked, it was said, of turnips, turnips and nothing but turnips, an obsession which was pilloried in a popular skit:

If a person 'turnips' cries,
On the day his father dies;
Tis no proof that he would rather
Have a turnip than a father.

Progress is nevertheless usually made by men with single-track minds like his.

Forty or fifty years later, in the same part of Norfolk, Thomas Coke, later the Earl of Leicester, became the second of the great landowners to pioneer the new style of farming. On succeeding to his estates at Holkham in 1776 he set about improving them with characteristic enthusiasm. His extensive

Viscount Townshend, pioneer of the Norfolk four-course crop rotation.

estates were mainly on light, heathy soils, very similar to those of Lord Townshend. Their condition at the beginning of his reign was described as 'one blade of grass and two rabbits fighting over that'. The Norfolk four-course rotation suited them admirably, and Coke reinforced it by frequent heavy marling. He grew impressive crops of the newly introduced swedes, employing the newly invented seed-drill to sow them, and fed them to Southdown sheep and Devon cattle stocked at unheard-of rates.

Coke had a home farm of 3,000 acres, and around it were tenanted farms totalling very much more. He soon succeeded in making his tenants as enthusiastic for the new methods as he was. Their tenancies were based on the strict observance of rules of husbandry which he himself laid down and practised, and in return he gave them long leases and provided them with splendid farmhouses and buildings. During his forty-year régime he raised the rent-roll of the estate from £2,200 to £20,000, but his tenants were well able to afford to pay the increase, for they made fortunes. They loved him, says the by no means sympathetic William Cobbett; they spoke of him 'as affectionate children speak of their parents', and when he died in 1842, at the age of ninety, the 'yeomen of Norfolk' started a fund for a memorial which was supported by farmers and landowners from Devon to Scotland and which raised sufficient money to erect the huge column, 125 feet high, that still dominates the Holkham countryside.

Thomas Coke, Earl of Leicester, did much to popularize new ideas in farming.

Besides being a highly efficient practitioner Coke was an effective propagandist. Early in his career at Holkham he initiated the custom of inviting his tenants and neighbours to a meal and a talk about farming matters every sheep-shearing. The fame of these summer gatherings spread so rapidly that soon agriculturists were flocking to Holkham from every part of Britain and some from overseas. The proceedings were extended over several days, during which Coke kept open house, and the overflow from his own mansion was accommodated in the spacious homes of his tenants. In 1821 the Holkham sheep-shearings, or 'Clippings' as Coke called them, were attended by no fewer than 7,000 guests. By day they inspected the crops and livestock; in the evenings, after dinner, they talked about them. The educational value of the gatherings was incalculable.

The example set by Coke and Townshend, and by others who have been not so well publicized, was followed far and wide. It did, after all, offer landowners an opportunity of vastly increasing their capital and income—in the case of Holkham, tenfold—simply by improving their land. By and large, they played fair with their tenants. The rents were only raised in relation to the tenant's income, and not only were the terms of leases greatly extended but at the end of them compensation was offered to the retiring tenant for improvements he had made. No wonder that many independent farmers, owning their land, sold out to the local capitalist landowner. They realized that they would be far better off working the farm with the help of his capital than trying to run it with their own limited resources.

As has been stated, the Norfolk four-course system on which the new farming was founded had as an essential feature a root crop, usually turnips, which provided valuable winter food for livestock, especially sheep, and enriched the soil through sheep being folded on them. In addition, once they were sown in rows and hoed by the new machinery, described below, they abolished the need for a summer fallow.

During the second half of the eighteenth century when an improved type, the Swedish turnip, or swede, was introduced, Coke thought highly of it. His method was to lift the roots in autumn, top them, store them in clamps and use them, sliced, for sheep food in winter. After a time it was realized that their greater hardiness made having them in the ground, where sheep could nibble them, possible in all but the severest winter.

Mangolds were introduced from France at about the same time but for a long time were regarded as only a novelty. At first only the leaves were used, the roots being thrown away, until farm pigs were observed eating the discarded roots. Less hardy than the swede and most varieties of turnip, the

155

mangold is also less nutritious, but it can produce very heavy crops and eventually was widely grown for cattle food in the south of England.

Cabbages, which had been cultivated as a field crop for feeding cattle at Wimborne St Giles, Dorset, in the 1660s, were now widely grown. In the early years of the nineteenth century cabbages averaging 13 pounds apiece are recorded at Danby, Yorkshire, and a crop of 54 tons an acre was grown near Grantham, in Lincolnshire. Several varieties, including the still popular Drumhead, are mentioned. Around Grimsthorpe, Lincolnshire, farmers specializing in ram-breeding grew cabbages in preference to turnips. Another brassica crop, kohl rabi, still regarded as something of a novelty by many twentieth-century gardeners, was introduced as a field crop by a Mr Reynolds, of Addisham, Kent, in 1767. He gave the tops to his cows and allowed pigs to eat the roots.

Rape was grown for its oil-producing seed but also as fodder for sheep and cattle, and in Yorkshire at this time public 'rape-threshings' apparently almost vied with Coke's sheep-shearings in popularity, people from miles around gathering to watch and assist in the communal threshing with flails. In Kent and Surrey hop-picking also assumed the nature of a social occasion, with battalions of hop-pickers already making it an annual holiday from London slums. Some places staged a hop supper at the end of the hop harvest, marked by wild scenes of revelry.

Hemp and flax, though still quite widely grown, were diminishing in popularity. One estimate put the profitability of hemp in Lincolnshire at from £5 10s. to £6 10s. per acre; of flax from £2 3s. to £4 10s. per acre. Although this compares quite well with other crops, both required a tremendous amount of labour, and now a wider variety of less exacting crops was available. Potatoes, for instance, were now being grown for human consumption, though many still grew them for cattle and pigs.

Wheat yields were steadily improving. Nathaniel Kent, reporting on the agriculture of Norfolk in 1796, states that on some of the best land in the reclaimed Fens farmers were taking harvests of six quarters (about 29 cwt) per acre, though he estimated the average for the whole county at about 14 or 15 cwt per acre. The seed used was mostly of local varieties, carefully selected. In 1732 William Ellis mentions four that were commonly grown in Hertfordshire, of which Old Red Lammas was the best, though suitable only for the more fertile soils. Yellow Lammas, which had a red ear and white straw, came next on the list; Pirky wheat was 'the most convenient for our Chiltern lands'; and Dugdale wheat was a hardy, square-headed type grown on 'sour soil'.

The method of selection and multiplication of cereal varieties is well exemplified by the account, written by that great agricultural publicist, Arthur Young, of the breeding of Chevalier barley, which from about 1825 onwards achieved national status and indeed dominated the barley scene for the next seventy years:

> About the year 1820 John Andrews, a labourer of Mr Edward Dove, of Ulverston Hall, Debenham, in Suffolk, had been threshing barley and on his return home at night complained of his feet being very uneasy, and on taking off his shoes he discovered in one of them part of a very fine ear of barley—it struck him as being particularly so—and he was careful to have it preserved. He afterwards planted the few grains from it in his garden, and the following year Dr and Mrs Charles Chevallier, coming to Andrew's dwelling to inspect some repairs going on (the cottage belonging to the Doctor), saw three or four ears of the barley growing. He requested it might be kept for him when ripe, The Doctor sowed a small ridge with the produce thus obtained, and kept it by itself until he grew sufficient to plant an acre, and from this acre the produce was 11½ coombs (a coomb is the equivalent of four bushels, or 240lb). This was again planted and from the increase thence arising, he began to dispose of it, and from that time it has been gradually getting into repute.

In the early decades of the eighteenth century about 38% of the bread consumed in England was made, it is estimated, from wheat flour. The balance was made up of rye, barley and oats, in that order, rye being used chiefly in the north. Enormous quantities of barley were required annually for brewing, ale or beer being the unchallenged drink for men, women and children, except in the western counties, where cider took its place.

The enquiring spirit of the age is again illustrated by Arthur Young's account of the ingenuity of a Norfolk maltster:

> In 1800 Mr Gilpin, of Heacham, a considerable maltster, bought some beautiful barley that had not received a drop of rain, and, trying a small parcel of it, found it malted badly. He tried a most uncommon experiment, and founded upon an idea very contrary to all common ones on the subject; he kiln-dried it by a gentle heat, watering it lightly with a watering-pot twice or thrice, six hours intervening; dried it; after which operation it malted well, every grain sprouting, but no malt could be finer. Hence observes the very intelligent gentleman from whom I had this account, it is evident that a good shower of rain in harvest, or a sweat in the stack, is beneficial to the maltster.

Would a maltster in earlier centuries have had the inspiration and initiative to experiment with an idea 'contrary to all common ones on the subject'? Would a successful experiment on those lines have received favourable publicity and been quickly adopted far and wide? The essence of this progressive century was that everyone was willing, indeed eager, to try out new things, to experiment with anything that promised an 'improvement'.

Arthur Young also found that one of the most prominent farmers of Lincolnshire, a Mr Cartwright of Brothertoft, had a decidedly modern approach to grassland husbandry:

> Hay-seeds, so-called, abound in general with seeds of various plants unfit for either pasture or meadow, with troublesome and pernicious weeds, and even with grasses deserving no better appellation. Hence it seems best wholly to abandon the use of hay-seeds and to lay down land with nothing but such grass-seeds as can be obtained separately and pure; trusting to Nature for a supply of such other grasses as the soil may peculiarly affect. We therefore want cultivators of distinct and separate grass . . .

This, of course, is the principle on which modern grassland farming is based.

The new farming demanded new techniques and new tools, and the century soon began to produce the necessary inventors. The affair of Jethro Tull and his *Horse-houghing Husbandry* (the title of a book which he published in 1731) is a strange one. Seldom can such immense practical benefits have resulted from such erroneous theorising, yet it was his work which made possible the successful field cultivation of turnips and the Norfolk four-course rotation. Tull was a product of his age, a gentleman of means who retired early from the Bar in order to enjoy country life. In 1699 he retreated from the London scene to his family home at Howberry, Oxfordshire, later moving to Prosperous Farm, Hungerford (a farm he himself named) where he demonstrated to critical and hostile neighbours the practical application of his ideas.

Of the two great inventions with which he is usually credited—the seed-drill and the horse-hough—the former had actually been in existence for a long time: both the ancient Babylonians and the Chinese (as early as BC 2800) used a type of seed-drill and in Europe one was invented in 1566 by a Venetian, Camillo Torello. From 1623 onwards several were patented in England, though they did not catch on. One, described in a book published in 1646, was designed to sow dry manure and seed side by side in the same furrow, after the manner of the modern combine-drill, and John Worlidge in his *System Agriculturae* of 1669 describes and illustrates a similar machine which used pigeon-dung as the dry manure. However, there seems no reason to doubt Tull's claim that he had read none of these books or indeed any

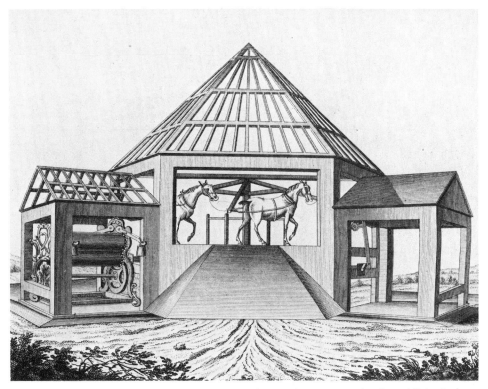

Horse-powered grinding mill plan from Annals of Agriculture *written by the publicist Arthur Young, 1799.*

other works on the subject before inventing his own machines.

Tull began by considering the basic problems of plant growth. Plants must obviously derive their nourishment from some source, he reasoned, so what were the options? According to the scientific knowledge then prevailing, matter was composed of five elements, namely, earth, air, fire, water and nitre. Previous investigators had already formed tentative ideas about nitre and air being largely responsible, but Tull decided that earth was the all-important factor. So, if plants fed on soil, he argued, it was essential for them to be provided with it in tiny and easily assimilable particles, and preparatory ploughing was not thorough enough. After-sowing cultivations were necessary, and broadcast sowing would make this almost impossible. But Tull had seen women dibbling in beans and peas in rows by hand, and he reasoned that if corn also could be sown in rows sufficiently far apart, a machine with blades and coulters could be drawn between the rows, reducing the soil to a fine tilth. But how to sow corn in rows without planting each grain? Among his recreations was playing the church organ on Sundays, and it was when thus engaged that inspiration came to him: his seed-drill was based on the battery of organ pipes. Seed was placed in a box from which equally spaced pipes guided it into the soil.

Some of the early mistakes he made may strike us as quaint. For instance, although his rows of root crops were sensibly spaced at thirty inches apart, the space between his corn rows was five feet! Presumably he felt he needed plenty of room between the rows to allow his horse-hoe to work efficiently, but five feet is ridiculous. Some of his other ideas were a trifle eccentric, too. For instance, he sowed turnip seed at two levels, one lot at four inches deep, the other at only half-an-inch, so that they would germinate at different times, giving him two chances of a crop in an unfavourable season. He called his new system of cultivation 'horse-houghing', but on his own farm he adapted the horse-hoe for use with oxen, walking in single file. Already among farmers in the eighteenth century an axiom, 'there's nothing like muck,' was in common circulation, but Tull thought nothing of it. The only benefit of farmyard manure was to dissolve some of the soil particles by its acids, or, as he called them, 'salts'; otherwise it simply contaminated the soil.

Nevertheless, his two inventions, the seed-drill and the horse-hoe, rank with those of the plough, the scythe, the combine-drill, the threshing machine and the combine-harvester as among the great contributions to world agriculture. Tull's eccentricities did not endear him to his contemporaries but they were quick to appreciate the tools he bequeathed them. Without them, the tremendous achievements of Townshend and Coke in Norfolk would hardly have been possible.

In other farm machinery progress was mostly a matter of improving existing types rather than inventing new ones. At the beginning of the period ploughs, for example, were made locally by blacksmiths, but in about 1730 a factory was set up near Rotherham, Yorkshire, to make a standardized type henceforth known as the Rotherham plough, with a wooden frame but iron share and coulter and iron plate on the mould-board. Soon after its foundation in 1754 the Royal Society of Arts began to offer awards for new plough inventions, one of which was won by John Brand of Essex, about 1770, for the first all-iron plough. From 1785 onwards Robert Ransome of Ipswich, who founded the manufacturing firm which still bears his name, brought out a series of inventions for improving plough-shares, by using self-sharpening, chilled iron, and in 1808 he produced a plough fastened together by bolts, enabling worn parts to be easily renewed. He also supplied

160

sundry attachments, such as hoeing tines and subsoiling tines, which saved farmers the expense of buying complete new implements for seasonal jobs. By 1840 his factory was turning out eighty-six different types of plough, and the age of manufactured farm implements had truly arrived.

Haymaking and harvesting was still dominated by the scythe, the hand-rake and the pitchfork. The invention of the horse-rake is unrecorded, though Arthur Young saw one at work, raking bean straw, in Essex in 1807. Threshing machines were, however, an important introduction in the latter part of the period. A Mr Ilderton of Alnwick (Northumberland) is thought to have been the first inventor of a threshing machine based on the principle of rubbing out the grain from the chaff and straw between two rollers, instead of bashing it out by means of flails. His machine appeared about 1776. Once the breakthrough in ideas had occurred, progress was rapid. Andrew Meikle, of East Lothian, who is credited with some of the most successful and widely used types of threshing machines, obtained an English patent in 1788. Arthur Young, surveying the agriculture of Lincolnshire in 1813, notes that at Riseholme he saw 'one of Mr Parsemoore's (of Sheffield) threshing-mills . . . I have seen so many of these machines, which do everything well except barley, that I enquired particularly about that grain . . . His thrashers assured me that it thrashed barley cleaner than they could; and did ten quarters a day, with two horses, four men, one woman and one boy.' The early threshing machines were invariably worked by horse-power, a horse attached to a circular gear driving it by walking in a circle. By 1830 threshing machines were becoming so common that they sparked off the labourers' revolt, characterized by smashing and burning of the hated machines, which the farm workers feared would rob them of their traditional winter employment.

Among other innovations of the period were the chaffcutter (which first appeared in the 1760s), the turnip-slicer (patented in 1839) and the barrel butter-churns, or tumbling churns, which were apparently invented in the 1750s.

But for all the ingenuity of the inventors and the enthusiasm of the protagonists of the new system of farming, the application of the new ideas remained patchy. While the new threshing machines, for instance, were performing efficiently in the more progressive counties, in Devonshire were farmers who apparently had not even heard of the flail. They still knocked out the grain from the ears by hitting the stalks against barrels. They then carried the corn 'on horseback to the summit of some airy swell, where it is winnowed in the wind by women'. William Marshall, who recorded the practice, also commented that the Devon turnip-fields were 'a disgrace to British agriculture', being foul with charlock. Even in counties near London, where farmers were consciously following Tull's methods, they too often neglected to carry out the hoeings which were an essential part of the system.

Improvements in cropping techniques and farming practice were paralleled by the advance in livestock breeding. The principle of the selection of the best to be parents of the next generation was already understood. For this reason Henry VIII had imported large stallions to improve the size of English horses. For this reason, too, the largest and heaviest grains of corn were selected for sowing, as already described. The great livestock breeders of the second half of the eighteenth century were therefore not venturing into entirely unknown territory. What was new was their vision in working out in advance the characteristics they wanted to emphasize and their persistence in a ruthless and sustained programme of culling. It is a programme still followed by all livestock improvers. When a higher milk yield from cows is the target, the breeder chooses cows that are giving more milk than their contemporaries and a bull whose daughters are registering a similar performance. These are the parents of the next generation. Those of their progeny which perform better than their parents are in their turn selected for breeding; those which fall short of the predetermined standards produce no successors. Similarly breeders obtain better fleeces from sheep, more piglets per litter from sows, more eggs from hens, quicker maturity from table poultry, exaggerated visual characteristics in dogs, more colour varieties in budgerigars.

All this may seem axiomatic to us, but the application of these principles in the eighteenth century represented a giant step forward. Credit for first applying them to the breeding of cattle and sheep is generally given to Robert Bakewell, a Leicestershire farmer whose career extended from 1760, when he took over his father's farm, to his death in 1795.

More successful with sheep than with cattle, Bakewell used as his foundation stock animals of the old Leicester type, which were big, coarse-woolled sheep closely related to the Lincoln. He planned to breed for meat, expressing his belief that 'small bones, thin pelts and the barrel shape are soonest and most productive of fat at the least expense of food'. Adhering to rigid standards of selection and culling, he used his rams not only on his own ewes but on those of his neighbours, thus greatly increasing the progeny on which he could base his assessments. This arrangement was also highly profitable: in 1789, when his work was well known and his reputation high, he received fees totalling 1,200 guineas for the use of one

Robert Bakewell, pioneer of modern livestock breeding.

ram alone—a celebrated animal known as Two Pounder.

Although he achieved what he set out to do, his Dishley sheep (named after his native village) would not have been to our liking. A visitor who dined on a leg of Dishley mutton and was told it weighed seventeen pounds, commented: 'The fat which dripped in cooking was measured and it amounted to between two and three quarts; besides this, the dish was a mere bag of loose, oily fat, huge deep flakes of which remained to garnish that which we called, by courtesy, lean.' Still, that was what Bakewell was aiming for, and he knew his market.

For his cattle-breeding programme Bakewell chose the local type of cattle, the Longhorns, then multi-purpose animals the chief common characteristic of which was their very long, curved horns. As with his sheep, Bakewell

Bakewell's prize ram, Two Pounder, earned 1200 guineas in breeding fees.

planned to breed for meat, and again he partially succeeded. His improved Longhorns matured quickly and amassed great quantities of fat on their carcase, especially on the rump. One of his bulls, Twopenny, achieved national fame and was let at high fees.

Bakewell was the first of a new type of breeder who specialized in breeding to the exclusion of other farming activities. Before this time breeders had bred primarily to improve the performance of their own flocks and herds. They were interested in the extra meat or milk or whatever that the improved animals would produce. Bakewell's aim was to sell or let breeding stock to other farmers, to improve *their* herds, his profits coming from sales and letting fees.

Geniuses such as Bakewell do not arise in a vacuum. There were other breeders before him, operating on somewhat the same lines and in the same district, from whom he derived certainly some of his ideas. When Bakewell was a young man, a Mr Webster who lived in the same area was using the methods Bakewell later adopted, and so apparently, from the little evidence we have, was Sir Thomas Gresley, of Drakelowe, near Burton-on-Trent.

Early type of Longhorn, a breed improved by Bakewell.

Gresley is said to have brought in Longhorns of an improved type from Westmorland and Lancashire early in the century, and Webster bought many of his best animals from him. It was from Webster that Bakewell purchased some of his foundation stock. Gresley and Webster hence both precede Bakewell as pioneers of the new breeding theories and practices, and Robert Fowler, of Little Rollright, was engaged in parallel work at the same time as Bakewell. His Rollright herd was so excellent that, when dispersed in 1791, it averaged the remarkable price of £85 per head, including nine calves. Fowler also bred one of the greatest of Longhorn sires, the bull Shakespeare, from a Canley dam. But Bakewell had Arthur Young to carry his torch.

In the end Bakewell seems to have paid the penalty of pioneering, for he is said to have gone bankrupt and died in poverty. And, although the value of the principles he tested and established is inestimable, the work he actually achieved with Longhorns, and, to a lesser extent Leicester sheep, was short-lived, for the criteria he applied were too narrow. To achieve the fat, quick-maturing, meaty beast he had in mind he sacrificed almost every other quality of the Longhorns. Milking capacity was neglected, prolificacy and mothering qualities went by the board, hardiness and high food conversion rates counted for little. The result was an excellent single-purpose breed which lacked fecundity and did not fit in at all well with conditions on an average farm. Within a few decades it had become a rare breed, and still remains so.

The New Leicesters could have foundered like the Longhorns, and indeed, as a pure breed they are now not at all common. They proved, however, to have a wonderful potential for crossing. All their good qualities the rams could transmit to their progeny from ewes of other types. And so the New Leicester achieved pre-eminence as a superlative crossing breed used for improving the Lincoln, the Teeswater, the Cheviot, several of the Devon breeds, and subsequently the Kerry Hill, Shropshire and others.

The path that had been pioneered by Bakewell and his contemporaries soon became a broad highway trodden by multitudes. Every progressive livestock breeder cast an appraising eye over his local animals and formulated plans for their improvement. The comparative failure of the improved Longhorn left the way open for competitors, of which one of the strongest and earliest was the Shorthorn.

Cattle of Shorthorn type were predominant all along the eastern coasts of England, from Northumberland to Kent. Commonly known as Holderness cattle, they were also referred to as 'Dutch stock', which indicates where at least some of their ancestry lay. Writers who saw them before improvement state that they were ungainly, heavy-boned, badly-shaped animals which gave large quantities of low-grade milk. The breeders most successful with these nondescript Shorthorns were Robert and Charles Colling, brothers who farmed near Darlington, in county Durham. Pupils of Bakewell, they acquired, on returning home in 1784, a bull named Hubback, of uncertain ancestry but whom they decided possessed the right qualities. By a sustained programme of inbreeding and rigid culling, based on his progeny, they succeeded in altering the old Shorthorn type almost out of recognition. Twenty years after the start of their experiments they produced the celebrated bull Comet, the first ever to sell for the magic figure of 1,000 guineas. Like Bakewell, they were breeders rather than farmers and were slack about their farming, but they laid such solid foundations for the Shorthorn breed that thereafter it dominated the English cattle scene for well over a century.

Following the fashion, Devon breeders, notably Francis Quartly of Molland, took in hand their native red cattle and established a number of very fine improved herds. They had quite good stock to start with and were helped by the publicity given to their cattle by Coke, who stocked Holkham with red Devons and offered prizes to the exhibitors of the best beasts.

The early Devons were not bad milkers, but the prototype Herefords were said to be some of the country's worst for milk production. They were primarily draught cattle though capable of fattening readily when their working life of about six years was at an end. Above all, they flourished on poor pastures and were exceptionally docile, qualities which eminently suited them for the pastures which were soon to be opened in new lands overseas. The white face and finching which are the visual hallmarks of the modern Hereford were becoming established by the end of the eighteenth century.

The career of the Sussex breed was more or less parallel to that of the Devon, though the Sussex was less widely known. Norfolk also had red, beef-type cattle, low in milking qualities, but these seem to have become almost obsolete by the 1830s. The likelihood is, though some controversy exists about it, that they and the Suffolk Duns next door were both superseded by a new Red Poll type derived from crosses between them.

Throughout the eighteenth century cows and heifers were being regularly shipped into England from the Channel Islands. The annual average from the 1770s onwards was about 900 head, of which about two-thirds came from Jersey, though all were known indiscriminately as Alderneys. Naturally they were most numerous in the south-western counties but found their way to most other regions and did valuable service in improving the quality of milk from dairy cows.

Although in the second generation of cattle breeders an increasing number became interested in milk production, the early improvers were largely obsessed with beef, and with vast quantities of it. For most of them the criteria of a good animal were size, weight and fat. The crowning achievement of Charles Colling's career was held to be the breeding of the celebrated Durham Ox, which for six years toured the fairs, markets and showgrounds of Britain, displaying to admiring audiences its 27 hundredweight of flesh.

Breeding for milk came when lessons had been learned from earlier errors. The pioneer breeder of Dairy Shorthorns, the breed which supplied most of the milking cows of England for the next century, was Thomas Bates, who farmed at Kirklevington, Yorkshire, from 1830 to 1849. He wisely attempted to breed back into the Shorthorn stock, improved for beef by the Colling brothers and their contemporaries, some of the milking qualities they were in danger of losing. So the Shorthorn breed split into two types, beef and dairy, the latter being regarded as dual-purpose.

The sheep scene was far more complex. To begin with, there were far more regional and district types than there were of cattle. But four main groups can be identified, namely, the primitive mountain types, the unimproved shortwools, the unimproved, coarse-fleeced longwools, and the better types of longwool, derived probably from old Roman stock. Within this broad framework, about forty distinct local types can be distinguished, which is almost exactly the same as the number of sheep breeds in Britain today.

Throughout the Middle Ages sheep had been valued mainly for wool. Their milk and its butter- or cheese-making qualities were of secondary importance. As with other farm animals, sheep were eaten when they were too old or ill for other purposes, and Bakewell and his contemporaries had made a radical departure from tradition by breeding for meat. Due to shorter gestation and maturing periods, it is of course possible to get results with sheep more quickly than with cattle, but the improvers encountered also a major obstacle. Sheep become acclimatized to their environment, building up over generations resistance to the local ailments and diseases, and every sheep farmer knew, and still knows, the dangers of introducing entirely new stock. The safer procedure is to bring in an improved ram to mate with indigenous ewes.

In the sheep world, therefore, controlled breeding eventually resulted in a number of new breeds represented primarily by first-class ram-breeding flocks, from which commercial sheep-breeders drew their rams. The policy still holds good. The achievement of the pedigree breeders was therefore to perfect and perpetuate the new super-sheep.

The ramifications of this programme are too numerous to trace here. Each breed has its own fascinating story. Each experienced its ups and downs. The old Wiltshire Horn breed, for instance, was initially so successful that in 1811 there were over 500,000 of them on Salisbury Plain alone, yet by 1840 only one flock remained in Wiltshire. Its hardiness and stamina had been largely bred out by its 'improvers'. The breed survived through the establishment of a few ram-breeding flocks on farms on the drovers' route from Wales to London. The ancient Cotswold breed came very near to extinction, and the once-numerous Norfolk Horn experienced a dramatic decline while the Shropshire survives only in a few ram-breeding flocks. Scottish and Welsh sheep, notably the Cheviot, Scottish Blackface and Welsh Mountain, have become popular in the English lowlands, while the Dorset Horn, now paradoxically represented by a polled type, has been experiencing an exhilarating revival.

Because of their extraordinary fecundity, pigs show the results of improvement programmes even more quickly than sheep and for that reason the fortunes of the breeds tend to fluctuate with corresponding rapidity. The work of the eighteenth-century breeders with pigs is much less well-documented than with sheep and cattle. The earliest breed or type recognized by name seems to have been the Berkshire, which was apparently a very different animal from the modern Berkshire as it was not only a different colour but was described as a long, heavy-boned pig, whereas the modern Berkshire is a short-bodied, snub-nosed porker.

It is evident that by this time pigs were regarded as genuine farm stock, worth a little care and pampering instead of scavengers turned loose in the forests. In particular they were valued in the dairying districts, where they could fatten on the by-products of butter and cheese. Improvements came largely by inter-breeding with imported pigs. John Evelyn had a Portuguese pig in the seventeenth century, and by 1770–80 considerable numbers of Chinese pigs were being brought in. There was also a trade in Neapolitan pigs, which were apparently bred in Italy from stock originating in China. The Essex Saddleback was also a well-defined type by about 1830, and the Yorkshire, or Large White, by 1835. No breed society or herd book was, however, formed for any breed until 1884.

Bakewell himself may have had a hand in the development of the Shire Horse as a farm animal, and certainly his contemporaries used his methods in improving it. The earliest known stallion was the Packington Blind Horse, which flourished at Packington, Leicestershire, between 1755 and 1770, and became a celebrated sire in his time. Bakewell's contribution seems to have been to make the type rather lighter and more active, an improvement for which there seems to have been scope, for Marshall (1789) referred to them as the 'black snail breed' and asserted that they were 'better calculated for eating than working, and whose tendency is to render their drivers as sluggish as themselves'. Probably Bakewell's main achievement in this sphere, however, was to help to popularize the breeding of farm horses. In his own county by the end of the century there were 'great numbers of mares kept for breeding, all of the large black kinds'. Considerable distances were evidently travelled by stallions on their rounds, for in 1813 Arthur Young noted that 'Mr Wright's horse from Dishley covers at Spilsby twenty black mares a year'.

Similar improvement was being made in Suffolk horses, of the old type of which Arthur Young observed, 'an uglier horse could not be viewed'. Every animal of the breed now alive is said to be descended from a stallion foaled in 1760, though a lighter type of trotting horse, introduced by Andrew Blake, a

Suffolk farmer, in 1794, had a considerable influence on the breed. So, too, may imported horses from Flanders, of which 'great numbers were brought over to this country last year', according to a writer in 1792.

As regards other stock, breeds of poultry began to emerge at this period. The Dorking and the Hamburg were among the earliest. They flourished near towns, where a growing market existed for eggs and table birds. Turkeys and geese also increased in numbers. Muscovy ducks, originating in tropical America, appeared, and the Aylesbury district was already noted for its table ducks. Peacocks and domestic pigeons now had a very minor role in the farm economy, but rabbits were still kept in warrens for profit, and William

The Yorkshire Hog, painted in 1809: 9'10" long, 8' in girth, he weighed 1344 lbs. Viewers paid nearly £3000 in three years to see him.

Marshall mentions deer displayed for sale in Sussex markets, like cattle.

A measure of the improvements in livestock effected by Bakewell and his contemporaries can be found in a comparison of the weights of cattle sold at Smithfield in 1710 and in 1795. In the first of the two years beef cattle averaged 370lb, calves 50lb, sheep 28lb and lambs 18lb. In 1795 beef cattle averaged 800lb, calves 143lb, sheep 80lb and lambs 50lb.

But perhaps the best measurement of the achievements of the agricultural revolution in the eighteenth century is that while the population of England and Wales rose from 5,500,000 to 9,000,000 during the period, the people were in general much better fed at the end than in the beginning. In this context it should be remembered that throughout the century a rapidly increasing population movement from country to town was in progress, removing workers from the farms and increasing the number of consumers who were no longer engaged in producing food. Also that, during the latter part of the period, Britain was fighting against Napoleon and subjected to a blockade which meant that England had once again to produce almost all the food needed.

As the non-food-producing population of the new industrial towns increased, markets expanded beyond all precedent and produce had to be transported to these customers. With livestock this was done by making the animals walk. A traveller riding across England in the eighteenth century would have marvelled at the immense herds, flocks and droves of livestock he saw on the march. In the third quarter of the century it has been estimated that around 100,000 head of cattle and 750,000 sheep were sold annually at Smithfield. Nor were some of the provincial fairs and markets much less busy. As late as 1887 Barnet attracted 50,000 head of cattle and 50,000 horses, besides other stock. At Stagshaw Bank, Northumberland, more than 100,000 sheep frequently changed hands at the great fair held there on July 4th, in the 1790s. A similar figure is quoted for Malham Fair, Yorkshire, in the 1830s, whilst in the 1840s the annual average number of sheep sold at East Ilsley, on the Berkshire Downs, was 400,000. At Weyhill Fair, in Hampshire, at about the same period, 140,000 sheep were sold on the first day, and the fair lasted for a further five days. At least 100,000 cattle and probably more than 150,000 sheep crossed the Scottish border every year, bound for English markets.

These enormous flocks and herds were entrusted to drovers, who had to be 'mature men, over thirty years old, of good character and tempermant'. Their journeys were highly organized, following well-established routes, along which farmers provided pasture and other food, while inns and alehouses did a good trade with the men. A Norfolk drover who had occasion to send his dog back from London to Norfolk alone, turned the dog loose with a note attached to its collar and instructed the dog to go home, which it did, calling at every familiar inn en route and being well cared for there by innkeepers who read the note. Cattle and sheep normally covered about fifteen miles a day, though less in hilly country. On long journeys the sheep were supposed to rest twice a day and for a whole day every third day. Pigs averaged only six to ten miles a day. Yes, pigs were among the

Boston, May sheep fair. Imagine the noise!

long-distance travellers. In 1830, 14,500 pigs from Ireland passed along the turnpike road at Beckhampton, Wiltshire, on their way to London, and many others, from both Ireland and Wales, trotted over to Somerset and Dorset where they were fattened on whey and buttermilk before resuming their journey some months later.

Turkeys and geese in immense flocks also walked across England. Defoe, early in the century, reported that the turkey flocks which crossed Stratford Bridge, over the River Lea, on the north-eastern approaches to London,

Sheep fairs vary little through the centuries: Findon Great Fair, 1948.

numbered from 300 to 1,000 birds, and that 300 such flocks passed that way during the season. Droves of geese could be met with with equal frequency, numbering from 1,000 to 2,000 per drove. 'They begin to drive them generally in August, by which time the harvest is almost over, and the geese may feed on the stubbles as they go. Thus they hold on to the end of October, when the road begins to be too stiff and deep for their broad feet and stiff legs to march in.'

These geese came from Norfolk, especially from the Fens, but some originating there were marketed at Nottingham Goose Fair, which lasted for twenty-one days and during which up to 20,000 geese were sold. Geese also made the journey to London from the West Country, and at Ilchester, Somerset, 'a saddler and harness-maker made boots of soft leather for the travelling geese. These boots were carried by the drovers and placed on the feet of geese that became lame or suffered damage to their feet in the long walks.' In 1740 Lord Orford backed a flock of geese to walk to London in a shorter time than a flock of turkeys backed by the Marquess of Queensbury. The geese won, chiefly because they grazed by the roadside as they walked, while the turkeys had to stop at intervals to be fed; also the turkeys insisted in roosting in trees, from which they were sometimes loath to descend in the mornings.

The routes by which the drovers and their charges travelled were the old green tracks of England—directions over open country rather than actual roads. But as the century advanced they became more and more restricted. The Enclosure Acts which multiplied during the second half of the century were matched by the Turnpike Acts, ostensibly to provide England with better roads, which were certainly needed. Even on the approaches to London 'the constant tramping of droves of cattle, herds of sheep and pigs, and flocks of geese and turkeys; the incessant stream of walking pack-horses; the galloping relays of post-horse and fish-carriers, all tended to keep the track in a perpetual slough of mud'.

The turnpike trusts were capitalist ventures, designed to improve the road system by private enterprise. A trust, generally formed by share-holding local gentry, contracted to make and maintain a section of road in return for the right to charge tolls for the use of it. In practice, once the road had been constructed and the toll-gates erected, the rights to collect the tolls were often put up for auction and bought by investors who made a good thing out of them. Surveyors, lawyers, clerks and of course the low-paid toll collector all had to have their share, and the amount of money left for road maintenance often turned out to be minimal.

174

By 1840 there were 22,000 miles of turnpike roads in England, with 8,000 toll-gates, averaging a toll-gate at every 2¾ miles. Some towns were so hemmed in by toll-gates that it was impossible even to take a horse out for exercise without passing one and paying the toll. The turnpikes which ringed the town of Aylesbury belonged to no fewer than seven independent trusts, each of which maintained an expensive board of officials, whereas, as an exasperated resident complained, one would have been sufficient for the lot. Public disapproval of the system, or rather its abuse, culminated in the Rebecca Riots of 1839, when men with blackened faces and dressed in women's clothes methodically destroyed the hated gates. But the doom of the turnpikes came not from the actions of disgruntled toll-payers or government legislation but from the arrival of the railways.

Another aspect of transport which suddenly achieved prominence was the canal. In 1750 there were some 1,300 miles of canals in England. Eighty years later there were more than 5,500. They, like the turnpikes, were constructed by private enterprise. One of the canal pioneers, the Duke of Bridgwater, who created the Bridgwater Canal to take his coal the ten miles or so from his mines at Worsley to Manchester, invested more than £3,000,000 in the project. His example was quickly followed by observant contemporaries, especially as he had made a profit on the investment. Canals had the important advantage of making possible the transport of heavy loads cheaply, where there was no urgency for delivery, and much grain and other farm produce became waterborne.

In addition to the long-distance traffic, virtually every farming community was served by local markets and fairs, which were thick on the ground. The relatively small county of Dorset had no fewer than 26 weekly markets (it has only five now) and more than 50 annual fairs. The markets tended to be collecting centres where farmers traded their produce to middlemen, who passed it on to customers in the distant towns. Trading licences were required by these entrepreneurs, though apparently they were not normally difficult to obtain.

The inventions and innovations of the second half of the eighteenth century and the first half of the nineteenth produced an England radically changed from that of earlier times. The impact was largely beneficial, in that the changes made possible a tremendous increase in food production at a time when it was urgently needed by an expanding urban population. They fostered the rise of a rural hierarchy in which the upper echelons enjoyed almost unprecedented comfort and luxury but in which the poor were worse off than when the revolution started.

10. Victorian High Farming

The high summer enjoyed by farmers in the mid-Victorian era was preceded by a wild and stormy spring. The spate of Enclosure Acts continued, so did both the beneficent revolution begun by the great improvers of livestock and arable husbandry, and the industrial revolution which would take Britain from a simple rural economy to the complexities of urban manufacture. Then, too, the country was engaged in a major European war, and nothing like the menace of the Napoleonic blockade had ever before been encountered. Each new problem had to be met by improvization, or, in many instances, ignored in the hope that it would go away.

One of the most pressing problems was feeding the hugely increasing urban population. During the eighteenth century imports of grain and other farm products from Europe had had a stabilizing influence on prices. In 1704 wheat fetched 41s. 4d. per quarter; in 1794 the price was 49s. 3d. per quarter—not a remarkable rise in ninety years. Thereafter, with a few fluctuations, the upward rise was steep, until the price reached a peak of 126s. 6d. in 1812, the year the French armies marched to Moscow. Unfortunately wages, both urban and rural, failed to keep pace with the fluctuating prices of food, and when wheat reached the phenomenal level of over 100 shillings a quarter some of the poorer citizens literally starved. Price controls would seem to us to have been the obvious remedy, but Parliament saw no reason to institute any remedy at all. Why interfere? Bad harvests had often caused distress and even starvation in times past, and the poor were always around. Out of the 11,000,000 people in Britain at that period, only 400,000 possessed the vote, and most of them were men of substance living in rural areas. No political advantage could be gained by catering for ('pampering' would be the word more likely to be used) the urban poor.

England during those war years was effectively divided into two nations. The tribulations of the poor contrasted dramatically with the idyllic existence of the rich, who, in the words of a Prime Minister of a much later time, had never had it so good. Rocketing prices for corn, and everything else produced on English farms, filled with cash the pockets of the rural gentry

Harrowing—a one-horse team.

and the wealthier farmers, while the watchful Navy ensured that the physical realities of war stayed safely on the far side of the seas. It was a golden age, too, for literature, art and gracious living—the Age of Elegance, as Sir Arthur Bryant calls it. It is difficult to appreciate that Wordsworth, Constable, Jane Austen, Sheridan, Sir Walter Scott, Byron, Charles Lamb, Burns and Coleridge produced their cultured masterpieces against the background of a wrecked Europe relapsed into barbarism and a grimy industrial England racked by the economic severities of war. Their public was, in fact, a leisured class which was not only virtually immune to the hardships of the age but which, in many instances, was quite unaware that they existed. Battles were exciting events to be read about in the newspapers, but hunt balls, summer picnics, race meetings, shooting parties and gossip about the neighbours and the royal family were the real pattern of the fabric of life.

Into such a cosy community the American author, Washington Irving, found himself enjoying Christmas in 1820, in an atmosphere which had doubtless changed not at all through all the exigencies of the war. In the country house to which he had been invited he wandered along the lengthy corridors to his bedroom, outside the door of which three small carol-singers aroused him at sunrise on Christmas morning. Almost immediately he was summoned to family prayers in a private chapel in one wing of the great house, a service attended not only by the family and guests but by footmen, butlers, maids and servants of every grade, saving only those who were busy preparing breakfast in the kitchen. The family sat 'in a kind of gallery, furnished with cushions, hassocks and large prayerbooks; the servants were seated on benches below'. After breakfast they all walked about half-a-mile to the parish church, just outside the park wall, where they sat through another service which included an extremely long sermon.

The parson, making the most of his opportunities, delivered yet another homily in the form of a long-winded grace in the early afternoon, as the family sat down to dinner. The *piéce de resistance* at this meal was a boar's head brought in on a silver dish, to the accompaniment of harp music. Additional dishes included sirloin of beef, roast turkey, a pheasant pie adorned with peacock feathers and gravy from fat sheep. The house was decorated with evergreens, and the dining room illuminated with enormous wax tapers. A Yule log, lit on Christmas Eve, burned all day on the hearth.

During the afternoon, as darkness was falling, they received a visit from the Morris Dancers or Mummers, who performed their ancient play and were rewarded with 'brawn and beef and stout home-brewed'. Further entertainment was provided by the household and guests during the evening, including a drama on the lines of a masque. The games played included 'hoodman blind, shoe the wild mare, hot cockles, steal the white loaf, bob apple and snap dragon.' During the evening a punch bowl, 'a huge silver vessel of rare and curious workmanship', was frequently replenished with a concoction based on wine or ale and containing 'nutmeg, sugar, toast, ginger and roasted crabs' (crab-apples).

It is an attractive picture of an affluent, gentle, devout and secure society, entirely content with itself and happy to extend Christian charity to its poorer neighbours, provided they, for their part, were willing to keep to their allotted places. According to Squire Lambton, to maintain this standard of living a man could 'jog along' on £40,000 a year. The foundations of his prosperity would be a flourishing home farm, a large estate with a high rent roll, and probably City investments or a stake in West Indian plantations.

A step downwards in the social scale finds the yeoman farmer enjoying a degree of opulence. Mary Mitford, observing her farming neighbours in the Hampshire village of which she writes, notes that 'everything prospers with him; money drifts about him like snow. There is a sturdy squareness of face and a good-humoured obstinacy, a civil importance. He never boasts of his wealth or gives himself undue airs, but nobody can meet him at market or vestry without finding him the richest man there.'

Nor did the more numerous class of peasant farmer suffer any particular hardship. Blessed with a few acres of land, they could produce almost all the food their families needed, without recourse to a shop. Geese, turkeys, fowls, mutton, butter, cheese, milk, ale, home-baked bread, vegetables and honey appeared on their table, and many of them supplemented their income with earnings from some craft, such as blacksmithing, hurdling, woodwork, wickerwork and cobbling. This was a class considerably reduced in numbers by the impact of Enclosure Acts, to the impoverishment of social life in the countryside.

Until now, labourers had also enjoyed a good standard of living for the reason that many of them had received part of their wages in the form of food. They ate at their master's table, and their diet, if lacking delicacies, was at least substantial. As Sir Arthur Bryant comments, 'The English ate as though eating were an act of grace; the very sick were prescribed beefsteak and port. They ate more than any people in the world, because they grew more.' He quotes from a survey made by Sir Frederic Eden, giving details of the budget of a Leicester woolcomber in 1795 and 1796. Although this man, with an income of only £47 a year including a grant from the Poor Law guardians, may be reckoned a member of the poorest classes, he 'was able to buy weekly ten pounds of butchers' meat, two pounds of butter, three-and-a-half of cheese, and about nineteen pints of milk, as well as potatoes, vegetables, tea, sugar and beer. He was not even a particularly industrious man, for he was said to spend several days every month in the alehouse lamenting the hardness of the times.'

But though agricultural progress could hardly have been made without enclosures, the consolidation of rural property into the hand of lords of the manor and the larger farmers vastly increased the numbers of peasants who now became landless labourers. High-priced food on top of this wrought hardships. In the absence of work, some migrated to the new industrial towns, some went overseas and some stayed behind in their native villages where they became a poverty-stricken and oppressed class. One of my grandfathers, born in the 1840s, belonged to that class. When he died at an early age, my grandmother had to rear three small children on five shillings and two loaves of workhouse bread per week.

Although Parliament had professed itself unable to do anything to alleviate the hardships caused by high prices during the war, as soon as prices came toppling after the battle of Waterloo (1815) it passed a protective Corn Law, designed to keep the prices of corn artificially high by prohibiting the import of any corn until the average price of English wheat reached 80 shillings per quarter. Bitterly resented by the town populace and their representatives, the Act was steered safely through a Parliament composed predominantly of rural landowners looking after their own interests. From that time onwards a state of undeclared war existed between town and country. Despairing of ever getting redress for their grievances and becoming increasingly conscious of their own numerical and economic strength, the urban populace agitated and at times rioted until at last they managed to force through the series of Reform Bills which, beginning in 1832, eventually produced a universal franchise and abolished for ever the domination of Parliament by the country gentry. One of the early acts of the reforming Parliaments was to repeal the Corn Laws (in 1846).

That piece of legislation, contrary to some expectations, did not immediately spell ruin for rural and agricultural interests. Instead the countryside settled down to thirty years of peaceful prosperity, but the portents of doom already existed, if few discerned them. Through those middle decades of the nineteenth century the English farmer, and England in general, prospered as never before. It was indeed a glorious high summer. This respite resulted from the phenomenal growth in the population, especially in the towns. Even in the austere years 1801 to 1831 the population of Great

Above: pastoral scene on a summer evening in Kent. *Overleaf:* winter frost helps with the cultivation of an English farm.

Top: summer in the Yorkshire Dales. *Above:* farming follows the setting sun to the far west of Cornwall.

Pedigree hens appreciate the warmth and shelter of a deep-litter house in winter. Intensive poultry production methods used today make this a comparatively old-fashioned scene.

Below: a disc plough buries the debris of last year's rape crop.
Right: a splendid crop of winter wheat begins to ripen.
Far right: frost-free storage is required for potatoes in winter.
Below right: Herdwick sheep from the Cumbrian mountains at the Troutbeck sales.

Top: powerful modern tractor with heavy harrows prepares to pulverize soil to make a fine seed–bed. *Above:* unlike most pigs, these are living outdoors.

Britain increased from 11,000,000 to 16,500,000. By the end of the century it had reach 32,500,000. The census of 1851, more detailed and comprehensive than any hitherto, revealed that already half the population lived in towns, a situation without precedent in the world's history. The population of London alone swelled from about 900,000 in 1801 to 2,363,000 in 1851.

As early as 1793 Thomas Malthus had published his penetrating investigation of population, demonstrating that a population inevitably outpaces its food supply until or unless it is checked by famine, disease, war or some other catastrophe. His prophecies certainly seemed about to work out in the England of the mid-nineteenth century. Only the vast improvements in agricultural techniques and production enabled the diminishing numbers of farmers and farm workers to feed the non-food-producing urban populace, and thoughtful observers foresaw a time fast approaching when they would find the task impossible. In fact, the landowners and farmers of the early decades of the century unknowingly engineered the means of salvation, though at the expense of ruin for their successors.

Let us look again at the sequence of events. As the century opened the enclosure movement was in full flood and so continued for ten or twenty years. Between 1802 and 1844 nearly 2,000 enclosure acts changed the fate of about 2,500,000 acres of land. It was accompanied by the inevitable drift to the towns. At the same time, the manufacturing towns were producing by improved factory methods artefacts which had formerly provided a living for village craftsmen and craftswomen. Weavers, shoemakers, furniture-makers, glaziers, garment-makers, brickmakers and their fellow-artisans migrated to the towns, sometimes leaving the village blacksmith as almost the sole surviving representative of the multifarious trades which once flourished in the villages. In other communities located far from the new manufacturing centres the artisan families multiplied in accordance with the general population trends and, lacking the initiative or information that led to migration, over-supplied the local market with their goods and so had to accept a lower standard of living. For example, in the Dorset village of Bere Regis by 1841 there were no fewer than eighteen cobblers in a population of 1394. In that same year the village had four dressmakers, but by 1851 there were sixteen of them. There just could not have been enough trade to go round.

In earlier centuries these crafts would have been plied by peasants who derived some of their livelihood from the land and particularly from the common rights they exercised, but the enclosures had put an end to that. Moreover, although the new farming was producing so much more food, it

The village shoemaker, a craftsman found in most Victorian villages.

required progressively fewer men, as new machines appeared. The fact is that, in spite of the large numbers of workers migrating to the towns, the countryside was overpopulated.

It was a concept against which William Cobbett, that grand old yeoman demagogue, instinctively rebelled. A champion of the good old days, he exploded with indignation at what he saw on his famous *Rural Rides*. He conducted a study of a sample parish, Milton, where he estimated that enough bread for 800 families, enough mutton for 500 families and enough bacon and beer for 207 families, each family consisting of five persons, was being produced by only 100 families—100 working men and their wives and young children. 'So here are about one hundred families to raise food and drink enough, and to raise wool and other things to pay for all other necessities, for five hundred and two families!' he rants. 'Aye, and five hundred and two families fed and lodged, too, on my liberal scale. Fed and lodged according to the present scale, this one hundred families raise enough to supply more, and many more, than fifteen hundred families, or seven thousand five hundred persons! And yet those who do the work are half-starved! . . . What a handful of people to raise such a quantity of food! . . .'

It is an early example of a benevolent autocrat coming face to face with the now familiar problem of surplus labour. Even the hundred families were more than the economy really needed. On another ride his indignation reached boiling point (always low with him) when, in the valley of the Avon in 1826, he encountered an Emigration Committee. His anger was particularly aroused by an instance in which parish overseers were about to transport an orphan lad to Canada because he had become chargeable on the rates. 'What impudence and insolence these base wretches must have,' he said, 'who propose to transport the labouring people as being too numerous, while the produce which is obtained by their labour is more than sufficient for three, four, or five, or even ten times their numbers!'

The situation had its origins in the so-called Speenhamland System, a well-meaning measure which was designed to relieve distress but which went awry. In the famine year of 1795 the magistrates of Berkshire met at the village of Speenhamland to try to protect the low-paid farm labourers from the worst effects of fluctuating prices. The price of wheat had shot up from 49s. 3d. per quarter in 1793 to 78s. 7d. early in 1796; a leap which a labourer on a low, static wage could not cope with without considerable hardship. The obvious solution was a statutory wage linked to the price of corn, but the magistrates had natural doubts as to whether such a measure,

Above and below: two views of nineteenth-century tenant life.

which would obviously be unpopular with farmers and landowners, could ever be enforced. So they worked out a compromise whereby the amount which a labourer and his family received did indeed fluctuate according to the price of a quartern loaf, but that when the price rose the difference should be made up not by increased wages but out of the parish rates.

It was a system which at first commended itself to the farmers and so was adopted by most of the southern counties of England, which were chiefly affected by the enclosures. But the results were deplorable. In the first place, wages were kept permanently low, for farmers knew that when necessary they would be supplemented out of the rates. For their part, the workers were reduced to the level of paupers. Then, as nowadays with social security payments, there was a means test, making it necessary for a family to divest itself of any savings and property before it could qualify for the help it so urgently needed. Prudence and providence flew out of the window, for the more mouths there were to feed, the more relief a family was entitled to. No incentive remained for a farmer to retain the services of his whole labour force throughout the winter. He could keep his carter, his shepherd, his dairyman and perhaps one or two other key workers, discharging the rest after harvest in the knowledge that they would exist on parish relief all though the winter and be available for re-engagement in spring. Many of these 'surplus' labourers did find winter work at threshing with flails in the barns, and it was the introduction of threshing machines, which threatened them with complete winter unemployment, that triggered off the Machinery Riots in the late autumn of 1830 and so led to the affair of the Tolpuddle Martyrs six years later.

The farmers themselves, after the early euphoria wore off and the good days of the Naploeonic Wars were left behind, came bitterly to resent the increasing burden on the parish rates. A deep wedge had been driven between the rural employers and the employed. The employers came to see that their interests lay in reducing the local surplus population to as low a level as possible. In the instance quoted above, arithmetic had evidently shown that it was cheaper to pay the lad's fare to Canada than to keep him on the rates. Hence the Emigration Committees.

Now this preoccupation with the plight of the rural labourer is by no means irrelevant in a book on the English farm. It led directly to the disaster which befell farming in the last quarter of the century. For, as well as departing for the new industrial towns of the North and Midlands, very large numbers of villagers voyaged to the new lands overseas. And it was some of the best who went. Fed up with conditions at home they were glad to try a freer if harsh life in Australia, Canada, America and New Zealand. There they created their own farms out of wilderness and became the pioneers who founded the great dominions that formed the British Empire.

Nemesis took quite a time to materialize. By the early 1870s the problems of England's food supplies were becoming more and more acute. The country's farms were producing more than ever before, and the farmers benefiting correspondingly, but thoughtful observers were aware that there had to be a limit to what was possible and that that limit was fast approaching. It was beginning to look as though the gloomy prophecies of Malthus were about to be fulfilled.

Then, in the nick of time, it happened. Those emigrants from English villages to farms overseas had done their work well. By hard work, thrift, ingenuity and boundless enterprise they had tamed the virgin continents. Now their children and grandchildren were producing a surplus of food from the fertile acres. Where to dispose of it except back to the Old Country? After a few tentative shiploads the imports of grain from the prairies of America and Canada became, from 1875 onwards, a torrent. A few years later, they were joined by the wholesale shipment of refrigerated meat, from Australia, New Zealand, South Africa, Argentina and again from America and Canada.

A new generation of English politicians, when they realized what was

Workers assemble for teamwork for seasonal jobs on the farm.

186

happening, was relieved and delighted. The looming problem of diminishing food supplies had been banished for ever, or at least for their lifetimes, which was the same thing as far as they were concerned. Moreover, it was cheap food, produced at lower cost and therefore at a lower price than the age-old fields of England could match. The overseas farmers who produced it were an obvious and valued market for the manufactured goods which British factories were turning out at an ever-increasing rate. This sudden reversal of fortune cut away the economic basis on which the squire and farmer operated and so destroyed their political power. Thenceforward agriculture plummeted and wallowed in a morass of depression from which it emerged only temporarily in time of war. Between 1875 and 1885, because of the cheap food imports, the wheat acreage in England declined by nearly 1,000,000, and by the end of the century by a further 1,000,000. Prices of farm produce in general fell by some 25%. Farm rents showed a similar decline, and much marginal land fell into dereliction. Good farmers went bankrupt.

A typical example is a downland farm in south-west Wiltshire. Here in the 1830s and early 1840s, when the times were troubled and farmers were fearing calamitous consequences from the threatened repeal of the Corn Laws, a farmer named Henry Baker took a lease on a large farm which had been allowed to go semi-derelict. The great estate to which it belonged was

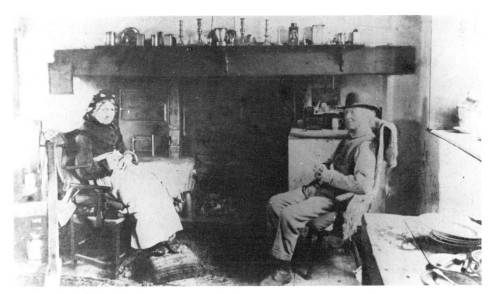

A cottage home at the turn of the century.

187

glad to get anyone of good character to occupy it. For the next twenty-five years Henry farmed the land well and prospered. The landlord was delighted with him, and he achieved a sound reputation among his fellow-farmers. As his two sons grew up they worked the farm with him and eventually, when he felt the time had come to retire, took it over from him and continued to farm by the well-established system which had served their father so well. They were in no way worse farmers than their father, except perhaps that they were not quick enough to adapt, but they were unlucky in the period in which they had to work. They had enjoyed only a few good years when the spate of imported food hit the market, and before the end of the century they had opted out, financially crippled if not actually bankrupt.

That, repeated a thousandfold, was the pattern of English farming in the last quarter of the nineteenth century and the first fifteen years or so of the twentieth. A modest amelioration occurred around the turn of the century, partly through British involvement in the Boer War and other minor wars and partly through an increasing demand for fresh farm produce, such as milk, poultry, eggs and vegetables, but in the national economy farming was still very much a minority interest. When the haemorrhages of the First World War demanded new armies of men, factory workers and farm workers alike were conscripted. Of the vulnerability of the country's food supplies there was no appreciation at all until the U-boat wolf-packs in the Atlantic approaches began to take their toll.

Food prices soared, as always in time of war, and the Government was forced to take note of the needs of home agriculture. Large numbers of women were recruited to take the place of the conscripted men on the farms, a minimum wage for farm workers was guaranteed for the first time, and, as the war neared its end, a Corn Production Act was passed to bolster farm prices against the flood of imports which was likely soon to be resumed. During the war the corn acreage was increased by well over 2,000,000 acres and the number of cattle and sheep (which could live largely on grass, without recourse to imported foodstuffs) multiplied. Farming emerged from the holocaust in a reasonably prosperous state.

Reaction came swiftly. In the competitive post-war world Britain's prosperity depended on its manufacturing industries, for whom cheap food was an essential factor in keeping down costs. Only three years after its introduction the Corn Production Act was repealed and home farming was left to fend for itself. By 1924 the industry was in rapid decline. The Great Depression which shattered the world in 1929 hit the English farm at least five years earlier and land went out of cultivation at an even greater pace than in the late 1870s. Millions of acres relapsed into dereliction. The splendid old sheep-and-corn, or Norfolk four-course, system of high farming foundered completely, sending those farmers who tried to adhere to it bankrupt in large numbers. Sheep almost disappeared from large areas of southern and midland England, to be replaced by unprofitable millions of rabbits. Land came to be regarded as just space out-of-doors.

As a young man in 1934 I was offered a tract of downland, 230 acres, for £750. When I went to try to borrow the money from a bank manager I was laughed out of the office. 'You've got your eye on the rabbit-shooting,' he told me, which was true though not the whole story. 'If you want to borrow money, buy something useful, not that useless stuff.' The same block of land, now bearing superb crops of cereals, changed hands in the early 1980s for just short of £2,0000,000. As a matter of fact, my father and I were able to rent the land for half-a-crown per acre, which the purchaser found perfectly satisfactory, for thousands of landowners had farms on hand which they were unable to let at all. We paid the rent in rabbit carcases for the first few years but during World War Two reclaimed all those derelict acres.

From the 1880s onwards many of the great rural landowners tended to divest themselves of large chunks of their estates, despairing of their ever becoming profitable again. In the village where I was reared this happened in 1912, when much of the land was purchased by the recently formed County Council Smallholdings Committee. My father began his farming by renting 90 acres from that Committee. After the brief boom in the latter years of World War One, survival proved to be possible only by introducing dairy herds to these basically unsuitable farms, which had formerly operated on a sheep-and-corn economy. So we milked cows, trundled houses of free-range hens round the fields and produced vegetables for direct sale to suburban housewives. It was a peasant-style agriculture, not vastly different from that prevailing on farms within reach of town markets in previous centuries. We killed a pig or two every November; my mother made a weekly batch of butter and baked a weekly batch of bread; we sold trussed and dressed table poultry and on our own table ate rabbits. We had very little money but needed very little. The taxman had never heard of us, for, by a benevolent clause in the tax laws, our rent was reckoned to be the equivalent of our income, and there was not a soul in the village whose income was high enough to bring him to the notice of the Inland Revenue. Happy days!

Successive governments in the inter-war period based their policies on the concept of free trade, as the late Victorian and Edwardian governments had done. As the Depression bit deeper the countries which had a surplus of food

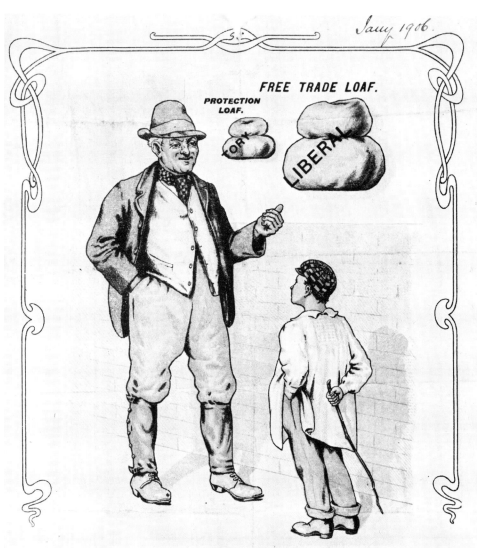

Electioneering poster, 1906; the recurring debate on free-trade.

for sale, becoming increasingly desperate for markets, began to subsidize their exports. At the same time they were finding protective tariff barriers raised against them in some of their former markets, notably Germany and Italy, where new nationalist governments were encouraging self-sufficiency. So more and more surplus subsidized food was diverted to complacent Britain, until at last it dawned on the Government that what they were supporting was something very different from free trade.

As the 1930s progressed they began to rectify matters by a series of protective Acts. The Import Duties Act of 1932 proved to be an almost useless and half-hearted attempt, for it excluded both meat and wheat from import duties and also did not apply to any imports from the Dominions. Agricultural Marketing Acts in 1931 and 1933 did a little better, especially as they provided for the setting up of marketing boards to regulate home-produced supplies. One of the first boards to be established was the Milk Marketing Board in 1933, an organization which, viewed at first with suspicion by farmers, proved itself invaluable and has been largely responsible for the huge market in liquid milk in Britain, unequalled in any country in today's world. In 1934 a Wheat Act offered a small subsidy on home-grown wheat, paid for out of a small import levy on imported grain. The 1937 Agriculture Act extended the subsidy to oats and barley, increased the payments on wheat, and offered subsidies on lime and basic slag.

So, when war broke out in 1939, the framework existed for an expansion of home agriculture, though little recovery had so far been registered. The

Very early tractor priced at 200 guineas.

acreage of derelict land had decreased hardly at all, the livestock population remained at a low ebb, the Victorian buildings with which most farms were equipped were falling to pieces, hedges were untrimmed, fences broken down, 60% of the total farm area was ostensibly devoted to grass (which included the roughest of rough grazing), few farms had as yet acquired the recently introduced tractors, and virtually every farm in the country was starved of capital. In that summer less than 30% of the country's food was being produced on English farms, and more than 70% was being imported. The task ahead of the farmers was at least to reverse that ratio.

The development of Chevalier barley, described in the previous chapter, marked the emergence of nationally recognized cereal varieties, as opposed to local ones. Throughout the middle years of the nineteenth century it dominated the barley-growing scene. Other new varieties began to appear in the 1890s. One of the earliest was Goldthorpe, a barley variety developed from a single outstanding ear grown in a field of Chevalier at Goldthorpe, Yorkshire in 1889, much as had happened with Chevalier. Around the same time Dr E. S. Beaven started to collect the best barley ears he could obtain from various parts of England, Ireland and Denmark. By 1905 he had, by cross-fertilization, produced the parents of Plumage-Archer barley which, with the closely related Spratt-Archer barley, soon took over from Chevalier. When in the late 1880s barley competitions were organized and staged in a Brewers' Exhibition, 83% of the entries of named varieties were of Chevalier, but in the decade 1926–36 Chevalier accounted for only 2%, and none of the entries was awarded a prize. By 1939, of the samples of seed tested by the National Institute of Agricultural Botany no fewer than 88.9% were of Plumage-Archer, Spratt-Archer or some nearly allied variety.

Parallel work in wheat-breeding, employing similar methods but producing results at a rather later date, was conducted by Sir Rowland Biffen. It was 1916 when, using genes of the hard Canadian and Australian wheats as well as British varieties, he introduced the outstanding wheat, Yeoman. It and its derivative Holdfast soon achieved the same popularity as Spratt-Archer and Plumage-Archer among barleys, though in the 1920s and 1930s the older varieties, Red Standard and Squarehead's Master, were still extensively grown. The traditional ten sacks (25-cwt) an acre were still considered a satisfactory yield of wheat, and many farmers harvested less.

Most farms grew a field or two of oats for feeding their own working horses. Grey Winter oats for autumn sowing and Black Tartar for spring were the standard varieties, though in 1892 Dr John Garton of Warrington introduced the first hybrid oat, a variety which achieved some popularity under the name Abundance.

The one new major crop of the period was sugar beet. This was first developed in France in Napoleon's time to replace the West Indian sugar supplies cut off by the British blockade. Vast improvements were effected by Louis de Vilmorin in the 1880s, resulting in sugar beet accounting for about half the world's supply of sugar. The first English sugar beet factory was, however, not established until 1912, though within the next thirty years it was followed by sixteen others, the sugar beet acreage ultimately reaching nearly 500,000.

While Victorian high farming flourished, adherence to the four-course rotation and its variations continued to produce excellent grassland which was efficiently used. Seed catalogues listed many species of grasses and leguminous plants, recommending some for one purpose, some for another. Some silage was even being made in the 1880s.

Grass, because it is so easy-going, was one of the first crops to suffer in the collapse of Victorian farming. It was, after all, the natural vegetation of much of England. It would spring up and eventually cover old arable land left derelict without the trouble and expense of sowing. Often the grass resulting from such neglect was poor, unproductive stuff, but no one cared. The very principle of alternate husbandry was forgotten so completely that in the mid-1930s Professor Sir R. G. Stapledon had to preach it again as an entirely new doctrine. Ley farming, he called it, as from 1919 onwards he worked quietly at the Welsh Plant Breeding Station at Aberystwyth where he was the first director. Under his direction the Station became the major source of new and improved grasses and clovers, on which the recovery of derelict farmland was based during and after the Second World War. One of its triumphs was the superb white clover hybrid, S 100, and many of the leafy varieties of perennial rye-grass on which modern leys are based originate from Aberystwyth.

Of course, all plant-breeders owed much to the pioneer research undertaken by the monk Gregor Mendel in his Moravian monastery in the mid-nineteenth century. It was he who established the principles of heredity and pointed the way to hybridization, though in his lifetime his discoveries were unappreciated and neglected. It was not until 1901, fifteen years after his death, that his papers were rediscovered and their value recognized.

Of equal importance to plant-breeding was the study of plant foods. As already noted, Jethro Tull thought, erroneously, that plants fed on tiny particles of soil, and his celebrated horse-hough was designed to assist in breaking down the soil particles to aid their absorption. In the 1830s a French farmer, M Boussingault, discovered by experiments in his own fields in Alsace that plants fed on nitrogen from the soil and carbon from the air, and between 1824 and 1873 the great German chemist, Justus Liebig, who is generally agreed to be the founder of the science of agricultural chemistry, experimented with the proportions of the various elements needed for plant growth and the best available sources for them. Though some of his findings were later shown to be in error, they constituted the basis for other experimental work, notably that carried on by John Bennet Lawes at Rothamsted. Nitrogen, he discovered, was absorbed via the soil, not from the atmosphere as Liebig had postulated; he also established the great importance of potassium and phosphates.

From earliest times farmers had appreciated the value of certain waste products in replenishing soil fertility. In the Bronze Age and perhaps even in the Neolithic period they had recognized the value of animal droppings and farmyard manure. In the Middle Ages and later they experimented with such surplus material as bones, ashes, blood, soot, fishmeal and rags. Now the new industrial processes began to make available new by-products containing plant foods. Sulphate of ammonia, a by-product of the gas industry, could supply quantities of nitrogen; superphosphate was obtained by treating bones with sulphuric acid. It appears that sulphate of ammonia was in steady demand on farms as early as 1833, and superphosphate about ten years later. Another industrial by-product, basic slag, which derives from the Bessemer process for producing steel, was not used as fertilizer until after 1885, when its value as a source of phosphates was demonstrated. Thereafter it achieved wide popularity, and experiments on old pastures at Cockle Park, Northumberland in 1906 showed its power to stimulate the growth of wild white clover and greatly increase their stock-feeding capacity.

Parallel with these developments were those of mineral sources of fertilizers. In the present century a controversy has arisen between the champions of organic or 'natural' fertilizers and those of chemical or 'artificial' fertilizers, but it is difficult, if not impossible, to draw a line of demarcation. One of the earliest manures to be imported into England was guano, from the accumulation of bird droppings on rainless islands off the coast of Peru. Shipments started to come in as early as 1840. Guano is beyond doubt an organic manure, but how, then, shall we define the coprolite deposits of the east Midlands, the mining of which began in 1847? Coprolites are animal droppings which have become fossilized; they are a valuable source of phosphates. Many countries are now engaged in mining phosphate-bearing rocks, some of animal origin like the coprolites and some not. Potash is also mined, and the first great stratum of potassium-bearing rock to be exploited was in Germany in 1875.

But farmers in general took little part in the arguments about 'natural' and 'artificial' manures and appreciation of the value of these new aids to better crops was slow in spreading. The depressed economic climate was against their rapid acceptance. I remember that on our farm during the late 1920s we grew such a satisfactory crop of barley that in the following year we decided to double the barley acreage. At harvest-time the price of barley had fallen to about half its level in the previous year. There was no incentive to increase production of anything.

From time to time, though, we experimented with these new chemicals. In the early 1930s I sowed sulphate of ammonia over many an acre, trudging

Berkshire mangold heap, winter feed for cattle.

with a seed-lip slung over my shoulders and spraying the damp, crystalline stuff over the soil by hand. Or, rebelling against the sores it made on my fingers, I shovelled it out from the back of a cart. Basic slag was even worse, for I used to go home black as a sweep, covered from head to foot in black dust. The potassic manure, kainit, was the one which impressed us most, for it certainly helped us to produce heavier crops of mangolds.

One of the most welcome improvements, which we began to hear about in the 1930s, was the development of compound granulated fertilizers, in which the three major plant foods were blended in proportions scientifically matched to the needs of the crops to which they were supplied. They came into commercial production and use just in time to play a major role in the reclamation and cropping of formerly derelict land during World War Two.

The story of livestock in the Victorian era and thereafter is that of steady and sustained building on the foundations laid by Bakewell, Collings and the other great improvers. One after another of the types which had now become recognized breeds established a breed society, each with its herd book or flock book and rigid rules for keeping the breed pure. Before the end of the nineteenth century almost all of them were thus organized.

The notable exception was the British Friesian, which did not possess its

breed society until 1909. In the second half of the nineteenth century enormous numbers of Friesians were imported from Holland, though it is true that most of them were intended for slaughter. In 1892 this trade was prohibited, through fear of disease, but by then numbers of breeding herds were well established, particularly in the eastern counties. When, in the great inter-war depression, erstwhile arable farmers turned to dairying for salvation, the high milk production and greater dependability of the Friesian soon became widely known. Until then cattle of Shorthorn type predominated in ordinary English herds, the preference being for fine-looking roan animals. As noted earlier, the Shorthorn breed split quite early into beef and dairy types but, unfortunately, the two looked alike and a lot of indiscriminate crossing took place. Consequently a farmer buying a Shorthorn-type cow in market on her looks alone could well find himself landed with a handsome animal which produced very little milk. With Friesians, on the other hand, he could be reasonably sure, and so, steadily but inexorably, the Friesians gained the ascendancy.

The confusion applied, of course, only to non-pedigree animals. The top

Rich cream-producing Jerseys (far left) were to be eventually outnumbered by Friesians (left and below), who give a lot more milk.

breeding herds and flocks were kept scrupulously pure and were continually being improved by rigorous selection, culling and interbreeding. In consequence, British livestock gained a very high reputation internationally. Individual animals, and especially sires, were sold for phenomenal prices to overseas buyers to improve their own stock. Even today the flocks and herds of Australia, Canada, the United States, New Zealand, South Africa, Argentina, Chile, Brazil and many other countries are based predominantly on British breeds. The traffic still continues.

During the century a revolution in veterinary knowledge and practice occurred. Although several major epidemics among livestock were a feature of the period, that was no new thing, for calamitous losses through 'murrain'—a term applied indiscriminately to almost any livestock ailment—had continually been recorded throughout the Middle Ages. This time, however, they were effectively tackled.

In 1791 a veterinary college had been founded, and gradually veterinary surgeons became thicker on the ground. It took a long time, for even by the middle of the century the old horse-doctors and cow-leeches with their traditional and generally useless remedies were all that most farmers had to rely on. New diseases also arrived to plague the stockbreeder, for in 1839 an epidemic of foot-and-mouth disease was first reported in England, to be followed two years later by one of pleuro-pneumonia, originating in The Netherlands. This latter disease is said to have killed more than 12,000 cows in the town dairies of London alone.

Then in the summer of 1865 rinderpest, which had been devastating the cattle herds of much of Europe, struck, again appearing first in the London dairies. Commendably, the Government took swift action, quickly initiating a slaughter policy which suppressed it within a year. Lesser outbreaks subsequently occurred, but the disease was finally eradicated by 1871, though not before it had caused the death of well over 200,000 animals. Pleuro-pneumonia was abolished by 1900.

Research into animal diseases resulted in the discovery of the bacilli of contagious abortion, bovine tuberculosis, sheep scab and other diseases, the virus of foot-and-mouth disease, and the responsibility of liver fluke for liver rot in sheep. The long uphill warfare against many of these enemies is not over yet, but the identification of one's adversary is a major step towards winning the conflict, and the present century has seen the eradication of bovine tuberculosis and contagious abortion. Meantime the development of a nationwide veterinary service meant that by the end of the century almost every farm was within reach of a qualified vet.

Yet another major advance was in the study and determination of the nutritional requirements of farm animals. Farmers in earlier centuries were not unaware of what was good for livestock. Coke of Holkham, for instance, had been well versed in the art of fattening cattle and sheep on turnips, clover and rye-grass leys. Lambs of the Dorset Horn breed were in the eighteenth century being fattened on oats, peas and meal, in order to catch the early spring market in London. The use of linseed and oilseed cake for fattening beasts was widely appreciated, and pigs throve on whey and buttermilk sometimes mixed with brewery swillings and bran or with boiled carrot, turnips or potatoes.

What the chemists of the ninteenth century did was to analyse foodstuffs and state their nutritional value in terms of carbohydrates, proteins and other components. The carbohydrate value of food became known as its starch equivalent, the protein value as its protein equivalent, and these equivalents, precisely calculated (by computers nowadays), are the foundations on which modern livestock rations are based.

Around the middle of the century farmers were experimenting with mixing their own livestock rations, with such things as roots, hay, chaff and culms as the bulk part and oilcake or meal as the fattening ingredient. Quite a cult developed for boiling the oil or linseed, pouring it over the other items and encouraging the mixture to ferment. Although the process was probably not worth the trouble, the principle was an important one. It was that of producing a compound and properly balanced ration, an idea which was in due course taken up and developed by the larger millers. One of the pioneers was Joseph Thorley, who founded the firm which bears his name and who produced a compound cattle cake in 1856.

A decade or two later millers began to import exotic ingredients from overseas. Such items as decorticated cotton cake, locust beans and maize were soon being incorporated into the compounds, the proportions of each calculated according to the needs of the animals they were intended for.

The Industrial Revolution, by which machines replaced men, had its parallel on the farms of England. Inventors in due course turned their attention to ideas for making farm work easier, quicker and, in the end, less costly, largely by saving labour. The Machinery Riots of 1830—the last despairing revolt of the old peasantry—was a futile protest against the inevitable. The smashed and burned threshing machines were the heralds of a mechanical revolution destined to transform agriculture as it had other industries.

These prototype threshers were stationary machines, powered by horse-gear. The horse was hitched to a horizontal, disc-like platform and made to walk in a circle, the power generated being harnessed by a series of cogs to drive mills, turnip-slicers and chaffcutters as well as threshing machines. An ox was sometimes employed instead of a horse. Within twenty years of the Machinery Riots, however, steam engines had appeared on farms. By 1853 manufacturers were supplying steam traction engines for agricultural use, and by the early 1900s most arable farms either possessed one of these or relied on the services of a contractor who did. In the 1920s and 1930s one contractor would undertake all the threshing on all the smaller farms in a group of perhaps a dozen or twenty villages, thus filling out the entire winter. The local farmers used to rejoice when the smoke of the threshing engine appeared over the approach road to our village, for at last the ricks in which the sheaves had been stored ever since harvest were about to be dismantled, to fill the waiting sacks with red-gold grain which could be sold. Money in the bank! My feelings were otherwise, for the arrival of the threshing machine on our farm meant a week of purgatory for me, living in a hell of dust at the end of the machine which spewed out the waste. The threshing machine usually brought a team of three men, of whom the driver lived in a hut on iron wheels trundled along behind the machine, and the farmer provided the rest of the team—an additional five or six men. The equipment

Steam ploughing employing a stationary engine.

provided by the threshers also included an elevator, a device introduced in 1863 and in common use by the end of the century. Its use here was to carry threshed straw to men who were making a rick of it.

The replacement of horses by steam as the farm power unit was an idea that occurred early to inventors. As early as 1769 a London draper who also farmed, Francis Moore, invented what he termed a 'fire engine' which he claimed would so revolutionize farming that horses would be redundant. Matching practice with precept, he sold all his own horses and advised his farming neighbours to do the same, while prices held.

Throughout the first half of the nineteenth century ideas for using steam for farm work multiplied, encouraged by prizes for practical inventions. The first effective steam plough appeared in 1833, and for the rest of the century experiments and demonstrations were frequently in progress on the larger farms. But the techniques employed had certain serious defects. The steam engine did not chug across a field, drawing a plough behind it, but was

Threshing team, working with portable steam engine, circa 1930.

anchored at one corner. It supplied the power for a cable, to which the plough was attached, along a square marked by pulleys. When the plough arrived back at its starting point, the pulleys had to be pulled up and carefully reset, a time-consuming task and expensive of labour, even though the inventors tried to economize by using multi-furrowed ploughs. Nor was the system very efficient. Comparing the amount of fuel consumed with the amount of work done, it had an efficiency figure of only about 6%. However, it retained many adherents until it was superseded by the much more efficient petrol and diesel tractors.

Improvements to ploughs continued to multiply, as the very large number of patents registered during the nineteenth century testify, but mostly they were minor improvements. Around the middle of the century there was quite a vogue in rotary cultivators, for use with steam tackle, but really efficient rotary tillage had to wait for the arrival of the tractor.

Early McCormick reaper, 1831.

Much corn and hay was still being reaped with scythes at the end of the nineteenth century, but from about 1840 on reaping machines were available. Credit for their invention is shared by the American, Cyrus McCormick, who after several decades of experiments, produced a successful machine in 1840, and the Rev Patrick Bell, a Scotsman, who built his prototype in 1826 and was awarded a prize of £50 for it by the Highland and Agricultural Society. Several models of this machine were working in Scotland in the 1830s and some were exported to other countries, but, as so often happens with British inventions and discoveries, no manufacturer could be found to take up the idea, so all the commercial advantages went to McCormick.

The early reaping machines did nothing but reap, depositing the cut corn or grass in swathes. Men and women had to follow behind, gathering up the stalks into sheaves and binding them, as they had done when the reaping was by scythe. McCormick now turned his attention to inventing a self-binder which would collect the severed stalks into sheaves and bind them automatically. He solved the problem by 1879, and by the 1920s self-binders were almost universally employed on English farms for harvesting corn, though reaping machines were still used for cutting hay. In America and Canada at that time work was in progress to combine a reaper with a threshing machine, but the combine-harvesters which were the result did not come into common use in England until after World War Two.

'A bit of good hay' has always been popular with farmers. It smells nice, has good feeding value, and making it successfully gives a lot of satisfaction. This is because it is so hazardous, depending as it does on a week's fair weather in June or July, when such blessings are rare in the English climate. Techniques of haymaking have therefore always been directed to speeding up the process of drying the cut grass. After the grass has been allowed to lie wilting for two or three days, it is turned and tossed again and again till it is dry enough to be carted to the barn or built into a rick, hopefully before the next rainstorm. The traditional tools for turning and tossing were the prong or hay-fork and the hand-rake, but naturally the ingenious Victorians thought out mechanical methods. In 1846 the Royal Agricultural Society organized its first demonstration of haymaking machinery, at which an award was made to the inventor of a horse-drawn tedding machine, capable of being raised or lowered by a gear lever. Other machines for turning the swathes and fluffing up the drying hay soon followed, and in the early years of the twentieth century the side-rake, which soon had its place on almost every farm, was perfected. In spite of every aid, however, haymaking in England is still a bit of a gamble.

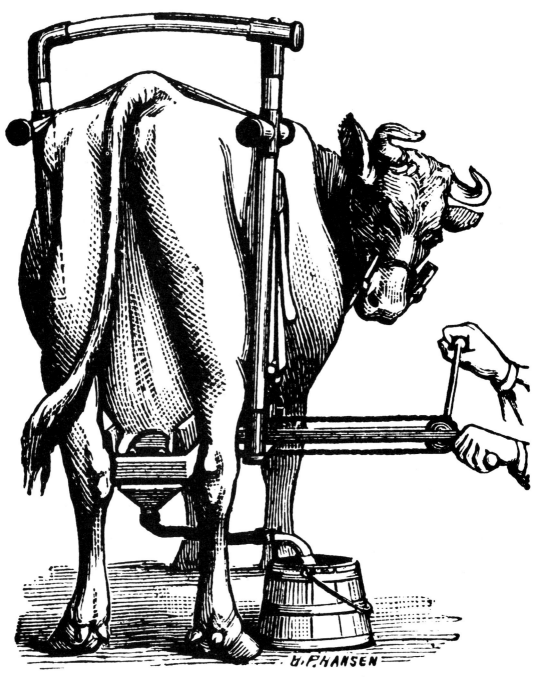

Victorian inventiveness seemed to stop at nothing, and, in milking cows, achieved amazing results. Above right: town dairies distributed to customers from churns carried pannier-fashion. Below right: the portable milking bail enabled farmers to use fields distant from buildings for grazing and milking cattle.

204

Interest in machinery for use with livestock did not have any notable successes till towards the end of the nineteenth century, the first milking machine operating on the pulsator system appearing in 1895. Even then it was far from perfect, and it was not until about 1910 that machines of modern types were available and came into widespread use. Cream separators were invented in the 1870s. When the downland farmers of southern England—forced to abandon their ancient sheep-and-corn tradition because of the importation of cheap grain—turned their attention in the 1920s to dairying, they had to solve the problem of keeping and milking cows in fields far from the farmyard. Their answer was the portable milking bail, a milking machine for four or six cows in a shed on wheels which could be moved around the pastures. A. J. Hosier, of Wexcombe, deserves much of the credit for this.

Wool had long since ceased to be a major reason for keeping sheep in England, so it was natural for the first mechanical shearing machine to be invented not here but in Australia. Specimens were sent over for exhibition in 1893 but the machines were not widely used until the 1920s.

Two other inventions of major importance on the farm might not occur to a non-farming reader: rubber boots and barbed wire. I can remember wearing lace-up leather boots with leather gaiters. Putting them on in the mornings was quite a major operation and they were never as efficient as Wellingtons. As for barbed wire, though many country-lovers have wished it had never been invented, it proved an admirably cheap method of fencing during the long years of depression. Instead of taking the trouble to maintain a stock-proof hedge, a farmer could mend gaps with a couple of strands of barbed wire anchored to trees. He could even make rough-and-ready collapsible gates of barbed wire. The visual effects, however, were deplorable.

The outside world now began to impinge more and more on rural life. Many medieval peasants never strayed from their manor or had any knowledge of the outside world, and even in more recent times life for many villagers was virtually sedentary. In 1826 Cobbett asked the way of a young woman he met near Chute, in north Hampshire, and learned that she had never been more than $2\frac{1}{2}$ miles from the place where she was born. The Victorian era not only opened the doors of the world to isolated farming communities but also began to bring the outside world to their threshold.

Associated with the development of the turnpike road system already described, was the stagecoach. By the 1820s traffic on the new macadamized roads was able to travel at a spanking pace, and formerly remote and

Trimming a Hampshire Down ram preparatory to export.

isolated country places found themselves in reasonably direct contact with the metropolis. Staging inns, established at seven-mile intervals along the highways, became points of rendezvous for countrymen of all classes, who enjoyed the opportunity of exchanging gossip with the coachmen and passengers.

The impact of the railways, which had allowed the stage coach era a career of less than a century, was even greater. The numbers of countryfolk who travelled by stage coach was strictly limited but almost anyone could afford the fare for a train journey, and London became a feasible destination for farmers and even labourers whose parents had never ventured farther than the nearest market town. A class quite dramatically affected was that of the daughters of farmers and farm labourers, from those of peasant status to the ranks of tenants of several hundreds of acres. Domestic work on their fathers' farms until they got married had been their lot in the past, and those who were considered too genteel for such mundane tasks must have often found life tedious in the extreme. Now London lay open to them. The wealthier country gentry and the larger farmers had town houses or belonged to town clubs, and the daughters of the less affluent 'went into service' with them. From the 1840s onwards innumerable country girls spent several years in service in London, travelling to and fro by train, and some of them rising high in the domestic hierarchy before coming home to marry the sons of local farmers and labourers. A veneer of gentility was thus extended even to cottage homes. In a perusal of parish registers it is noticeable that before about 1840 a high proportion of village brides were illiterate. They signed the register with a cross by their names. Few needed to do so after that date.

Another revolution for which the railways were responsible was the transport of goods to and from the farms, and no aspect of it was more important than the milk train. Instead of having to make most of their milk into butter or cheese, dairy farmers now had an almost unlimited market for liquid milk at their disposal. Milk collected in churns from the farms by day was despatched to the big cities by train overnight, to arrive in time for distribution early the next morning.

Earlier in the century town dairies had assumed considerable importance. The cows were kept in sheds in back-street yards and food for them fetched in from farms just beyond the suburbs. Some cows were milked in the streets. By the 1850s a number of city dairies had assumed impressive proportions and were highly organized. One of the outstanding examples was William Harley's in Glasgow, which at its peak housed 1,700 cattle, 1,000 of them in milk at any one time. They were milked three times a day by a battalion of dairymaids, gave an average daily total of 1,500 gallons and were fed on scientifically balanced rations. The dairy was even equipped with a viewing balcony, where visitors could watch the milking at a charge of a shilling a head. Unhappily this, like other town dairies, was badly hit by rinderpest in the 1860s, paving the way for the milk trade to be taken by the milk train.

Railway transport also made possible the proliferation of organizations which would have been hardly feasible in previous eras. Attention has already been drawn to the numerous breed societies which were preceded by the Smithfield Club in 1798, and the Royal Agricultural Society of England in 1839, one of whose major activities was organizing the Royal Show. In the decades which followed numerous other regional, county and local shows were founded and have flourished ever since. Politically, agriculture had to wait until 1908 before it became officially represented by the formation of the National Farmers' Union.

As the twentieth century began to unfold, therefore, it revealed an agriculture which, although retaining its time-honoured status as a way of life, was emerging as an alert industry, intent on staking its claim for equal consideration to mining and manufacturing.

A scene almost entirely vanished from the English country side.

11. *The Age of Specialization*

In the 1890s my father possessed the first bicycle the villagers had ever seen. Standing on the lawn of our Wiltshire farmhouse as a small boy some time before 1920, I saw the first aeroplane ever to fly over the village—a flimsy biplane circling overhead. I saw, too, the first motor car ever to test the roads of the village. We ourselves bought, in 1921, a Ford van—a lefthand-drive vehicle surplus from war duties in France—to replace our pony and trap for deliveries of farm produce to town customers. In 1934 our farm was the first in the parish to acquire a tractor. Much time and ingenuity were spent during the war years in adapting sundry horse-drawn farm implements for use with this new power unit. I remember helping to devise a very serviceable potato-planter from a double-furrow plough, some blacksmith-made funnels and an old saddle. My father (by then quite a prominent farmer locally, and a member of the War Agricultural Executive Committee for the district) was allocated one of the new American combine-drills when they began to come over under the Lease-Lend arrangements towards the end of the war.

When the war at last drew to its close we gave up the tenancy of our downland farm, effectively halving our acreage. My father's reasoning, which led to this step and which I accepted, was entirely logical but erroneous. His arguments were terse and persuasive: 'Twice in only just over a hundred years farming has been thrown overboard as soon as a war has ended,' he pointed out. 'It happened when the Corn Laws were repealed after the wars with Napoleon, and it happened even more quickly in 1921 when the Corn Production Act was jettisoned. It will happen again. The Government has no real option.' He observed that the top-heavy urban population would have to be fed as cheaply as possible, so there would soon be free trade again, 'and farmers can go hang. The towns have the votes'. When the decline started, the land that would go derelict first, he reasoned, would be the hill land and the downland, as happened before. The soil was too poor and the fields too far from home. 'Within ten years that land we've reclaimed will revert to a rabbit warren.' So we gave notice and quit, and events proved that it was a completely wrong decision.

Modern egg-packing station using conveyer belts.

Why didn't history repeat itself, as my father predicted? The reasons were threefold. In the first place, the international situation remained in a state of armed peace. With the Cold War dominating international affairs, successive governments had a powerful incentive to keep agriculture moderately prosperous and efficient. This they did by subsidies, controlled prices and various other monetary inducements. Secondly, Britain was no longer a dominant and relatively wealthy nation able to take the pick of produce in the world's markets. Many of the emerging nations possessed increasing purchasing power and could compete with us for available food. The third factor was that the thin hill soils, of which our downland farm was a typical example, were no longer the poor relations of the rich valley fields. We ought to have realized that. Having reclaimed almost the entire farm from dereliction, we had harvested good crops not only of barley and oats but also of the more exacting wheat, turnips and potatoes. We were inclined to attribute the excellence of the crops to the fact that we were cashing in on the reserves of fertility which had accumulated during the long period of dereliction. If we had been more farsighted we would have realized that the techniques we were using and the aids to agricultural efficiency now available would keep the soil in good heart indefinitely.

Several other developments that have occurred since then were not generally foreseen in the immediate post-war years either. In the course of one year, 1938, our farm and village had been supplied with electricity, telephones and piped water, but the war was on us before the implications of these innovations became evident. No one who did not rely on the village farms and fields for a livelihood had wanted to live in a place where such amenities were lacking. You lived in a village because you worked there. It had always been so.

But now we had to face the fact that the town, the journey to which by carrier's cart had taken two-and-a-half hours when I was a small child, was only a quarter-of-an-hour distant by motorcar. A family could enjoy the spaciousness of country life while the father commuted to town every day. For countless villages the future lay as commuters' dormitories. No lack of amenities, either, now deterred elderly folk from settling there in their retirement.

Of course the demand for houses from these new quarters developed only gradually. Between the wars thatched cottages could be bought for £100 a pair. I myself bought a couple for £200 in the late 1940s. Such cottages, however, tended for a time to be rather more of a liability than an asset, for they did not conform to the building standards which the newly appointed

212

planning authorities were applying. The ceilings were much too low, the windows were too small, the winding stairs dangerous, the walls lacked damp courses, the lavatory was a box-like edifice in a far corner of the garden. Half the cottages I knew well from my boyhood days were recklessly demolished because of such defects, though today they would be regarded as treasures.

When the property price explosion occurred in 1972, prices which had been rising gently over the years rocketed. Everyone was taken by surprise. I remember a would-be purchaser arguing, at the beginning of that year, that the £5,000 he was being asked for a three-bedroomed thatched house with about half-an-acre of land was a ridiculous exaggeration of the true value. He refused to buy, but before the end of the year the property had been sold for nearly £20,000, after a building plot had been extracted from the half-acre. Now, tastefully remodelled into what it is fashionable to consider a country cottage should be, it would easily fetch £70,000. The modern farm worker lives either in a council house or in a farm cottage that goes with the job or, increasingly, in a house he is buying on mortgage. Not that there are many farm workers left. Their numbers have been steadily diminishing ever since the war.

To cope with the work on our 450-acre wartime farm we needed ten regular workers, besides the three able-bodied men in our family, and more in busy seasons. The other farms in our village were similarly staffed. How many men, excluding the farmers themselves, are employed there now? None. Each surviving farm is a one-man unit so well-equipped with modern aids to efficiency that the farmer himself can run it.

During wartime maximum production had priority almost regardless of cost. Our beleaguered island was hard-pressed to feed its population. Every imported cargo had to run the gauntlet of lurking U-boats, besides occupying shipping space urgently required for other purposes. Every acre had to contribute its quota of food. In the late 1940s and 1950s the emphasis changed. Farmers were still urged to aim for maximum production, but with due regard to costs. Indeed, costs soon assumed paramount importance.

The 1950s saw the rise of 'agribusinesses', which have since come to dominate many aspects of agriculture. An agribusiness is simply a farm to which the business principles that govern factories and shops are applied. Its master is its accountant. Production is planned to provide an excess of income over expenditure—in other words, a profit.

During the years of depression in the 1920s and 1930s, the village in which I was brought up would be, by modern standards, termed poverty-stricken. Farm workers were then being paid about thirty shillings a week, but the small farmers on our thin, impoverished chalk soil managed on about the same. Even though no one had wealth enough to pay any taxes, no one went short of food, shelter, heating or clothes. Most of the milk produced in the village was consumed there. Bread from the village baker cost only a few pence, though many housewives baked their own. Almost every family cultivated a large vegetable plot, kept a pig to be killed for winter bacon, and had a pen of poultry. Rabbits galore could be had for the killing and constituted our main meat supply. We had a village shoemaker and a village dressmaker. When, in snowy winters, the sunken road over the downs to the town was blocked by drifts for weeks, we suffered no hardship. It was the town which was cut off by snow, not us.

Though the farmers produced, ostensibly, to make a profit—selling their grain in autumn to find money for the rent, and disposing of surplus calves, lambs and pigs when cash was required at other season—the village flourished on what was still very largely a subsistence economy. Our own farm, then about 140 acres, was typical. Like most farms always had, it produced a little of everything that could reasonably be expected. After all, we did aim to have a varied diet. We grew fields of wheat (for sale to pay the rent), oats (for feeding the horses) and barley (for feeding pigs and chicken). We had a dozen milking cows, from whose milk we made butter. We reared their calves and kept them on till they were old enough to have calves of their own, unless we ran short of ready cash in the meantime. We ran a flock of about fifty sheep. We kept two sows and usually had a few sties of fattening pigs. About 300 laying hens lived on free range, roosting in portable houses which were moved around the farm, being parked on pastures in spring and summer, on stubble-fields after harvest, and in rickyards throughout the winter. The poultry flocks were replenished by chicken hatched under broody hens every spring. We also kept ducks (including Muscovies), geese, turkeys and even guinea-fowl. We grew turnips for the sheep, kale and mangolds for the cows, and all manner of vegetables partly for our own use and partly to send to the produce market in the town. Later, when the countryside began to fill up with suburban-type houses, we had a milk round, and washed up the bottles daily in the kitchen sink.

All this was not only farming in the traditional style but also seemed to provide us with the best possible programme for a settled life. 'Don't put all your eggs in one basket,' was a favourite proverb of my father. 'There is never a year when every crop succeeds or when every crop fails,' he used to add. 'Play safe.' That sounded reasonable enough, and it had always served

214

us and our ancestors quite well. It was not going to do so for the future.

In a cost-conscious economy, the essential equation in the production of any commodity is cost per unit. A high cost per unit necessarily dictates a high price to the consumer. The lower the cost, the more competitive can be the price. All factory production is based on that truism. In agribusinesses, and indeed in all successful modern farming, the unit is not the farm but the actual commodity being produced. The economist in charge of an agribusiness works out the cost of producing a dozen eggs, a gallon of milk, a pound of bacon, a hundredweight of potatoes, a table chick to the age of ten weeks, and so on. He then seeks ways of reducing costs.

Portable range shelters for growing pullets once featured on most farms.

One method is by increasing the number of units. The first motor cars, made by metal workers with a mechanical bent in back-street workshops, were more substantially built than their modern successors, for they were put together by one or two craftsmen doing the whole job. Consequently they were correspondingly much more expensive than factory-made models put together on an assembly line. The factory could charge lower prices because, by producing a very large number of cars, it could accept a smaller margin of profit on each. So the future of car manufacturers lay with factories, and the backstreet workshop closed down.

It was the same with farm commodities. Even in the days of the depression we needed to make a charge for table poultry that gave us several shillings a head above costs. Otherwise, with only a dozen or two chicken to sell, they would hardly have been worth keeping. As a result, in those days table chicken were something of a luxury. Instead of a dozen cows, as our farm once had, a modern dairy farm has a herd of between 100 and 200. Specialist sheep farms keep well over 1,000 ewes; specialist pig farms 3,000 or more fattening pigs. A modern arable farm aims to increase its quota of acres. The larger the acreage, the lower the acceptable margin of profit per acre.

To attain the super-efficiency required, the modern farmer has to equip himself with all the available devices to cut costs. The specialist producer of table poultry, for example, keeps his chicken in batches of ten thousand, or multiplies of ten thousand, in one house. This economizes in space and hence in building costs. In such a house, lighting, temperature, ventilation and humidity are all automatically controlled. Food, in the form of pellets of a specially balanced ration, and water are supplied automatically. The chicken arrive as day-olds, straight from the incubator, and never leave the building or see the outside world. Their lives are less than three months. Skilled geneticists manipulate cross-breeding so that these cockerels reach slaughter weight in less and less time. The shorter the period, the less food they eat and therefore the lower the price at which they can be sold to the public.

Similarly, fattening pigs are kept in a series of pens in purpose-built buildings, in which the same factors—lighting, temperature, ventilation and humidity—are automatically controlled. Twice a day the pigman presses a series of buttons and the correct rations for each pen surge along pipelines from the storage tanks and pour into the feeding troughs. The pigman even has the use of a computer to work out the most economical food for each pen.

Hens in an egg-laying battery; eggs are collected from wire trays.

216

Above: combine-harvester automatically transferring its load.

Below: the driver's view of a combine harvester at work.

Milking cows also have their rations calculated by computer. The amount of nutrition they are obtaining from grazing or silage is accurately measured and the balance, if any, is made up of scientifically blended ingredients fed in the form of cubes at milking time. The cows are milked by machine in parlours of ever-increasing sophisticated design.

The arable farmer has to invest not only in tractors but in combine-drills, spraying machinery, cultivating machinery, combine-harvesters, drying facilities and storage bins. It all represents a very heavy outlay. No one farm could afford to modernize the entire range of farm products such as used to be produced on a mixed farm. The successful farmer has had to be selective. He has had to choose his specialities.

Pigs are fattened indoors but are often reared in outdoor shelters.

Ideally, a farm should have one arable enterprise and one livestock enterprise. Then it can operate a proper crop rotation in its fields, devoting each field to livestock for a few years and then, when the soil has been thoroughly manured, switching to crop production. In practice, that is not always possible. Many arable farmers find that they have invested so much capital in machinery and equipment that to introduce a livestock department would put too great a strain on their resources. Or a livestock farm simply cannot get hold of enough acres to run an adequate system of alternate husbandry.

One result of the vast investment programme required on modern farms is that big economies can be made in labour. Modern farm workers are highly skilled specialists, but there are few of them. One man can milk and manage a herd of 100 to 200 cows. One man can do all the essential work on an arable farm of 100 to 200 acres. One man can look after 3,000 fattening pigs or, alternatively, a hundred or more breeding sows. One man can take charge of 40,000 or 50,000 table chicken and still have half the day free for other tasks.

Management, too, is an important factor. The modern farmer or farm manager is a specialist not necessarily in general farming but in one particular branch of it. He may be expert at running a wheat-growing farm but know very little about dairy cows. The tendency therefore is for an agribusiness to grow ever larger. If such a business which already has four big dairy herds acquires another farm it does not branch out into pig-keeping, poultry-keeping, potato-growing or some other type of agriculture; it installs yet another dairy herd. So agribusinesses grow ever bigger. And that means that they become, or should become, ever more efficient. The more units they produce, of whatever commodity they have chosen, the lower the price margin they can accept. So each agribusiness is in competition with every other agribusiness devoted to the same commodity. In some branches of the industry, notably in poultry and turkeys, the competition has been so intense that most of the smaller practitioners have been forced out of business, leaving the field to a few giant combines, some of them operating on an international scale.

Even in what may be termed a conventional type of farm the same forces are at work—one example is a farm of 2,400 acres on the chalk downs, operating today on a modification of the old sheep-and-corn system. Before the war 900 acres were derelict; the other 1,500 acres were divided into ten small farms. Now the entire area is farmed by a limited company, which employs ten persons, including the farm manager and the farm secretary.

Every year about a third of the land is devoted to sheep, including the grassland cut for hay and silage. The rest of the farm grows cereal crops, and a crop rotation is followed which allows each field to enjoy a period of two or three years under grass at regular intervals, thus ensuring that the fertility of the soil is replenished by the sheep manure.

There are 1,600 breeding ewes, which produce a lambing average of about 160%, so when the lambs are running with their mothers there are 4,160 sheep on the farm. One shepherd, aided by his wife and one of the other workers at lambing-time, looks after the lot. The arable fields produce about 4,500 to 5,000 tons of grain per year. Each worker has the use of machinery and equipment worth, on average, £30,000 and is responsible for a gross output of something over £40,000.

Inflation has made monetary comparisons between the two periods almost meaningless, but before the war the 1,500 acres then being farmed would, by the yields then obtainable, have produced no more than about 1,200 tons of grain and, if all the ten farms were each keeping a small breeding flock of ewes, perhaps 500 to 750 lambs. The contribution of the 900 acres of downland would have been a few heifers and a ton or so of rabbit carcases.

Judging from the labour force in my own village, mentioned above, the average in the 1930s was one man to about 30 acres. The 1,500 acres then comprising ten farms would have provided employment for 50 men, including the farmers. Using the same ratio, the 2,400 acres now under cultivation would be employing 80 men, whereas, in fact, they need only ten, of whom two can be reckoned as primarily office staff. Such calculations provide fodder for the arguments of those who maintain that the modern agricultural revolution has depopulated the countryside, but workers whose ancestors were peasants ploughing in the fields are now busy in factories, making machinery for the farms. Today, workers in factories in Coventry and Peterborough, for instance, could stake a legitimate claim to be part of the staff of many an English farm.

Certainly the countryside *has* been depopulated, as far as agriculture is concerned. A few statistics will illustrate that fact. Since World War Two the number of farmers in England and Wales has declined from 695,000 to 382,000. The number of farms has dropped from 525,141 to 234,200, but the average size of farm has climbed from 23.9 hectares to 51.5 hectares. The total labour force, comprising full- and part-time farmers and farm workers, is now 633,000, compared to 1,331,000 in 1950.

The reduction in the number of farms since the war is far greater than would be accounted for by normal wastage—that is, by farmers retiring and leaving no heir to carry on the farm. By far the greater proportion of the vanished 313,000 are farmers who have failed—a fact worth bearing in mind by any who think that farmers have had an easy time over the past forty or so years. Pressure has been intense, and the weakest have gone to the wall. Weeding out the inefficient is how this process has been described by successive governments. What it has amounted to is that the winners have been those quick to adopt modern intensive methods of farming, with their over-riding criterion of producing for profit, whereas the failures are those who were content with the old part-subsistence economy.

Size has had much to do with it but, as already noted, size reckoned in other units than acres. In that respect the figures of the average size of farms, quoted from Ministry of Agriculture statistics, can be misleading. For an arable farmer growing crops of cereals, an acre is indeed a valid unit and his prosperity will depend largely on how many acres he farms. For a poultry farmer housing his stock in modern, purpose-built, factory-like edifices, acreages are almost meaningless. He needs only a few acres for his hundreds of thousands of poultry, which are the true units of his agribusiness.

I happen to know a lot of failed farmers, or the sons of failed farmers and so can give examples. Some were tenants of small farms of the western hills (where 'small' means anything less than about 120 acres). Their sons, who in former times would have carried on the family farm, are now working as foremen, tractor-drivers or dairymen for larger enterprises. They fare far better than they would have done running their own faltering businesses and, because of their experience, background, expertise and habit of hard work, are highly appreciated by their employers.

There are others who chose the wrong speciality, notably those who went in for intensive production of pigs or poultry. These are enterprises that need to be fairly heavily capitalized and have the disadvantage that pigs and poultry have to be fed largely on purchased foodstuffs. Competition in both of these branches of farming has been intense, and production is now largely in the hands of huge agribusinesses.

A smaller though interesting category of failed farmers comprises those who engaged in too much pioneering. These were progressive farmers who tried every new device and idea as it came to their notice, ignoring the time-honoured axiom that it pays to let someone else do the pioneering and to come in with the second wave, after most of the initial mistakes have been made. Though they have fallen by the wayside, they deserve well of agriculture, and they are in good company. Robert Bakewell, Arthur Young, William Cobbett, King George III and many others who were in the forefront of farming progress all made financial failures of their farming.

Of course, most farming is now financed by borrowed money. Another interesting statistic is that since 1960 the total borrowed by farmers from the banks has risen from £315 million to over £4,000 million, though the significance of the figures is somewhat obscured by the change in the value of money. What is clear is that the farmer who has ample collateral for security is at an advantage for borrowing money at crucial times. Which brings us back to rural estate-owners.

As the 1875 depression became deeper and more prolonged, and tenants more and more difficult to obtain, profits from farming were so low that few landlords had been tempted to try farming themselves. Under the exigencies of war, however, every available acre of land *had* to be cultivated, and landowners with no tenants were forced to take their neglected acres in hand. To their delight and often surprise, they found themselves making money out of it. So when the war ended they continued to be farmers. They proved to be highly efficient, too. They had no traditional ideas and methods to forget, they had no high opinion of their own technical ability, but they did possess money or the wherewithal to borrow it. So they obtained the best advice, employed the best managers and stocked their farms with the best animals and latest machines.

The programme proved so successful that, as opportunity offered, they enlarged their farming enterprises. When a tenant died or retired, the estate took his farm in hand rather than let it to another tenant. Legislation in the 1970s accelerated the process. The laws enacted to safeguard tenants against eviction meant that, once in possession, a tenant was safe for life. It even became possible for a farmer to pass on his farm to his son, without permission from the landowner. Although from the tenant's point of view this has provided valuable security, it has caused farm and house tenancies to dry up almost completely. Very few landlords, with one exception to be quoted shortly, will relet land of which they have managed to regain possession. So the estate farms have become larger and more prosperous. Many of them are organized on a limited company basis and are operated as agribusinesses. And they have an immense advantage in that the ever-increasing value of their land provides them with ample collateral for whatever money they wish to borrow.

This matter of the capital appreciation of land deserves a little attention, as it accounts very largely for the myth of the rich farmer. A householder coming from a town to reside in the country learns that the farmer whose cows he can see over the hedge has a hundred acres of land. As the land is

All commerce in livestock ceases when foot and mouth disease strikes. Opposite: a modern milking parlour; cows are washed automatically on entering.

now worth about £1,000 an acre, this farmer must be a millionaire if he owns the land. And he does share in the general appreciation of property that affects any owner of house or land in a time of inflation. If he is a tenant, however, he is dependent on his profits from farming, and, on the whole, these have not been large. Monty Graveley typifies the former. He inherited his 500-acre farm in the late 1940s. As he also inherited a modest but adequate income and had little interest in farming, he decided to opt out of the business. He allowed his land, which had been reclaimed and cropped during the war, to relapse into dereliction, or, to be more precise, he sowed it all with cheap grass-seed, put a ring fence around it, and for the next thirty or forty years grazed a few score cattle on its indifferent pasture. The land, which was valued at about £50 an acre when he inherited it, is now worth more than £1,000 an acre, which makes him a millionaire several times over. By doing virtually nothing, he has been presented with an increase in the capital value of his assets of around 2,000% in forty years. Put another way, his assets increased by about £13,500 a year, which is probably more than he would have made by farming the land properly and certainly more than the neighbouring tenant who, going all out for full production, went bankrupt. And Monty Graveley has the satisfaction of being the toast of every conservationist within miles, for his agriculturally neglected farm is a naturalist's paradise.

I mentioned above an exception to the prevailing reluctance of landowners to let farms. It is provided by the institutional landlords. Since Victorian times, and in some instances earlier, the Church Commissioners and the Oxbridge colleges have invested in agricultural property, relying on the rents for a large slice of their income. No doubt they were motivated like Mark Twain, who reputedly advised his son to 'buy land, my boy. They stopped making it long ago!' It is true that in times of depression the institutional landlords suffer with the rest, but in the present economic climate land seems as sound an investment as any. Many shrewd long-term investors think so, for over the past twenty years the Church and the colleges have been joined by insurance companies, pension funds and oil-rich Arabs. They see agricultural land as an investment likely to hold its own in times of inflation, but few of them want to farm it. What they want is a good, efficient farmer in occupation, capable of paying his rent promptly, and their preference is naturally for a mature farmer of proved ability. Under their régime an established farmer is doubly safe in his tenancy and is more likely than a beginner to receive an offer of a further tenancy on any land that becomes vacant. So the tendency towards larger and fewer farms is given yet further impetus.

Paradoxically, the annual return on rented land is low. For land for which a purchaser has paid £1,000 an acre he will be lucky to get £50 an acre rent, which is 5%. Investors evidently consider that this, together with the appreciation in land values in a time of inflation, together with certain tax concessions, make the proposition worthwhile. If ever the inflationary trend is reversed, it will not look so attractive.

In the war years and the following decades agricultural prices were regulated to some extent by the government, and adjusted annually in a price review. As a rule, a minimum price for each commodity was fixed. A farmer could sometimes get above the minimum for quality, but in general the minimum price proved to be the standard. Farmers who had operated in the uncontrolled situation between the wars welcomed the element of security.

Since Britain joined the European Economic Community in 1973 a somewhat similar arrangement has been in force—controlled by the Community's headquarters in Brussels instead of by Parliament in London. The theory is that in each member country of the Common Market the prices of the various agricultural commodities and the costs of producing them should be the same. When that ideal is attained, completely free trade in those commodities between the member countries should be possible. In practice that is far from being the case. The governments of the member countries tend to protect their farming population in accordance with the value they place on the farm vote. The measures by which this is achieved are generally subtle and surreptitious, so that lip service can still be paid to the Common Agricultural Policy. There are hidden subsidies on feeding stuffs for farm animals, or specially low prices for oil used in commercial glasshouses, or unduly stringent restrictions on the import of commodities likely to compete with the products of the home farms.

The importance of the farm vote is far greater to the politicians of most other Common Market countries than Britain. The agricultural revolution which transformed the British countryside in the late eighteenth and early nineteenth centuries had no counterpart in most continental states. That is not to say that there are now no efficient large farms as in Britain, but the peasant on his smallholding is still predominant. His political power is multiplied by the laws of inheritance that prevail in most European countries. In most of continental Europe inheritance is divided equally among the sons of the family, and the result is a continual fragmentation of holdings. The process can be pushed to such extremes as a man inheriting an eighth share of a cherry tree or a walnut tree. Pragmatic peasants do not of course fail to see the absurdities to which the process can lead. So in practice a family meeting decides which of the sons is going to carry on the farm, often long beforehand, and one of the boys stays at home with his father while the others take jobs elsewhere. But they still retain their financial interest in the family farm, so any political decision affecting farm finances has repercussions far beyond the farm boundaries. Politicians are well aware of this and treat agricultural matters with the utmost caution.

The basis of the Common Agricultural Policy of the EEC is a system of intervention prices. Most farm commodities are permitted a free market, but if the price falls below a certain level the government concerned intervenes and buys that commodity at the intervention price. But the intervention prices are fixed at levels which allow a peasant farmer, operating to standards which in Britain would be thought inefficient, to make a profit. If a peasant growing, say, ten acres of wheat can make a comfortable living, how much greater will be the profit of an efficient modern farmer cultivating a thousand acres?

It is this which gives rise to the 'milk lakes', 'wine lakes', 'butter mountains', 'wheat mountains' and the other gigantic hoards of produce that attract the attention of the press from time to time. Production surplus is purchased at the agreed intervention prices and stored, eventually to be disposed of as bargain lots to eastern European countries, amid much controversy. Britain, of course, is a non-producer of wine (at least, in any considerable quantities) and makes relatively little butter. For milk we have developed a home market that is the envy of all our neighbours, but the commodity which we tend to accumulate in surplus is grain, and in Britain the marketing system is vigorously criticized by producers of pigs and poultry, who are large-scale buyers of grain to feed their livestock. A surplus of grain used to force down the price, enabling them to buy cheaply, but now that the price of grain is kept artificially high to protect the grain growers, the EEC sells masses of it cheaply to countries such as Poland, which feed it to their pigs and then, complain British pig farmers, 'export the bacon to us at prices with which we can't compete'.

There has been some justification for their laments, though gradually such problems are being ironed out. Meantime there can be no doubt that cereal-growers in Britain have in recent years been doing better financially than many of their colleagues in other branches of the industry. One reason has been the vastly increased yields achieved since the war. In the 1920s and 1930s farmers were quite content with yields of 25 to 30 cwt of wheat per acre. In 1982 one harvest survey gave an average of 58.25 cwt per acre for 720 random records. In that summer a field at Tidworth, Hampshire, produced a world record crop of 127 cwt per acre. Several factors contribute to this impressive performance. Balanced fertilizers have undoubtedly played a large part; so have selective fungicides and insecticides. But the biggest share of the credit probably goes to the plant-breeder.

The plant-breeder sets about his business much as Dr Chevalier did 160 years ago. He selects the best seed for the next generation, and from that crop the best seed for the following generation, and so on until he has achieved a variety far superior to its original parents. In Chevalier's day, best meant biggest, but now breeders work for many characteristics—resistance to specific diseases, early or late ripening, the ability to withstand harvest storms, length of straw, protein content, use on certain soils or in certain climates, and sundry other qualities. Moreover, the original seed no longer depends on chance discoveries. Skilled geneticists crossbreed from selected parent stock, as with domestic animals.

Most of the more progressive countries now have their plant-breeding stations and plant-breeding scientists, and much of the work is done on an international basis, notably that of CIMMYT (Centro Internacional de Mejoramiento do Maiz y Trigo) which, based in Mexico, now operates in more than sixty countries. Earlier in the century pioneer work tended to be concentrated in certain European countries, among which Germany, Sweden and The Netherlands were prominent. Britain had its own programme but was inclined to lag because the law prevented worthwhile financial advantage by allowing anyone to trade in a variety once it became available. The introducer was forced to make all his profit in the first year. However, a vigorous campaign resulted, in 1964, in the Plant Varieties Act, which gives a breeder or introducer of a new variety permanent rights in it and allows him to collect royalties. Since then British plant-breeders have forged ahead and are now among the foremost in the world.

Among the exciting material which one of the plant collectors, Joseph Nickerson, found in Bavaria were several promising strains of winter barley. In Britain the cereal crop traditionally sown in autumn was wheat, and in spring, barley. In the 1950s one or two useful varieties of spring wheat were marketed, but nobody had had much success with autumn-sown barley. Nickerson, however, brought home some of the most promising varieties he could find on the Continent and, at the research and breeding station he had established at Rothwell, Lincolnshire, set about improving them further and adapting them to English conditions. After a lengthy gestation period he launched on the British market in 1975 a new winter barley, named *Sonja*, to be followed in 1977 by a stable-mate, *Igri*. By 1981 the winter barley crop in

Britain had expanded, from nil just after the war, to around 2,500,000 acres, of which the two Nickerson varieties accounted for 83%.

Their introduction coincided with a period of fine, mild autumns and late, wet springs, which further encouraged the switch from spring-sown to autumn-sown crops. The result has been a dramatic change in the pattern of life on the farm. For arable farmers, harvest—once the grand climax of the year—has been downgraded to an incident in the circle of the seasons. While

in one field a combine-harvester (engaged in work which would have occupied at least ten men in previous eras) is busy with harvest, another team is sowing next year's crop elsewhere on the farm. The figures already quoted demonstrate that the yields from autumn-sown crops are higher than those for spring-sown, so naturally farmers strive to get as much land as possible sown in autumn.

A fleet of combine harvesters making short work of the harvest.

Progress with breeding new plant varieties is now so rapid and sustained that last year's prizewinners are soon superseded. Each year the National Institute of Agricultural Botany at Cambridge issues a recommended list of varieties of almost all farm crops, and it is surprising how quickly a popular variety is accorded an 'O', meaning 'Outclassed'. New varieties emanate not only from British plant-breeding establishments but from overseas as well—the trade is truly international.

But even though farmers continually experiment with new crops, not many innovations have been widely adopted. In the 1950s and 1960s maize, grown chiefly for silage, seemed about to become a major British crop. But a series of late springs made establishment of the crop hazardous and deterred growers, and now interest in it, even for silage, is declining. Oilseed rape is increasing though, and in late May and June it enlivens the pattern of the countryside with huge rectangular patches of vivid sulphur-yellow, to the delight also of bee-keepers, for the flowers are rich in nectar. Often it poses problems of uneven ripening, and, as these are overcome, new diseases and pests are appearing. However, the crop proves reasonably profitable in most years.

Protein peas, recently developed as a crop for feeding livestock, are becoming popular, and, now that seed (which cannot normally be produced in Britain) is readily available from other countries, lucerne is widely grown.

Grass continues to be cultivated as a specialist crop, with great emphasis on leafy strains of perennial ryegrass. Livestock farmers sow temporary leys of this variety alone, using it intensively (by grazing and cutting for silage) for one, two or three years and then ploughing the sward and cashing in on the accumulated fertility. It is sound farming practice, on the 'up-and-down' or alternate husbandry principle, though I doubt whether total reliance on one variety of grass is wise. The realization will probably come before long that a mixed herbage, with at least some deep-rooted species to tap the mineral resources of the subsoil, would be better for animals' health.

In the late 1950s and early 1960s techniques for the extraction of leaf protein seemed to hold much promise and machines were being developed to break up the cellular composition of green matter and release the protein content as a valuable concentrated food. But interest has subsided in Britain, though certain tropical countries have carried the process farther and are now producing food for human consumption. Taken to its logical conclusion, it could lead to the cultivation of a whole new range of crops, such as nettles, nasturtiums, comfrey and a number of exotic weeds. This will almost certainly be an important future development.

Monoculture has an inevitable weakness. Where large areas of one plant are grown they are bound to attract the attentions of parasitic organisms, which multiply to match the available food supply. The Colorado potato-beetle provides a familiar example. Originally it was a rather pretty and harmless beetle living on Solanoid plants in the foothills of the Rockies. Accidentally introduced to the world's potato-fields it has multiplied prodigiously and is now a major pest, though so far kept out of Britain by stringent controls.

Fungus, virus and bacterium pests are even more difficult to control, and the farmer wages an endless war against them. The problems vary with the weather, the temperature and other obscure factors. Sometimes the chief enemy of the cereal grower consists of vast clouds of aphids drifting over to southern England from continental Europe; sometimes it is a fungoid disease such as septoria or rhynchosporium. As fast as scientists get the measure of one adversary another looms large, or an immune strain of an old enemy is bred. Chemicals are now the chief weapons in the farmer's arsenal, and throughout the summer wide-boomed crop-sprayers are busy on most arable farms—to the accompaniment of widespread public apprehension.

Because pests and diseases strike rapidly and at inconvenient times, farmers have often to choose between losing a proportion of their crops to them or controlling them by sending in tractor-mounted spraying-machines, whose heavy wheels themselves cause damage. An alternative is to spray from the air with fixed-winged aircraft or helicopters. The latter are more efficient but also more expensive. Therefore in England most aerial spraying is done by small fixed-wing planes. These planes are also used to spread fertilizer and even to sow fodder turnips, rape and other quick-growing, leafy crops in standing corn just before harvest. When the grain is harvested, the green-crop seed has already started to sprout and so has a flying start. Within a month or two it makes a valuable green crop for grazing.

Each new invention, each new development, has brought its problems. When, for example, on our farm we acquired, soon after the war, one of the early combine-harvesters from America, we failed to appreciate that grain threshed in the field would not be as dry as that threshed after being stored in ricks for a few months. No one had realized what a splendid drying agent an old-fashioned rick of sheaves was. Those early combines dumped the sacks of grain in the field. When lifted, by manual power, the sacks proved heavier than they should have been, and, testing, we found that the moisture content of the grain was between 25% and 30%. The grain-driers belonging to the corn merchants to whom we sold our grain soon proved inadequate to deal with the ever-increasing quantities threshed by the combine-harvesters which were now becoming common. The merchants were compelled to ask farmers to hold their grain on the farms, and soon every farmer producing cereals on any appreciable scale had to install a grain-drier and storage bins. On the larger arable farms today the batteries of storage bins and siloes are reminiscent of similar facilities at major docks.

The installation of a grain-drier on a farm usually meant the construction of a new building to house it. And that was not the only new building that new technical developments demanded. The combine-harvester, for instance, was too expensive a machine to be left outdoors in the winter. Then there was the combine-drill, which was soon universally used for sowing seed and fertilizer at the same time: that needed to be housed when not in use. So did the manure-spinner, which spreads nitrogenous manures over grass and other growing crops; the baler; the tractor-trailers; the multi-furrowed ploughs; and, on specialist farms, the potato-harvester and the sugar-beet harvester, both of which are juggernauts. The farm building complex has

Latest technique for baling hay. Round bales weigh about 8 cwt.

thus moved a long way from the old style of barns, stables and cart-sheds, with most of the limited range of machines parked outside.

Keeping livestock on a large scale also demands specialized buildings and equipment. Dairy cows need not just a milking parlour but adequate collecting and feeding yards. When the cows are lying in in winter they are

Grain and hay silos at Andeversford, Gloucestershire

Modern farmstead near Ongar, Essex.

often provided with individual cubicles. In addition to the hay or silage supplied ad lib in the communal feeding troughs, each cow gets supplementary rations while she is being milked. She wears a plastic collar stamped with her code number, and as she enters her stall in the milking parlour her number triggers off an electronic device which deposits the appropriate ration in her feeding bowl.

One twentieth-century innovation, now taken for granted but which has, in a way, revolutionized the management of dairy cows, is the electric fence. Using it, a dairyman can ration efficiently the luxuriant grass which modern leys produce. A common method is to have a grazing fence long enough for all the cows to graze comfortably side by side and to move it a yard or two forward once or twice a day. The cows clear each strip as they advance and are prevented from straying over the rest and fouling the herbage by trampling and dunging. Another method is to divide a large pasture into small paddocks, by permanent electric fences, moving the cattle from one paddock to another as the grass in each is exhausted.

Yet another method is to keep the cows permanently in yards and transport their food to them, even in summer when it consists largely of fresh grass. The machine used for cutting the grass for this purpose is the forage-harvester, introduced from America in the mid-1950s. It cuts and lacerates the young grass and blows it into a waiting grass-box—a tractor-trailor equipped with high sides. This technique is known as zero-grazing. The forage-harvester is also used for cutting grass for silage.

236

Grazing is controlled by portable electric fence.

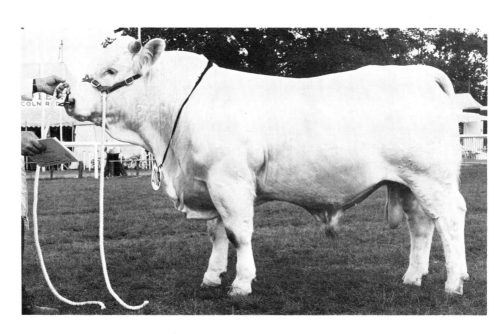

In the cattle world the dairying scene has been dominated for the past thirty or so years by the Friesian, which is a milk-producing machine *par excellence*. Second place in the affections of dairy farmers is held by the Ayrshire, which enjoyed a considerable measure of popularity because of their clean bill of health in the early days of the campaign for the eradication of bovine tuberculosis. The dainty Jerseys and golden-coloured Guernseys will always have adherents and are valuable producers of milk rich in cream. Though the Dairy Shorthorns have largely lost out to the Friesians, a nucleus of good herds survives. The Red Poll is in even greater decline, and the dwarf Dexter has a place almost exclusively as a smallholder's or country house cow.

More variety is in evidence among the beef breeds. The docile, distinctively marked Hereford is probably the most popular, though the Aberdeen Angus, the Galloway, the Devon, the Sussex, the Beef Shorthorn, the South Devon and the Welsh Black are all quite numerous. Among beef cattle large numbers of crossbreds are found, many of them imported as stores (for breeding or fattening) from Ireland, though most dairy herds are pure-bred.

In the decades which followed the end of the war a movement developed for producing 'beef from the dairy herd', it being argued that, as the surplus animals from our dairy herds supplied a large proportion of our home-produced beef, we might as well make it as good as possible. With that objective in mind, Charolais cattle were imported in the early 1960s from south-western France. Crossed with Friesians and other dairy breeds the bulls fathered progeny with such desirable qualities that more and more of them were introduced.

The experiment opened the gates to a spate of imports of continental breeds. In came the Simmental, the Limousin, the Chianina, the Romagnola, the Race Normande, the Danish Red, the Marchigiano and several others, each with its persuasive advocates. All have now been absorbed into the British scene, some making a greater impact than others, and there is certainly now a wider choice of sires for farmers seeking to produce beef from their dairy herds. The massive-framed Friesians, however, put on plenty of meat and produce good carcases without crossing, and whether the newcomers have really contributed anything which British breeds could not is doubtful.

Above left: Charolais bull, a French breed introduced to Britain in the 1960s.
Opposite: winter quarters for beef cattle.

The British breeds of both sheep and pigs have also been reinforced from the Continent. With sheep such an exercise seemed hardly necessary, for we already have over forty distinct breeds, between which the permutations are endless. The main purpose of the introductions, however, has been to increase fecundity. Sheep farmers reckon their success by lambing average, anything over about 160% being commendable. So their attention has turned to certain continental breeds, such as the Texel from Holland, which have a reputation for producing high proportions of twins and triplets.

The chief pig import has been the Landrace, originally from Sweden, which is a lean, long-bodied, white pig, noted for producing uniform carcases of the type demanded by bacon factories. Previously the fashion had been for shorter, stockier pigs—a favourite cross in the inter-war period being a white pig, such as the Large White, with a black one, such as the Saddleback or Large Black. The blue-and-white progeny were much esteemed, and the black sows were held to possess excellent mothering qualities. Now coloured pigs are out of favour, and the most popular type is a cross between the Large White and Landrace. The white Welsh breed has, however, been so improved that it is now very similar to the Landrace.

Pig farming has, of course, become specialized and highly industrialized. Pigs are kept in monster fattening buildings containing row upon row of pens with troughs connected by pipelines to supplies of food and water. As with dairy cows, rations are worked out by computer and delivered automatically when the pig-man presses the correct button.

Sheep do not lend themselves readily to intensive housing, though it has been tried. They do better outdoors. Early lambing flocks, however, were traditionally given the protection of lambing folds in late winter, and pens of hurdles and straw have now been replaced by pens in modern buildings, equipped with electricity and piped water, which certainly makes the lambing season more comfortable for everybody. Some farms have been known to hire huge marquees for the six weeks of the lambing season.

The lambing season itself has been extended. Farmers all over the country have become aware that in Dorset there is a breed of sheep, the Dorset Horn, which can mate at almost any season, instead of only in autumn, like most of the others. By skilful manipulation a farmer can get three crops of lambs in two years. Consequently, the Dorset Horn has become very popular.

As for poultry, the portable timber houses which used to be trundled round the harvest fields, for the hens to glean the stubbles, have now, as everyone knows, been replaced by the mass production methods which make table poultry one of the cheapest of meats, instead of the luxury it once was.

Broiler chicken, the unattractive technical term for young table chicken, are now killed at eight to twelve weeks, having spent their entire lives, with tens of thousands of their fellows, in the warmth and semi-darkness of specially constructed broiler houses. The main feature of the other branch of poultry-keeping—egg-producing hens—is the much-criticized battery house, in which the hens live in rows upon rows of wire cages, generally three to a cage. Moving containers supply food and water; the sloping floors of the cages allow the eggs to roll safely out of their reach; and the wire floors ensure that the droppings fall into a pit, from which they are conveyed automatically to a slurry tank. It is all highly efficient and looks uncomfortable and boring, but possibly the hens do not find it so. The sounds I hear as I enter such a house are those of contentment—and I speak as one with a lifetime of experience of poultry language, though I pass no final judgment.

We would look in vain in a modern broiler house or battery cage for Chaucer's Chaunticleer. Indeed, we would find it impossible to distinguish any recognized breed of poultry, for these birds belong to synthetic strains. Geneticists have evolved them from a wide range of basic stock. For the broiler chicken they have chosen parent stock showing early maturity, good carcase conformation and good food conversion rates. In breeding laying hens for the battery cages, they have selected, again, for good food conversion rates, early maturity and high egg-laying capacity. They have taken material (i.e. cocks and hens) from any breed that showed promise. The formulae used are valuable trade secrets.

The old breeds, from Victorian and Edwardian times, survive in limited numbers. Their role, apart from in the show ring patronized by fanciers, is to supply geneticists with material for still further improvements. They are thus of considerable importance and their future should be assured, though one cannot foresee them ever again coming into general farm use. (An exception may be the Marans, whose eggs attract a specialized luxury market because of the deep-brown shells.)

Geneticists are similarly busy on ducks and turkeys, also pigs, though here extraordinary precautions are taken to keep the foundation stock free from disease. Elite pig-breeding establishments are out-of-bounds to all visitors except those prepared to take a bath in disinfectant. The piglets are born by Caesarian section and are taken immediately from their mother, so that they stand no chance of picking up any infection from her.

Of course, mass production of any species invites the build-up of disease, and there are still plenty of infections to keep research scientists and veterinary surgeons busy. By sustained and carefully planned campaigns two

major diseases of cattle—bovine tuberculosis and contagious abortion—have been eradicated, and there has been, to date, no major outbreak of foot-and-mouth disease since the winter of 1967–8. Then the rigorous policy of slaughtering every animal which could conceivably have come into contact with the affected one worked, though at a cost of 208,811 cattle, 100,699 sheep and 113,423 pigs. The outbreak was contained in the north-western counties of Cheshire, Shropshire, Flint and Denbigh, and there has been no recurrence. At present a programme is being prepared to tackle Aujesky's disease, which, though unheard-of a few years ago, has developed into a major ailment of pigs. And cancer-like diseases affecting poultry seem adept at producing new strains capable of defying existing methods of control.

Whether or not we approve of the agricultural revolution of this second half of the twentieth century or the methods it employs, we cannot doubt that it has produced impressive results, as the following examples illustrate. Before World War Two, Britain imported most of its food, domestic farming contributing more than half of the products suitable to our climate. Now we are self-sufficient in seven major commodities, namely, wheat, barley, oats, milk, eggs, pork and poultry meat, and in barley, of which in pre-war days we produced only 46% of our requirements, we have built up a flourishing export trade.

There is, of course, a debit side to the account. The depopulation of the countryside, which has already been mentioned, would be far more serious were it not for the influx of newcomers. Though farmers and farm-workers are now a minority in a countryside where they were once supreme, the villages have been filled up by migrants from the towns, and turned into garden suburbs. The great rift between town and country which opened at the time of the Industrial Revolution and the Enclosure Acts is at last being healed. Farmers and erstwhile city folk have each other as close neighbours and, being for the most part sensible persons, are learning to get on together.

There are, of course, sources of friction. Living next door to Nature is a splendid theoretical concept, but not all newcomers to the countryside are prepared for its realities. A grunting, contented sow digesting her meal in a sty invites one to scratch her back or tickle her stomach, but living next-door to the all-pervading smell of pigs is not everyone's choice. Drifting spray

Barley field in Hampshire. Barley production in England has more than doubled since World War Two.

chemicals cause frequent trouble with gardeners, and a herd of a hundred or so cows strolling along their accustomed road to the milking parlour can be a sore trial to impatient motorists.

On the other hand, there are advantages in living near the source of food supplies. The days when the neighbours took their jugs and cans to the dairy farmer's back door are past, for the milk from local farms is, of course, carried away by tankers and returned to doorsteps in bottles, in the country just as in the town. Most villagers, however, can find a source of fresh eggs, from free-range hens if they are lucky. And vegetable gardens and orchards, which from time to time produce a glut, are a feature of country life.

Paddocks for pet ponies and riding horses are another commodity in strong demand by the new country residents, and there is usually no lack of farmers willing to oblige. Once they realize the existence of the demand they normally set aside a store of hay, too, for improvident owners who run short of keep during winter. Moreover, the farmer who possesses a few fields

adjoining a sea beach or a beauty spot is sitting on a gold mine, if he can obtain the necessary planning permission. The cult of holiday brings him a caravan crop which is easily the most lucrative use to which he can put his land.

While the problems of adaptation to country life which confront new-comers are well known, those of the old-time residents who cope with the influx have not been widely publicized. Until this present age farmers, except those on the fringes of towns, were used to having as neighbours either a subservient population of employees or at least fellow country folk who understood country ways. Many of them have found the attitude of some of their new neighbours as alien as Chinese.

The attitude of farmers to the general public varies too, in proportion to

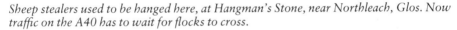

Sheep stealers used to be hanged here, at Hangman's Stone, near Northleach, Glos. Now traffic on the A40 has to wait for flocks to cross.

the distance of their farms from towns and motorways. Farmers near large towns often complain of vandalism. Farms near motorways fall prey to the modern poacher. Until the past decade or two the poacher was a local character, well known and frequently tolerated. The modern poacher is altogether more sinister. Because he travels along motorways from distant towns he is assured of anonymity unless caught red-handed. He strikes quickly and is gone. If deer are his quarry, yet when he arrives at the field he has earmarked for operations he finds no deer present, he is quite prepared to kill a vanload of sheep or a steer or two instead. Anything to make the journey worthwhile. The rustling of cattle, sheep and ponies, living or dead, is very much on the increase.

Yet these hazards have to be seen in perspective. Most people are law abiding and therefore welcome or at least tolerated. More and more progressive farmers are adopting a positive rather than a negative attitude towards the new urban pressures on them and their businesses.

Just as in the early 1860s William Harley opened his huge dairy in Glasgow to the public, charging a shilling a head, many farmers today are doing much the same. Often the public is invited to visit, free of charge, a farm for a farm walk or field day. Or schools 'adopt' a farm and visit it at intervals to learn about seasonal activities. Many such farms are interested in wildlife conservation as well. Almost every county has a Farming and Wildlife Group, and national competitions are organized with prizes for the best schemes for protecting birds and flowers. Some farmers try to integrate conservation with their farming; others set aside certain areas of their farms to be used exclusively for nature conservation, though stressing that the success of the arrangement depends on the continuing profitability of the rest of the farm.

It is in compromises and educational enterprises such as these that the future must lie. Healing wounds is always a longer process than inflicting them, but the healing of the old rift between town and country has begun. It is true that the number of farms is still diminishing, and here and there farmers are still going broke while their neighbours flourish, but there are no generalizations to which an exception cannot be found. The overall picture is of an alert, vigorous and progressive industry adapting itself well to the challenges of the age and moving with some confidence towards the twenty-first century.

Time comes to us conveniently in small parcels, each wrapped in darkness and sleep. Life on the farm, as elsewhere, has always been concerned with how we spend each package as it arrives. Life on the farm also establishes a set order in which the packages are presented, an order which we call the cycle of the seasons. It has not varied much since our neolithic ancestors sowed the first handfuls of seed or first assisted a lambing.

Early rising is still the order on most farms. When the family sits down to breakfast after the morning milking or the feeding of the livestock, conversation is inevitably of the work to be accomplished during the day. As the winter frosts are conquered by the south-westerlies laden with showers and warm air from Mediterranean latitudes, thoughts turn to the sowing. Our northern summer is so short that no time must be wasted.

The century has brought some changes in practice, of course. In addition to sowing spring corn, we now stimulate the autumn-sown crops and the grass-fields with top-dressings of nitrogen. But multitudes of lambs may be seen every spring cavorting in the meadows, though few people, even on farms, ever see a day-old chick.

In midsummer hay is made and silage consolidated for food for live-stock in the winter ahead. By skilful programming, modern fodder crops are made to extend the grazing season for cattle and sheep, but storing for the winter still remains the over-riding priority for the livestock farmer. Surplus animals, in excess of the stored provisions, are disposed of at the autumn fairs and sales. Sheep are mated again, cattle come into their winter quarters, and the countryside settles down to its winter rest, like a dormouse.

Could a farmer from any point of time in the ages which we have been surveying be transported to the present, he would find much to marvel at in our new techniques and skills. He would be impressed by our vastly improved animals, by the enormous yields from crops, the mechanical wonders at our service, and by the incredible comfort in which we live. But the seasonal pattern of life on the farm would be much the same as he had known. He would be able to join, quite knowledgeably, in the breakfast-time conversation. He would be able to walk the fields with his modern counterpart and by turning the soil with the toe of his boot, assess accurately whether it was ready for sowing. He could gauge, as accurately as his host, whether the mown hay ought to be gathered tomorrow or whether it would be better left lying for another day or two. And he would be able to read the weather as efficiently as any meteorological officer. If his life had been spent in a devout age he would take comfort in the abiding value of the things that have not changed, quoting, with satisfaction, the ancient promise: 'While the earth remaineth, seed-time and harvest, cold and heat, summer and winter, day and night shall not cease.'

Bibliography

ADDISON, William, *English Fairs and Markets*, 1953
Agricultural History Review, Vol. VI, 1958; Vol. XII, 1964
ALDOUS, Tony, *Battle for the Environment*, 1972
ANDREWS, S. W., *All About Mead*, 1971
ARCHER, Fred, *A Lad of Evesham Vale*, 1972
ARNOLD, James, *The Shell Book of Country Crafts*, 1968
ARVILL, Robert, *Man and Environment*, 1967
ASHE, Geoffrey, *From Caesar to Arthur*, 1960
ASHLEY, Maurice, *England in the Seventeeth Century*, 1952
ATKINSON, R. J. C., *Stonehenge and Avebury and Neighbouring Monuments*, 1959

BAKER, T. H., *Records of the Seasons, Prices of Agricultural Produce and Phenomena of the British Isles*, 1912
BARBER, Derek, ed. *Farming and Wildlife*, 1970
BARLEY, M. W., *The English Farmhouse and Cottage*, 1961
BEAVEN, E. S., *Barley*, 1947
BEDDINGTON, Winifred, and CHRISTY, Elsa B., *It Happened in Hampshire*, 1937
BERESFORD, M. W., *The Lost Villages of England*, 1975
BERESFORD, Tristram, *We Plough the Fields*, 1954
BETTEY, J. H., *Rural Life in Wessex, 1500–1900*, 1977
       The Landscape of Wessex, 1980
BIRLEY, Anthony, *The People of Roman Britain*, 1979
BLAKE, Michael, *Concentrated Incomplete Fertilizers*, 1967
BLANDFORD, Percy, *Country Craft Tools*, 1974
BLITH, Walter, *The English Improver Improved*, 1652
BLYTHE, Ronald, *Akenfield*, 1969
BOALCH, D. H., *Prints and Paintings of British Farm Livestock, 1878–1910*, 1958
BONHAM-CARTER, Victor, *The English Village*, 1951
BONSER, K. J., *The Drovers*, 1970
BOWEN, H. C., *Ancient Fields*, 1961
BRITTON, Denis K., *Cereals in the United Kingdom*, 1969
BROWN, Lester, *Seeds of Change*, 1970
BROWN, R. J. *English Farmhouses*, 1982
BRUNSKILL, R. W., *Traditional Farm Buildings of Britain*, 1982
BRYANT, Arthur, *The Age of Elegance, 1812–1822*, 1950
BUTLER, Lionel and GIVEN-WILSON, Chris, *Medieval Monasteries of Great Britain*, 1979

CAMDEN, William, *Britannia* (trans. R. Gough), 1789
CHISHOLM, Anne, *Philosophers of the Earth*, 1972
CHURCHILL, Winston, *A History of the English-Speaking Peoples*, 1968 edn
COBBETT, William, *Rural Rides*, 1853 edn
COOKE, G. W., *The Control of Soil Fertility*, 1967
       Fertilizing for Maximum Yield, 1972
COPPOCK, J. T., *An Agricultural Geography of Great Britain*, 1971
COULTON, G. G., *Medieval Panorama*, 1938
CRAMPTON, Patrick, *Stonehenge of the Kings*, 1967

CROMARTIE, The Earl of, *A Highland History*, 1979
CULPIN, C., *Farm Machinery*, 1969
CURWEN, E. Cecil and HART, Gudmund, *Plough and Pasture*, 1953

DARBY, H. C., *The Draining of the Fens*, 1940
DAVIES, William, *The Grass Crop*, 1960
DAVIS, Thomas, *General View of the Agriculture of Wiltshire*, 1811
DEFOE, Daniel, *A Tour through the Whole Island of Great Britain*, 1962 edn
DEXTER, Keith and BARBER, Derek, *Farming for Profits*, 1961
DIMBLEBY, Geoffrey, *Plants and Archaeology*, 1978
DONALDSON, J. G. S. and Frances, with BARBER, Derek, *Farming in Britain Today*, 1969

EDLIN, Herbert L., *Woodland Crafts in Britain*, 1949
EDWARDS, Angela and ROGERS, Alan, *Agricultural Resources*, 1974
ELWELL, F. R., *Science and the Farmer*, 1961
ERNLE, Lord, *English Farming Past and Present*, 1961
EVANS, George Ewart, *Ask the Fellow who Cut the Hay*, 1956
        The Horse in the Furrow, 1960
        The Farm and the Village, 1969

FIENNES, Celia, *The Illustrated Journeys of Celia Fiennes, 1685–c.1712*,
        ed. Christopher Morris, 1982
FIENNES, Richard, *Man, Nature and Disease*, 1964
FINBERG, H. P. R. ed., *The Agrarian History of England and Wales*, 1967
FITTER, R. S. R., *London Natural History*, 1945
FLEURE, H. J., *A Natural History of Man in Britain*, 1951
FORREST, Denys, *The Making of a Manor*, 1975
FOWLER, J. K., *Records of Old Times*, 1898
FOWLER, Peter, *Regional Archaeologies; Wessex*, 1967
        edn., *Recent Work in Rural Archaeology*, 1975
FRASER, Allan and STAMP, John T., *Sheep Husbandry and Diseases*, 1968
FRASER, Andrew F., *Farm Animal Behaviour*, 1974
FREESE, Stanley, *Windmills and Millwrighting*, 1957
FROISSART, Jean, *The Reign of Richard II*, 1907 edn.
FUSSELL, G. E., *The English Rural Labourer*, 1949
        Old English Farming Books, 1950
        The Farmer's Tools, 1500–1900, 1952
        Farming Technique from Prehistoric to Modern Times, 1965
        The English Dairy Farm, 1500–1900, 1966

GARNIER, Russell M., *Annals of the British Peasantry*, 1908
GAYRE, G. R., *Wassail! In Mazers of Mead*, 1948
GERARD, J., *The Herball of General Historie of Plantes*, 1597
GIROUARD, Mark, *Life in the English Country House*, 1978
GLOB, P. V., *The Bog People*, 1971

HAMMOND, J. L. and Barbara, *The Village Labourer*, 1911
HART, Edward, *Victorian & Edwardian Farming*, 1981
HARVEY, Nigel, *A History of Farm Buildings*, 1970
HAWKES, Jacquetta, *A Guide to the Prehistoric and Roman Monuments of England & Wales*, ed. 1973
HAWKINS, Desmond, *Avalon & Sedgmoor*, 1973
        Cranborne Chase, 1980
HAWKINS, Gerald S., *Stonehenge Decoded*, 1965
HOLE, Christina, *English Traditional Customs*, 1975
        English Custom and Usage, 1941/2

Bibliography

HOSKINS, W. G., *Devon and its People*, 1968
    History from the Farm, 1970
HUBBARD, A. J. and HUBBARD, G., *Neolithic Dewponds and Cattleways*, 1904
HUDSON, Kenneth, *Patriotism with Profit*, 1972
HUDSON, W. H., *A Shepherd's Life*, 1949
HUGGETT, Frank E., *A Day in the Life of a Victorian Farm Worker*, 1972

JACQUES, John H., *Rothwell* (published).
JEFFERIES, Richard, *The Toilers of the Field*, 1892
JEWELL, C. A., ed. *Victorian Farming*, 1975

KEILLER, Alexander, *Windmill Hill and Avebury*, 1965
KENCHINGTON, F. E., *The Commoners' New Forest*, 1944
KERR, Barbara, *Bound to the Soil*, 1968
KERRIDGE, Eric, *The Agricultural Revolution*, 1967
    The Farmers of Old England, 1973
KLOTZ, John W., *Ecology Crisis*, 1972

LEASOR, James, *The Plague and the Fire*, 1962
LOCKHART, J. A. R. and WISEMAN, A. J. L., *Introduction to Crop Husbandry*, 1975

MANLEY, Gordon, *Climate and the British Scene*, 1952
MANSFIELD, W. S., *The Farmer's Friend*, 1947
MARKHAM, Gervase, *Cheape and Good Husbandry*, 1623
    Farewell to Husbandry, 1625
MARSHALL, William, *Review and Abstract of the County Reports of the Board of Agriculture*, 1818
MCWHIRTER, Norris and Ross, *The Guinness Book of Records*, 1974
MINCHINTON, W. E., ed., *Essays in Agrarian History I and II*, 1968
MITCHELL, Ann, *The Tudor Family*, 1972
MITCHELL, R. J. and LEYS, M. D. R., *A History of London Life*, 1958
MOORE, Ian, *Grass and Grasslands*, 1966
MORTIMER, J., *The Whole Art of Husbandry*, 1707
MUIR, Richard, *The Lost Villages of Britain*, 1982

NATIONAL TRUST, *Chedworth Roman Villa*, 1960
NICOL, Hugh, *The Limits of Man*, 1967
NORTON-TAYLOR, Richard, *Whose Land is it, Anyway?* 1982

ORDISH, George, *The Constant Pest*, 1976
ORWIN, C. S., *A History of English Farming*, 1949
ORWIN, C. S. and C. S., *The Open Fields*, 1967 edn
OSBORN, Fairfield, *The Limits of the Earth*, 1954

PAISLEY, Keith, *Fertilizers and Manures*, 1960
PALMER, Joan Austin, *From Plough to Porterhouse*, 1966
PARRY, David, *English Horse-drawn Vehicles*, 1979
PARTRIDGE, Michael, *Farm Tools through the Ages*, 1973
PAWSON, H. Cecil, *Cockle Park Farm*, 1960
PEARKES, Gillian, *Growing Grapes in Britain*, 1969
PEMBERTON, W. Baring, *William Cobbett*, 1949
PIGGOTT, Stuart, *The Agrarian History of England and Wales*, Vol. I, 1981
PONTING, Kenneth G., *Wool & Water*, 1975
PORTER, Enid, *Cambridgeshire Customs & Folklore*, 1969
POWELL, T. G. E., *The Celts*, 1963
PUGSLEY, Alfred J., *Dewponds in Fable and Fact*, 1939
PULBROOK, Ernest C., *English Country Life & Work*, 1976 edn

PURTON, Rowland W., *Markets and Fairs*, 1973

REEVES, Marjorie, *Sheep Bell and Ploughshare*, 1978
RICHMOND, I. A., *Roman Britain*, 1958
ROBINSON, D. H., *The New Farming*, 1938
   edn., *Fream's Elements of Agriculture*, 1949 edn
ROUSE, John E., *World Cattle*, 1970
RUSSELL, Sir E. John. *The World of the Soil*, 1957

SALISBURY, Sir Edward, *Weeds and Aliens*, 1961
SEEBOHM, M. E., *The Evolution of the English Farm*, rev. edn. 1952
SORRELL, David and COULING, Frank, *Birdefelda* (Great Bardfield), 1951
STAMP, L. Dudley, *Man and the Land*, 1955
STAMP, Sir Dudley, *Nature Conservation in Britain*, 1959
STAMP, L. Dudley and HOSKINS, W. G., *The Common Lands of England and Wales*, 1963
STENTON, Doris Mary, *English Society in the Early Middle Ages*, 1951
STOW, John, *A Survey of London*, 1598 (1890 edn)
SYKES, Friend, *Food, Farming and Future*, 1951
   Humus and the Farmers, 1956
   Modern Humus Farming, 1959
SYKES, Geoffrey, *Poultry, a Modern Agribusiness*, 1963

TACITUS, *On Britain and Germany* (trans, H. Mattingley, 1948)
TAYLOR, Gordon Rattray, *The Doomsday Book*, 1970
THIRSK, Joan, *English Peasant Farming*, 1957
TOULSON, Shirley, *The Winter Solstice*, 1981
TRETHOWAN, H. M., *A Short History of Broadchalke*
TREVELYAN, G. M. *English Social History*, 1945
   A History of England, 1947
TROW-SMITH, Robert, *English Husbandry*, 1951
   British Livestock Husbandry, to 1700, 1957
   British Livestock Husbandry, 1700–1900, 1959
   Life from the Land, 1967
   Power on the Land, 1975
TURNER, Newman, *Fertility Farming*, 1951
TUSSER, T., *Five Hundred Pointes of Good Husbandrie*, 1753 (1878 edn)

VESEY-FITZGERALD, Brian, *The Book of the Horse*, 1947
VINCE, John, *Farms and Farming*, 1971
VIRGIL, *The Georgics*, trans. L. A. S. Jermyn, 1947
VOISIN, Andre, *Grass Productivity*, 1959
   British Grassland Sward, 1960
   Grass Tetany, 1963
   Fertilizer Application, 1965

WACHER, John, *The Towns of Roman Britain*, 1974
WALSTON, H. D., *No More Bread?* 1954
WELLER, John B., *Farm Buildings*, 1965
WELLER, John, *History of the Farmstead*, 1982
WILSON, John Dover, *Life in Shakespeare's England*, 1944
WOOD, Eric S., *Collins' Field Guide to Archaeology*, 1963
WOODMAN, Marian, *Food and Cooking in Roman Britain*, 1976
WOOLRYCH, Austin, *Battles of the English Civil War*, 1961

YOUNG, Arthur, *The Farmer's Kalendar*, 1771 (1973 edn)
   General View of the Agriculture of the county of Hertfordshire, 1804
   General View of the Agriculture of the county of Lincolnshire, 1813
   General View of the Agriculture of the county of Sussex, 1813

ZIEGLER, Philip, *The Black Death*, 1969

Index